PARTICIPATORY AND SUSTAINABLE DEVELOPMENT AMONG THE DIDAYI

Chief Editor:

Pyarimohan Mohapatra (b. 1940) was in the Indian Administrative Service from 1963 to 1998. During his administrative career, Mohapatra served in the tribal areas for over a decade and held several key positions, like Development Commissioner, Principal Secretary to the Chief Minister, Director General, Gopabandhu Academy of Administration, Secretary of Revenue and Education Departments, etc. He was the Chief Administrator of Dandakaranya Development Authority, Government of India. He has edited a number of books concerning current problems of Indian Society. He is the Chairman of Board of Governors of COATS, Koraput, Odisha. He is currently an Hon'ble Member of Parliament (Rajya Sabha).

About the Authors

Krishna Kumar Mohanti (b. 1940), obtained M.A. degree in Anthropology (1961) from Utkal University and Ph.D. Degree (1985) from Berhampur University. He was a Professor of Anthropology since 1984. He was the Director of the S.C. and S.T. Research and Training Institute, Nabakrushna Choudhury Centre for Development Studies and Academy of Tribal Dialects and Culture. He has worked as a consultant in the State Resource Centre for Adult Education for two years after superannuation. He is a member of the Board of Governors of COATS, Koraput. His areas of special interest are Social/Cultural Anthropology, studies of S.T., S.C. and other Caste Communities, Development Anthropology and Anthropology of Education.

Profullo Chandro Mohapatro (b. 1943) obtained his Post-graduate degree in Economics (1965) and Ph.D. degree (1982) from Utkal University. He has taught economics in a number of colleges in Odisha for about 33 years. He has a large number of research papers published in different journals. Mohapatro has presented a paper on the problems of weaker Classes in India at a seminar on Public Policy and Income Distribution in the University of Sussex, U.K. His areas of specialization include regional socio-economic development, tribal development and agrarian development. Mohapatro is currently working as the Director, COATS, Koraput, Odisha.

PARTICIPATORY AND SUSTAINABLE DEVELOPMENT AMONG THE DIDAYI

A Particularly Vulnerable Tribal Group of Malkangiri District of Odisha

Chief Editor
Pyarimohan Mohapatra

Authors
Krishna Kumar Mohanti
Profullo Chandro Mohapatro

Jointly Published
COUNCIL OF ANALYTICAL TRIBAL STUDIES (COATS), KORAPUT
and
CONCEPT PUBLISHING COMPANY PVT. LTD.
NEW DELHI-110059

ISBN-13 : 978-93-5125-005-0

First Published 2014

Published and Printed by :

Concept Publishing Company Pvt. Ltd.
A/15-16, Commercial Block, Mohan Garden
New Delhi-110059 (India)
T: 25351460, 25351794, *F*: 091-11-25357109
E: publishing@conceptpub.com, W: www.conceptpub.com
Editorial Office: H-13, Bali Nagar, New Delhi-110 015, India.

Cataloging in Publication Data--*Courtesy:* D.K. Agencies (P) Ltd. <docinfo@dkagencies.com>

Participatory and sustainable development among the Didayi : a particularly vulnerable tribal group of Malkangiri District of Odisha / chief editor, Pyarimohan Mohapatra ; authors, Krishna Kumar Mohanti, Produllo Chandro Mohapatro.

p. cm.
Includes bibliographical references (p.) and index.
ISBN 9789351250050

1. Didayi (Indic people)—India—Malkangiri (District)—Social conditions. 2. Didayi (Indic people)—India—Malkangiri (District)—Economic conditions. 3. Participatory rural appraisal—India—Malkangiri (District) 4. Sustainable development—India—Malkangiri (District) 5. Rural development—India—Malkangiri (District) I. Mohapatra, P. M. II. Mohanty, K. K., 1940- III. Mahapatro, Prafulla Ch. IV. Council of Analytical Tribal Studies.

DDC 305.800954133 23

Preface

The Present Study, entitled, **"In Search of a Strategy to Build a Field Model to Ensure People's Participation for Sustainable Development — Case Study of Didayi: A Particularly Vulnerable Tribal Group of Malkangiri District of Odisha"**, was sponsored by the Planning Commission, Government of India during March 2001 with the financial support through the grant-in-aid under the scheme of S.E.R. The study report is the outcome of intensive fieldwork among the Didayi tribe inhabiting in 39 villages under the jurisdiction of the Didayi Development Agency (D.D.A.), a micro project with its headquarters at Kudumulugumma. While publishing the study report in a book form it was decided to change the title as **Participatory and Sustainable Development among the Didayi of Odisha** to be more precise and meaningful.

The tribal societies are in a state of flux. They are experiencing socio-cultural change in their lifestyle, aspiration and value orientation. They need the development *in situ* and attainment of sustainability through optimum utilisation and conservation of local resources. Planned development intervention for the tribal people over half a century and more specifically, micro-level efforts for the Particularly Vulnerable Tribal Groups including the Didayi over nearly two decades have not achieved the desired result, and a hiatus has been created between the expectations of the tribals and achievements by the Government. Intensive efforts made by the Didayi Development Agency have not made perceptible socio-economic development among the Didayi. The development schemes and programmes have to be people-centred, eco-friendly and in consonance with their culture, to make a significant dent in their development process. The present study has made, within a limited time, an humble attempt to build a field model for participatory and sustainable development and its operationalisation in the Didayi community.

It would not be out of place to mention here that in response to the observations of the Planning Commission on the Draft Report submitted to them earlier, the recommendations of COATS regarding interventions of activities/schemes for different sectors for overall socio-economic development of the Didayi people based on their felt needs have been given at Appendix XV and the findings of an in-depth study on the traditional political organisation *vis-à-vis* the statutory panchayats have been incorporated in Chapter III, 'Political Life'.

On behalf of the Council of Analytical Tribal Studies (COATS), Koraput, we express our gratitude to Prof. (Dr.) L.K. Mahapatra, former Vice-Chancellor of Utkal and Sambalpur Universities, Prof. (Dr.) N.K. Behura, former Professor and Head of the Department of Anthropology, Utkal University, and Prof. (Dr.) S.N. Ratha, former Director, COATS for providing intellectual inputs to the present study.

We sincerely thank Sri V.V. Yadav, I.A.S., Collector, Malkangiri for his valuable suggestions. We also thank the B.D.O., Kudumulugumma, Special Officer, D.D.A. and his staff, Tahasildar, Chirtrokonda, Forest Range Officer, Balimela and several other officials connected with the D.D.A. for their cooperation during the study.

We thank Sri K.C.Panigrahy, Director, Tribal Museum, Koraput for his support in the completion of the study.

We express our hearty gratitude to the Didayi people living in our study area and without their cooperation the study could not have been completed.

Our sincere thanks are due to Professor (Dr.) Jagabandhu Samal, Professor of Tribal Studies, COATS, Dr. Nityananda Pradhan, Reader and Head, Department of Education, Ravenshaw University, Dr. K.K. Behera, Reader in Commerce, D.A.V. College, Koraput, who have prepared the initial draft of the report.

We thank enormously the Concept Publishing Company Pvt. Ltd., New Delhi for their painstaking efforts in publishing the present book.

Krishna Kumar Mohanti
Prophullo Chandro Mohapatro
Editors

Pyarimohan Mohapatra
Chief-Editor

Contents

Preface v
List of Tables xi
List of Figures and Charts xiii
List of Photographs xiv

1. Introduction **1**
- Theoretical Frame 1
- Methodological Perspective 12
- The Field Investigation and Research Technique 22
- Tools and Techniques of Data Collection 25
- Research Personnel 28
- Data Analysis 29

2. Socio : Demographic Profile **30**
- Population 30
- Decennial Variation 30
- Age-Sex Distribution 31
- Sex Ratio 34
- Marital Status 36
- Literacy and Educational Status 36
- Distribution of Population 39

3. Persistence and Change **42**
- Social Life 42
- Economic Life 48
- Cultivation 49
- Animal Husbandry 55
- Productive Factors and Production Decision 58
- An Analysis of the Consumption Expenditure 59

- Income and Expenditure — An Analysis 60
- Consumption 61
- Poverty 61
- Exchange and Distribution 62
- Monetization of Economy 63
- Distribution 64
- Political Life 64
- Religious Life 69
- Socialisation/Enculturation and Education 70
- Case Study of a Didayi Family 71
- Health and Sanitation 75
- Value Orientations 76
- Epistemological Issues 76

4. Planned Development Intervention **78**
- Block Development Effort 78
- Didayi Development Agency Efforts 81
- Ongoing Development Process 86
- Didayi Perception of Development 88

5. Participatory and Sustainable Development : Inventory of Resources and Resource Utilisation **94**
- Land Resources 94
- Forest Resources 95
- Water Resources 96
- Human Resources 96
- Resources Mobilisation 96
- The Challenge and the Response 98
- People's Sustainable Development 98
- Attitude towards Development 100
- Further Development Inputs 105
- An Empirical Model 108

6. Summary, Concluding Observations and Recommendations **125**
- Summary and Concluding Observations 125
- Plains Sub-Area 148
- Cut-Off Sub-Area 151
- Hills Sub-Area 151
- Recommendations 152

Appendices

I Research Personnel 156

II. Council of Analytical Tribal Studies (COATS), Koraput 158

III. Council of Analytical Tribal Studies (COATS), Koraput 165

IV. Council of Analytical Tribal Studies (COATS), Koraput 169

V. Case Study of Developmental/Poverty Alleviation Programme 173

VI. Proceedings of the Focus Group Discussion — 1 174

VII. Proceedings of the Focus Group Discussion — 2 178

VIII. Proceedings of the Focus Group Discussion — 3 181

IX. Proceedings of the Focus Group Discussion — 4 185

X. Proceedings of the Focus Group Discussion — 5 189

XI. Proceedings of the Focus Group Discussion — 6 192

XII. Proceedings of the Focus Group Discussion — 7 195

XIII. Proceedings of the Focus Group Discussion — 8 198

XIV. Council of Analytical Tribal Studies (COATS), Koraput 202

XV. Interventions of Activities/Schemes for Socio-Economic Development of the Didayi People based on People's Felt Needs as Recommended by COATS 206

XV-(I). Infrastructural Facilities to be created—Construction of Roads 224

XV-(2). Infrastructural facilities to be created—Bridges, Culverts and Causeways 225

XV-(3). Infrastructural Facilities to be provided 226

Bibliography 227

Index 231

List of Tables

2.1 [illegible]

2.2 [illegible]

2.3 [illegible]

2.4 Table showing [illegible]

2.5 [illegible]

2.6 Table showing Number of [illegible]

3.1 Table showing the Marital Status of the [illegible]

3.2 Percentage Break-up of Annual Income [illegible] Sub-areas to Economic Pursuits [illegible]

3.3 Average Annual Income Per Household [illegible] Economic Activities and the Total Income [illegible] Households in Different Sub-areas [illegible]

3.4 Table showing Annual and Monthly Average [illegible] per Household on Various Items and its [illegible] (131 Households, 2001-[illegible])

List of Tables

1.1	Sample of the Didayi Villages	25
2.1	Table showing the Population of the Didayi Tribe and its Decennial Variations in Growth Rate	30
2.2.1	Table showing the Distribution of the Didayi Population by Broad Age Groups.	31
2.2.2	Table showing Distribution of the Didayi Population by Broad Age Groups.	32
2.3.1	Table showing the Distribution of the Didayi Population by Broad Age-Groups and by Sex-Groups.	33
2.3.2	Table showing the Distribution of the Didayi by Broad Age-Groups and by Sex-Groups	35
2.4	Table showing Marital Status of the Didayi	37
2.5	Literacy and Educational Status of the Didayi as per 1961, 1971 and 1981 Census and Survey of 2001-02 by COATS, Koraput	38
2.6	Table showing Number of Households and Population by Sex in Didayi villages located in 3 Sub-areas	40
3.1	Table showing the Marital Status of the Didayi by Sex and Age-groups	45
3.2	Percentage Break-up of Annual Income of the Didayi in 3 Sub-areas by Economic Pursuits	56
3.3	Average Annual Income Per Hosuehold from Different Economic Activities and the Total Income of the Didayi Households in Different Sub-areas during 2001-2002	57
3.4	Table showing Annual and Monthly Average Expenditure per Household on Various Items and its Percentage (1,313 households), 2001-02	60

3.5 Table showing Sub-area-wise Annual Per Household (H.H.) Average Income and Expenditure (1313 Didayi households), 2001-02 61
3.6 Sub-area-wise Number of Households (H.H.) living below the Poverty Line 61
3.7 Enrolment of the Didayi Children at Primary School Stage from 1997-98 to 2001-02 by Sex 73
3.8 Didayi Villages of Malkangiri District by Population, access to Primary Education, Number of Teachers and the existence of School Building. 73
4.1 Statement showing Funds received and utilisation Certificates submitted to Government (Annual of Didayi Development Agency Kudumuluguma) since inception. 89
5.1 Showing the response of Beneficiaries on Developmental Programmes undertaken by the D.D.A. in different villages 100
5.2 Distribution of Respondents by Assistance received from the D.D.A. 103
5.3 Impact of Development Programmes on Different Aspects 103
5.4 Showing the attitudes towards value-orientations 104

List of Figures

5.1	A sociogram showing the bases of sustainable Development	102
5.2	An Empirical Model for Sustainable Development by Ensuring People's Participation among the Didayi of Malkangiri District (Odisha)	109

List of Chart

5.1	Classification of Resources	101

List of Maps

1	District Map of Odisha	122
2	Malkangiri (Odisha)	123
3	Muzumuli Map of Kudumuluguma Block District Koraput	124

List of Photographs

1.	Ploughing land at Purunagumma	113
2.	Preparing land for sowing seeds at Purunagumma	113
3.	A watch hut with indigenous device to protect crops from wild animals	114
4.	A tempotary hut near Podu land at Karkaguda	114
5.	The shrine of Bhirubhairo at Purunagumma	115
6.	Didayi woman bringing cereal from field to home at Jantry	115
7.	Focus Group discussion at Orapadar	116
8.	Investigators collecting data at Oringi	116
9.	Investigators on their way to Taber	117
10.	Head of the Household with his children	117
11.	Old woman husking suan at Badankiguda	118
12.	Grinding cereal by wooden grinder at Sanyasiguda	118
13.	Children at Orapadar	119
14.	Investigators with dance party at Orapadar	119
15.	Investigators greeted by dance party at Orapadar	120
16.	Discussion of Investigators at Orapadar	120
17.	Didayi woman with her children at Orapadar	121
18.	Didayi woman cleaning utensils at Orapadar	121

1

Introduction

THEORETICAL FRAME

Development approach is holistic. It includes both economic and non-economic phenomena in its process. It is a multi-dimensional process. In the development process, both economic system and social system are reorganized and reoriented. It encompasses both material progress and improvement of the quality of life. Additional income generation and increase in output in production witness concomitant changes in institutional, socio-cultural and politico-administrative fabrics of a community. It does not halt there; further changes are also noticed in people's attitudes, aspirations, ethos, ideologies, world-views and value orientations. Precisely, therefore, economic development and social development are complementary to each other both in theory and practice. Development envisions economic growth and upward social mobility along with social justice.

Economic Development

Ideas on economic development are so rich and varied that one definition of it will not be sufficient for comprehension. The classical economists, the Marxists, the neo-classical theoretician, Joseph Schumpeter and the post Keynesian theorists have made major contributions in the study of economic development. The classical school is represented by Adam Smith (1723-1790) and David Ricardo (1772-1823). According to Adam Smith economic development is cumulative, gradual and self-perpetuating and he emphasizes the significance of capital accumulation in the development process. Ricardo's analytical thrust on economic development hints on efficient allocation of resources and supports *laissez faire* of Adam Smith as the best policy for economic growth and asserts that the capitalist system can effectively maximize production. In the words of Meier and Baldwin, "classical economics is an outstanding illustration of dynamic, aggregate theory of development" (1961:44). Marxian analysis of economic development is unique and in this context Verma states, "A challenge to the theory of capitalism came from Marx, Lenin and others, but they also did not challenge capitalism as such. In fact, they indirectly supported it by taking the view that capitalism, in course of time and through logical steps, will be followed by Imperialism and ultimately by Socialism, nor did they challenge the concept of progress being identified with growth" (1989:18). Further in the words of Dube, "Marx, on the other hand, attempted to understand the dialectics of development in the civilizational process. His endeavour was to unravel the inner logic of development and to project a vision about whose certainty he at least was in no doubt. His economic determinism appears to have been overemphasized; and Marx's theory had an important ideational dimension also" (1989:3-4).

According to neo-classical economists and Alfred Marshall, in particular, economic development is gradual, continuous, harmonious and cumulative and it seems Darwin and Spencer's evolution theories influenced Marshall's economic views. Joseph Schumpeter (1883-1950) who rejects the neo-classical view of development process as gradual and harmonious puts entrepreneurial function as the central theme in the concept of economic development. Meièr and Baldwin write, "In summary the key individuals in Schumpeter's theory of development are the entrepreneurs. They are the initiators of significant advances in national product. And these interests do not occur through a smooth, continuous process; economic development is an uneven, disharmonious process. Cyclical swings are the cost of economic development under capitalism" (1961:91). J.M. Keynes in his admirable work, General Theory of Employment, Interest and Money (1936), did not justify *laissez faire* for better economic management but made dynamic contributions to the theory of economic development.

The post-Keynesian analysis is not simply an extension of Keynesian doctrine. It hinted at models of growth. R.F. Harrod and Evsey Domar provided model of steady growth or in other words continuous growth in real national income. Verma states, "The

Harrod-Domar model of growth became, in course of time, a basis for growth not only in planning strategies of the developing countries but also in shaping U.N. policies. The basic objection to the acceptance of models of economic growth based on Keynesianism is that they treat GNP as the basis of economic development. The GNP concept does not take note of many considerations, which are important elements in economic development" (1989:19). Further Myrdal and Singer pointed out that economic development was multi-dimensional and dualistic instead of unidirectional and monistic (*Cf.* Verma, 1989:19). One of the 'Stage' theories related to the study of economic development has been provided by W.W. Rostow who recognised traditional society, pre-conditions, take off, drive to maturity and high mass consumption as five stages. The traditional society stage is characterised by low output and backward technology. In the second stage, instead of traditional rigidity occupational, geographical and social mobility occur. In the third stage, political, social and institutional framework enkindles sustained growth. The fourth stage experiences increase in the per capita income and steady growth. The fifth stage witnesses increased allocation of resources for social welfare and security (*see* Mukherji, 1985:48-49).

Professor Amartya Sen, a Nobel Laureate (1998) for his outstanding contributions in welfare economics, has key thrusts in specialized fields, such as theory of social choice, human development indices, empirical studies of famines, economics of hunger, economic development, and social change, inequality and unemployment, population policy, measure of poverty, etc., to mention but a few. We may quote here excerpt from the citation of the Royal Swedish Academy of Sciences (*Yojana*, January 1999), "Sen has emphasised that what creates welfare is not goods as such, but the activity for which they are acquired. According to this view, income is significant because of the opportunities it creates. But the actual opportunities or capabilities, as Sen calls them also depend on a number of other factors, such as health. These factors should also be considered when measuring the welfare. Alternative welfare indicators, such as U.N.'s Human Development Index, are construed precisely, in this spirit". According to Professor Sen, world food problem has regional variations and calls for different types of concern although they have common predicaments. Professor Sen further emphasizes multi-dimensional aspects of problems of hunger and states, "Food production is indeed an important component of solving the problems of hunger in the modern world. But much else also needs to be done, including encouraging general economic growth, expansion of employment, diversification of production, enhancement of medical and health care, arrangement of special access to food on the part of vulnerable mothers and small children, spread of basic education and literacy, strengthening of democracy and the news media, reduction of gender-based inequalities and so on" (1999:9-14). Professor Sen calls for the integration of public policies in different fields, involving an active role for the public itself in the organisational level. In other words, Professor Sen equally weighs the roles of economic and social factors in the development exclusively meant for humans.

Sociology and Anthropology of Development

Earlier theorists and thinkers of great repute in the disciplines of Sociology and Anthropology have contributed their thoughts in conceptualizing 'progress', 'development' and 'change' in societies. Auguste Comte's formulation in ideological perspective speaks of intellectual development or progress from theological mode of thought through metaphysical mode to the positive mode of thought and depicts dynamics in societies through linear growth. Comte's three stages of intellectual development is more philosophical than empirical. To Herbert Spencer, progress of societies is a continuous process. Being influenced by Darwin's theory of organic evolution, Spencer conceived of social evolution and conceptualized cosmic progress in all societies from an 'indefinite unstable homogeneity' to 'definite stable heterogeneity'. L.T. Hobhouse stressed on social development based on mental development and it resembled Comte's development of moral ideas. As per Kuppuswamy (1972), "Hobhouse worked out five stages in the intellectual history of mankind, beginning with the preliterate societies and ending with the development of modern scientific thought from sixteenth and seventeenth centuries" (*see* R.S. Mann, 1987:35). Toynbee, a cyclical theorist, expressed his concept of growth of societies and their social structure over time. For Oswald Spengler, each civilization has a peak, declination, decay or disintegration. Further, in this context, "theory of circulation of elites' by Vilfredo Pareto; 'social culture and dynamics' by Pitirim A. Sorokin which speaks of three types of cultures..." Ideational, idealist and sensate," succeeding each other in cycles; are noteworthy. Max Weber's theory hinting at capitalism and development had a religious flavour and Verma states, " ..... Weber pointed out that Protestantism Calvinism had created certain values which formed the basis of all development ....." (1989 : 22).

Shifts in the Development Paradigm

It transpires from the foregoing discussions that theories of development have been constantly changing in order to make them more meaningful and pragmatic. After the Second World War when development was given top priority attention was given for both less developed countries and developed countries. The primary focus was on economic growth-oriented development paradigm. But economic growth alone could not solve the intricate problems of development and accomplish the goals of development. It led to disillusion and disenchantment with the economic growth. Subsequently another paradigm substantiating intricate inter-relationship between economic development and social change was pronounced. A link between economists and non-economic social scientists, e.g., sociologists and anthropologists was established. It was felt that economic development can only be achieved through changes in the society's institutional framework, Value orientations, attitudes and the like. As development is primarily a human concept, economic development should have restricted autonomy and take cognizance of both social and economic factors, which act either as stimulants or barriers to development process. The above paradigm had limitations and had lacked full proof predictability as the institutional transformation could not become explicit. The next paradigm, which emerged out of rethinking, is styled as the human-centred development, which emphasized mobilization of human resources and formation of human capital. In this context, putting people first in the development niche for ensuring people's participation or in other words conceptualizing Participatory Development came to the forefront. Further, environmental consciousness in the development process gave rise to a novel approach, known as Sustainable Development, which not only put stress on the socio-economic well-being of the present generation but also of the future generations too.

Development and Social Change

Societies have never been static. In the context of social dynamics, social theorists have conceptualized social/cultural change from various angles. It has given rise to multiple schools of thought in the perception of sociological analyses. Mann states, "More notable among those subscribing to single process theory can be included Auguste Comte (with intellectual based), Karl Mannheim (with educational base), Max Weber (with cultural, more religious and ethics based), Karl Marx (with economic contradiction base), Emile Durkheim and Znaniecki (with value crises base), Robert Redfield (with tradition base), Mahatma Gandhi (individual reformation and non-violence base) and Gary (moral development base)" (1987:42). Besides there are other multiple explanations regarding process of change or development keeping in view the context, types, process and conditions of social change, we may delineate two significant types of change, e.g., planned/purposed/directed/induced change as opposed to non-directed / spontaneous change. Invention, innovation, diffusion and culture contact create and accelerate the process of change in societies. Several processes, such as modernization, westernisation, sanskritization, universalisation, parochialization, interplay of great tradition and little tradition, etc., play vital roles in the field of social change.

India as a multi pluricultural, multiethnic and multilingual country has been experiencing social/ cultural change over time. Half a century old planned development interventions have been responsible for creation of directed or induced social change although its pace and content are not uniform. Further, the complexity of directed social change in rural India in general and tribal communities in particular can be endlessly documented. The tribal villages which were traditionally uniethnic, homogeneous and simple are facing the challenges of differentiation and disharmony in social, economic, religious, and political spheres consequent upon social change or social development efforts. Because of high incidence of abject poverty, illiteracy and unemployment, the tribal communities deserve special development measures for enhancement of their quality of life.

Tribal Development

Tribal communities constitute a significant segment of Indian society and civilization. In the recent past they were labelled as autochthonous people, *Jana Jati*, *vanyajati*, *Adima jati*, *Girijan*, Indigenous people, etc., and notwithstanding their rich cultural heritage, ethos, ideologies, values and worldviews they represented the weakest of the weaker sections because of their economic backwardness. During the colonial administration they were secluded, isolated, deprived and remained below the subsistence level of economy and faced the threats and challenges of survival. inaccessibility, eco-hostile habitat, poverty, illiteracy unemployment, etc., kept them away from the mainstream of national culture. Soon after the achievement of Independence and launching of Five-Year Plans for national development, welfare and development of tribal communities were given a new direction. The constitutional status of these communities as "Scheduled Tribes" under the article 342 and provision of protective measures and safeguards redefined the social identity of tribal communities.

Here, while we think of our national approaches for the welfare and development of tribal people and their shifts from isolationism to integration through assimilation, the Nehruvian 'Tribal Panchasheel' appears before us with its humane sentiments incorporating the vision of optimism and pragmatism and a reasonable model for tribesmen for tomorrow. We may quote the five fundamental principles written by Shri Jawaharlal Nehru, the first Prime Minister of Independent India in his preface to the book, entitled *Philosophy for NEFA*, authored by Dr. Verrier Elwin (1958) as follows;

- The Tribal people should develop along the lines of their own genius and we should avoid imposing anything on them but rather try to encourage in every way their own traditional arts and culture,
- Tribal rights in lands and forests should be respected,
- We should try to train and build up a team of their own people to do administration and development. Some technical personnel from outside will no doubt be needed especially in the beginning but we should avoid too many outsiders into tribal territory.
- We should not over administer these areas or overwhelm them with multiplicity of scheme, rather we should work through and not in rivalry to their own social and cultural institutions.
- We should judge the results not by statistics or the amount of money spent but by the quality of human character that is evolved.

The above policy enunciation, dispassionately speaking, was not adhered to in the tribal development process and our efforts, did not yield the desired results.

The socio-economic development effort during the First Five Year Plan (1951-56) for tribal people witnessed an humble beginning through community development approach. During the Second Plan (1956-61) period, Special Multi-Purpose Tribal Blocks (SMPT) functioned selectively in tribal concentrated areas. The principal objective of the Third Plan (1961-66) was to bring about comprehensive and integrated socio-economic development of tribal people through tribal development blocks by poolling together funds under the T.D. and C.D. sources. During the Fourth Plan (1969-74) period there was shift from area development approach to specific target group-oriented approach through introduction of special programmes, like Tribal Development Agencies (TDA), Small Farmers Development Agencies (SFDA), Marginal Farmers and Agricultural Labourers Development Agencies (MFAL), Drought Prone Areas Programme (DPAP), etc. The Fifth Five Year Plan (1974-79) as a landmark in the history of tribal development brought a new approach, which is known as the Tribal Sub-Plan (TSP) strategy. The development blocks with more than 50 per cent or more of tribal concentration were identified (e.g., 118 out of 314 Blocks in Odisha State) for launching massive integrated efforts for the all-round development of tribal communities. The Integrated Tribal Development Agencies (ITDA), as autonomous bodies, were introduced (e.g., 21 I.T.D. As in Odisha State). Funds for both infrastructure development and family beneficiary oriented schemes for additional income generation were made available. There was quantification of funds under the State Plan, Central Ministries including Centrally Sponsored Schemes and Special Central Assistance and Institutional Finance. In addition, beyond the TSP, Modified Area Development Approach (MADA), pockets and cluster area approach pockets were identified for implementation of development programmes. In Odisha State, 46 MADA pockets spread over 47 Blocks and 14 cluster approach pockets are in operation. Further, for the Particularly Vulnerable Tribal Groups (PTGs) identified on the criteria of declining/stagnant or near stagnant population growth, pre-agricultural mode of subsistence and low level of literacy. The Union Government provided the entire funds under Special Central Assistance (SCA). At present, in Odisha as many as

17 Micro Projects are functioning for 13 identified Particularly Vulnerable Tribal Groups for their overall development. During the Sixth Plan (1980-85) period, vigorous attempts were made for tribal development under the multisectoral approach. The Seventh Plan (1985-90) approach aimed at speedier development and reduction of socio-economic exploitation for ensuring social justice. The quantification of funds for tribal development was re-emphasized during the Eighth Plan (1992-97) and there was prioritisation of efforts based on the felt needs of the tribal people. The Ninth Plan approach cherished sustainable socio-economic development, women development/ empowerment, conservation of forests, preservation of ecology, etc. And it is expected that the focus of the Tenth Plan in this respect would be even more realisitc.

It may be summarised that the five-decade old tribal development intervention has brought out socio-economic transformation in the tribal micro- world, although our achievements are not in consonance with our aspirations. It opens avenues for further efforts in order to attain sustainability in the field of development, so that the tribal people become self-reliant, reasonably free from exploitation and enrich their quality of life. The enhancement of the quality of life *vis-à-vis* the enrichment of the quality of environment would develop people, fulfil their basic needs, promote self dignity and assure them freedom from servitude with empowerment and social justice. Special attention is needed for the development of tribal women who make all-out efforts not only in the upbringing of their children but also in contributing their mite for strengthening their household economic pool. Therefore, women empowerment, eradication of gender disparity, skill development, capacity building, etc., are considered as dire necessities for tribal women. There is the need for rethinking tribal development keeping in view the ground realities, so that integration and mainstreaming are achieved and assured and tribal communities are saved from the maladies of further deprivation, marginalization and exploitation.

Participatory Development

Rethinking development emphasizes human development through people's participation. As top-down approach in development planning could not deliver the desired goods, it was aptly thought that implementation of development programmes cannot be successful without people's participation at all levels, right from programme formulation to evaluation. Since development is human-centred, bottom-up approach based on the carefully expressed felt needs of the people is thought to be appropriate by planners, policymakers, researchers and development practitioners who are unanimous on this issue. Especially in the field of tribal development, the pertinent question arises as to how people's participation in the development process could be ensured. The tribal micro-world is traditionally relatively isolated, encapsulated, encysted and tribal people are relatively shy, inward looking and less modernized. Most of them intend to uphold their social/ethno-cultural identity, to maintain their own social boundaries and to replenish their heritage. In this context, they will not be able to internalize alien traits if imposed upon them through exogenous agents in the name of induced social change or development. Participatory development has enough scope for capacity building for acceptance of the new traits and it would further pave the path of crises management and of removal of barriers which act as stumbling blocks in the development process. Michel M. Çernea (1985) has emphasized the sociological issues in development process and enunciated the axiom, 'Putting People First'. Even in the context of the irrigation system, Cernea states, "The water flowing in irrigation system, is as much a social product of human organization as it is a natural commodity" and further, "the in-depth understanding of physical and agronomic problems of irrigation is impossible without the understanding of the surrounding social organization" (1985:23). Participatory development will certainly bridge the hiatus between the intended tribal beneficiaries and the development practitioners by ensuring mutual confidence among them. The people's perception of development would come to the surface in order to successfully implement the development programmes.

Sustainable Development

The attainment of sustainability has emerged as the principal theme and core- concept of the development process. Gupta and Gurjar write, "Sustainable development to meet the immediate needs of the present population, without hampering the requirements of future generations as well as endangering the ecology and environment as such, i.e., to take into account the local and global effects to arrive at an optimal solution for meeting the basic aspirations of the affected people."

Various U.N. publications, in an effort to define strategy for sustainable living and development, refer it as "improving the quality of human life while living within the carrying capacity of the supporting ecosystems" (1993:I:1). While ensuring compatibility between ecology and economy, a striking balance is maintained between the humankind as consumer and natural system as producer. Further, the goal of sustainable development pronounces certain cardinal features, such as equity and social justice, economic efficiency, ecological harmony and endogenous choices (see Khanna in Gupta and Gurjar (eds), 1993: I:24).

In discussing biotechnology as an opportunity of the sustainable future development, Heinrich Wohlmeyer quotes the first principles of the United Nations Conference on the Human Environment, June 1972 as, "Man has a fundamental right to freedom and suitable conditions of life in an environment that is so constructed that a life of dignity and well-being is possible. He has the solemn duty to preserve and improve the environment for this generation and for future generations [Wohlmeyer in Gupta and Gurjar (eds), II; 1993:266]. Michael Witherick quotes Drewnowski's well-being index and states that 10 indices under multivariate condition are able to measure the well-being of people. Under the somatic/physical development status, nutritional status, health status, life expectancy and Physical fitness are included. The educational/mental development status includes literacy, educational attainment, congruence of education with manpower needs and employment. Finally, the social status includes integration and participation (in Gupta and Gurjar (eds):I;1993:44).

It is understood that the sustainable development processes are to continue in such a way that the socio-economic order is maintained and a long term carrying capacity of land in a region is assured. In analyzing the ecological perspective of sustainable development, Misra outlines its goals, such as fulfilment of basic needs of humankind and the maintenance of ecological balance for the preservation of environment [Misra in Sharma and Chattopadhyay (eds), 1998:28]. Further, Chattopadhyay mentions the essential elements/objectives and premises of sustainable development, such as survival of human being, survival of all other life forms, satisfaction of basic human needs, maintenance of bio-physical productivity, economic efficiency and growth, preservation of environmental quality and ecosystem, inter- and intra-generational equity, social justice, self-reliance and people's participation, stabilization of human population and promotion of values and ethics [Chattopadhyay in Sharma and Chattopadhyay (eds), 1998:87].

It is apt to quote the Brundtland Commission (Our Common Future, World Commission on Environment and Development, 1987) which has given a fuller definition of sustainable development and mentions as follows: "Humanity has the ability to make development sustainable to ensure that it meets the needs of the present without compromising the ability of future generations to meet their needs. The concept of sustainable development does imply limits — not absolute limits but limitations imposed by the present state of technology and social organization on environmental resources and by the ability of the biosphere to absorb the effects of human activities. But technology and social organization can be managed and improved to make a way for a new era of economic growth. In the end, sustainable development is not a fixed state of harmony, but render a process of change in which the exploitation of resources, the direction of investments, the orientation of technological development, and institutional change are made consistent with future as well as present needs [Ghosh, Ray and Roy in Ghosh, Gabbay and Roy (eds), 1999:251].

Since humans are the cause and consequence of development, sustainability is the prime need in the socio-economic development process.

METHODOLOGICAL PERSPECTIVE

The present study on the Didayi, an identified Particularly Vulnerable Tribal Group (P.T.G.) of Malkangiri district of Odisha, aims at developing a strategy to build a field model to ensure people's participation for sustainable development. Pursuant to the evolution of the Tribal Sub-Plan (T.S.P.) strategy for intensive tribal development efforts during the Fifth Five Year Plan (1974-79) period, an autonomous agency or a micro-project, known as the Didayi Development Agency (D.D.A.) started functioning during the financial year, 1986-87. The D.D.A. has its headquarters at Kudumulugumma and includes a total number of 39 villages, out of which 6 villages are located in the foothills or plains area, 18 villages in hills or mountainous area and the rest 15 villages in cut-off area by the side of the Chitrakonda reservoir consequent upon the construction of

Balimela Hydro Electricity project. Thus, the Didayi constituting one tribal or ethno-cultural group are distributed in 3 distinctive habitats. The plain Didayis are more advanced than their counterparts in hills and cut-off areas because of culture contact, accessibility and the in-road of modernization process. The hills and cut-off area Didayis have retained their core-culture as they are more or less inaccessible and have experienced less culture contact. The plains Didayis are settled agriculturists whereas the hills and cut-off area Didayis are in the pre-agricultural stage pursuing shifting cultivation, food-gathering, hunting and fishing for their subsistence. Because of their pre-agricultural level of economy and technology, low literacy rate and declining or near stagnant population they have been identified as one of the PTGs as per Government of India criteria, norms and conditions. But appropriately they are to be labelled as one of the Particularly Vulnerable Tribal Groups. In the beginning of the Twenty-first-century, for the promotion of national integration, social cohesion and fraternity among various tribal groups it is desirable to eschew ethnocentric attitude and forge amity among people (*ref.* Behura and Mohanti, 1998:1-24). However, the Didayis have already experienced planned development intervention for a period of one and a half decades. The multi-sectoral special programmes launched for the development of the Didayi people and the investments made for the purpose have not yielded the desired result. It is a pertinent feeling of all concerned, i.e., the Government of India as investor of development inputs, and the State Government as the implementor of development programmes in the field and the people as intended beneficiaries that the achievements are meagre and not satisfactory. In spite of strategies and efforts benefits in real terms have not reached the Didayi beneficiaries although the D.D.A. was initiated with the promise to develop them. The hiatus between the expectations and achievement results in lamentable disappointment.

The above situation poses before us several pertinent questions, problems and challenges, which need answers, solutions and responses. The erstwhile strategies, approaches and implementation procedures have to undergo changes. Our principal objective is to evolve an appropriate mechanism to arrest differential flow of development opportunities and promote accrual of benefits to the poorest of the poor Didayi, so that their basic survival is assured. Prior to introducing a scheme or a programme among the intended beneficiaries it is necessary to know the culture of the people, or in other words, the total way of life, through which their societal articulation is possible. Since tribal societies are simple, tradition-bound, encysted, inward looking and relatively less prone to change, the new culture-traits induced through planned development process take time for acceptance and assimilation. In spite of their low techno-economic base they possess the repository of traditional knowledge and the cultural apparatus and unless the development approach is compatible with their culture, attempt towards the attainment of sustainability will prove to be futile. Moreover, every tribal community has its tenacity to fight out all odds in the perpetual struggle for survival since times immemorial and that tenacious grip is provided by its culture. Man lives through bio-cultural adaptation, which is continuous, but gradual especially in tribal societies. Both environmental and cultural adaptations have explicit and implicit interrelationship with three subsystems of culture, such as techno-economic, social-structural and ideological. The social-structural subsystem is based upon the techno-economic subsystem and both influence the ideological subsystem to function in the desirable manner. "Culture consists of patterns, explicit and implicit of and for behaviour acquired and transmitted by symbols, constituting the distinctive achievements of human groups, including their embodiments in artifacts. The essential core of culture consists of traditional (i.e., historically derived and selected) ideas and especially their attached values. Culture system may, on the one hand, be considered as products of action, and on the other as conditioning elements of further action (Kroeber and Kluckhohn, 1952:161). Culture is the integrated system of learned behaviour patterns which are characteristics of the members of a society and which are not the result of biological inheritance. Culture is not genetically pre-determined; it is non-instinctive. It is the result of social invention and is transmitted and maintained solely through communication and learning (see Behura and Mohanti, Unpub.). The development is ought to be culture specific in the context of tribal communities.

A purely anthropological approach in understanding development and social change comes from Professor Sol Tax who invented the phrase "Action Anthropology" and first used it publicly in 1951. Professor Sol Tax had his experiment among Fox Indians (in Fox Indian Reservation, U.S.A.) in a uniethnic social situation, in the micro-region, constituting their habitat. The Fox Indians had exclusive control over the natural resources and absolute right over management. In recapitulating some relevant aspects of Professor Tax's experiments, Mahapatra states that action anthropology did not seek "so much the application of general propositions as the development and classification of goals and the compromising of conflicting ends or values". The action anthropologist works for the community with community participation through his chief tool as education. Instead of the external imposition, the people themselves had the freedom of choice of action programmes and alternatives were open to them. Through the tool of education people had the opportunity of drawing expertise of others in order to manage their affairs. The decision making and prioritization in the pace, context, direction and sequence of social change and development were of the people themselves and action anthropologists acted as catalyzers (Mahapatra, 1986-87:3-4). In the words of Professor Tax, "A major characteristic of the action anthropologists in the same situation is that we have adopted what might be called clinical or experimental methods of study. We do not conceive of ourselves as simply observing what would happen 'naturally', we are willing to make them happen, or to help them along or at least to be catalyzers. We believe we can learn many things in this way that we could not in any other way. So we are anthropologists interested in anthropological problems but we pursue them in a context of action, hence the phrase action anthropology (1968:34). Further Professor Tax mentions three basic postulates of action anthropology, i.e., the value of truth, the value of freedom and the Law of Parsimony. The truth and knowledge are more constructive than falsehood and superstition. The value of freedom allows people to choose its way of life and that freedom lies with the community. The action anthropologists only provide genuine alternatives from which people are free to choose and avoid imposition of exogenous values if any and "it is programme of action not inaction, but it is programme of probing, listening, learning, giving in. A third value—or is it a principle of operation?—is a kind of Law of Parsimony, which tells us not to settle questions of values unless they concern us. This in a way, is a value to end for us the problem of values" (*Ibid.* : 38-39).

We are confronted with several hurdles in applying the Fox Indian model as such in the Didayi situation in the micro project area. All the Didayi villages are not uniethnic. The Didayis have no command over natural resources available in and around their habitats in the micro region. While thinking about evolving a plan for social inputs in rural tribal blocks with people's participation Professor Mahapatra suggests "a suitably modified Fox Indian Model". (1986-87:7)

Didayis are peace loving, hospitable, rational and gentle. They are innovative, ingenuous, industrious and sincere. They maintain inter-ethnic amity because of their conscientious attitude and sobriety. Do all these considerations promote people's participation in the development process? Notwithstanding age-sex variations in their value orientations they exhibit growth-positive, growth-negative, and growth-neutral traits in their culture. These traits provide clues for understanding their future plans, potentialities and aspirations. It is quite natural to observe that their value orientations have undergone transformation due to various factors, such as modernization, peasantization, monetization of economy, introduction of schooling and literacy intervention, implementation of development schemes, and programmes, etc. They need to develop their coping mechanism for better integration with the changing environment both physical and human and it would require capacity building through training. The training component would not be simply limited to the techno-economic sphere to handle a power tiller, to repair a bi-cycle and such other vocational skill development; they would also require training in the fields of decision-making, conflict resolution, leadership management, natural environmental protection, maintenance of health and hygiene, household management, child rearing and caring and management of supernatural world, etc. It appears that the space and not even the sky is the limit for human resources development and among the Didayi the effort is almost at the zero level. The human capital formation is a cry in the wilderness. It is easy to pronounce the phrase 'felt needs' of the people, but how difficult it is to assess the 'felt needs' of the Particularly Vulnerable Tribal Group, such as the Didayi in their humble setting. They are, no doubt, marginalised, lack of education and literacy but they are not less knowledgeable in life situations and about the micro-world around them. They are able to forecast, foresee, and visualize, if not far, the near future and take care for life sustenance for human beings, animals and plants. Like Fox Indians they need experts and consultants for enhancing or improving their way of life through their technical advice. By this their crises management becomes easier. In this context, a single window service is necessary as it would be a cumbersome process to run from place to place for expert advice and various related activities.

The Didayi women folk play a vital role not only in the household sphere but also assume responsibility in supplementing household income which goes a long way in upbringing of children. The marriage for a woman cannot be performed without her consent and her choice in this regard is respected by all concerned. Although they are mostly pre-literate they have the propensity to save for future in terms of cash and/or kind. At least a Didayi woman does not spend thrift unlike her male counterpart. Their latent leadership quality has been manifested in the assumption of roles under Panchayati Raj institutions and they have become reasonably vocal to express their ideas for betterment of the community as a whole. They have started actively participating in meetings organised by the Panchayati Raj institutions from time to time. It has given them the scope to come out of the cocoon of ignorance and indifference. Their awareness level has enhanced their zeal to organise Self-Help Groups (SHGs), promoting micro-financing network. In this regard, in addition to governmental efforts, the non-government organizations are motivating, creating awareness and looking through its success. Even in a patriarchal social situation, Didayi women's status is not inferior. There is need to create avenues so that they empower themselves without any exogenous interference. They have experienced starvation at the cost of their husbands and children and also deprivation at all levels of life situations. They have remarkable enduring tolerance and patience to overcome odds and the perseverance to go ahead without complaining. Of course, the trend is not uniform throughout. The Didayi women in the hill area and cut-off area are less advanced and there is need for special campaign for the enhancement of their awareness level. A woman after marriage leaves her family of orientation or parent's household and incorporated as a member of her family of procreation and lives with her husband in a lineal extended family or in a neolocal residence as per patrilocal residential rule. In case her, husband dies or quits her at young age she is free to go for a remarriage by leaving her husband's households with or without her children as per her choice. The destitute, impoverished and incapacitated widows/ widowers are taken care of during their old age till death by their lineage members. They follow junior levirate so that a young woman can remarry her deceased husband's younger brother and does not leave her husband's household. The polygyny or plurality of wives is practised by them and it often requires maintenance of two households instead of one in order to avoid co-wives unhappiness due to jealousy.

In a nutshell, the Didayi women are hard working, sincere and capable of shouldering responsibilities and given appropriate scope they would participate actively and equally as their male counterparts.

In the arena of health management, the Didayi still cling to their indigenous ethnomedicinal practices often coupled with magical practices with the help of their own medicinemen. The medicinemen are conversant with the aetiology of various diseases, diagnose the patients and give medicines prepared out of herbs, plants, animals and inanimate objects usually collected from local forests. It is not a fact that they are not aware of modern medical facilities but it is not available in their proximity and their income does not allow them to go for it. In case of serious health hazard a patient is often carried by men in a stringed cut to avail of modern medical treatment, often when the chance of cure is remote. However, the multi-purpose village level workers (MPWs) are distributing medicines among ailing persons for very common ailments. At times chances of cure are rare as there is no health check-up, proper diagnosis and follow up action. In such a situation their traditional medicinemen with their quackery continue still gaining confidence of the people. The slogan for medical facilities at the doorstep and health for all programme have not made any significant dent in the Didayi community.

A look into their economic activities to eke out their living reveals that in the plains area the Didayi households which are in possession of land practise settled cultivation as their primary occupation and in addition they grow seasonal vegetables and tobacco in their kitchen gardens. In the cut-off area where cultivable land is scarce, they have no other alternatives but to practise shifting cultivation which yields crops for 3-4 months sustenance and in addition, they pursue food gathering and fishing. The hunting as an economic pursuit has become rare due to depletion of forests. In the hill area, the Didayi practise shifting cultivation and pursue food gathering for earning their livelihood. It goes without saying that shifting cultivation has many adverse effects, such as deforestation, soil erosion, lessening of rainfall, decrease in the fertility of soil, etc. It is a pernicious practice which results in the creation of environmental hazards endangering humankind, wildlife and plant resource. It is considered a stumbling block in the path of sustainable development, but it is also felt that the practice should not be stopped unless and until viable economic alternatives are made available to the people and the shifting cultivators are adequately rehabilitated. In food-gathering pursuit, while collecting edible roots, tubers, green leaves, fruits nuts, etc., they do not empty the stock, thereby there is enough scope for rejuvenation and growth in future. In fact, they are not the destroyers but the preservers and protectors of natural resources and they possess the indigenous skill for environmental management. The joint forest management, social forestry scheme and wasteland development through plantation would certainly receive people's participation. Another economic venture is pisciculture in the cut-off area where plenty of fresh water is available in the Balimela reservoir. Of course, this would require necessary training of Didayi youth in the cut-off area in pisciculture. Currently they are utilising boats and nets for fishing in the reservoir and selling fish in local markets to earn their living. The pisciculture cherishes an optimistic future exclusively for the Didayi of the cut-off area and it would result in additional income generation. The non-timber forest produce collected by them in different seasons are exchanged in the markets at a lower price as there is no scope for value-addition through processing and semi-processing and there is lack of storage facilities and marketing avenues. The cooperative system is yet to develop in the Didayi area. Further, there is need for boosting animal husbandry practices in a scientific manner as they possess the indigenous skill for rearing and caring of animals. Their cattle wealth is insufficient for which they borrow plough bullocks for engaging them in cultivation and annual expenditure appears to be very high. In the Didayi opinion milk is meant for calves and do not utilise milch cattle for economic purposes. The younger generation realizes the significance of dairy farming and would join the milk run for additional income generation, provided opportunity is created for them. Like other tribal people, the Didayi lack entrepreneurial skill and capital formation is at the rudimentary stage. All these need careful probing at the field level.

The Didayi political organization traditionally was very simple and useful in the maintenance of the external and internal affairs of the community. They were never lawless. Their customary law was backed by sanction and physical force and the law was administered through oaths and ordeals and justice was available for the mass. The punishments were inflicted on the culprit for the breach of crime committed in the shape of cash, kind and there was provision for ostracism/social excommunication. The culprit after the lapse of time was readmitted to the community after offering a feast to the fellow tribesmen and undergoing prescribed rituals. The Naik was considered as the secular chief of the village and was assisted by the *chalan*, the messenger. The post of village secular leader was hereditary. The central assembly of all the village leaders in its headquarters at Kudumulugumma has become non-functional. The inroad of Panchayati Raj system recently has given rise to the emergence of new leaders, elected representatives instead of hereditary ones and the traditional politico-jural organization is fast weaning. The conflict between the traditional and the emerging leaders is not conspicuous among the Didayi. However, the older generation pines for the traditional organization.

The Didayi are polytheists, believers in a number of deities—benevolent, malevolent and ambivalent. The religious beliefs, such as animism, animatism, nature worship, fetishism, etc., are translated in various rituals and ceremonies. They worship the sun as the supreme deity, the earth goddess, forest deity and a host of gods and goddesses for their blessings. The deities are appeased with offerings and sacrifices on specific occasions. They believe in purity and pollution, especially while observing life-cycle rituals. They worship ancestral cults. The Hundi or village deity, who is believed to safeguard them from evil spirits, is propitiated regularly. The Palasi is the sacerdotal chief of the Didayi community. Another deity, called Bhirubhairo, resembling the *shakti* cult, installed under a tree in the hill at the outskirt of the village in plains area is worshipped, everyday and specially, once in a year by a non-tribal priest. The Didayi devotees of nearby villages assemble on the special occasion for worship with offerings. They surrender themselves to the supernatural beings and consider that their wrath may bring dire catastrophe, crop-failure, famine, psychosomatic disorder and disease.

They believe in both white and black magic, witchcraft and sorcery although magical beliefs, and practices are gradually weaning due to the inroad of modernization.

The Didayi social organization is simple, The tribe is divided into a number of clans and lineages under the unilineal principle. The clans are totemistic and besides other functions, play a vital role in regulating marriage in their community. The Didayis are patriarchal, patrilineal and patrilocal. Among other ways of acquiring mates, the marriage by negotiation appears to be very prestigious and significant. After marriage, the married couple lives in a separate house, which is called the neolocal residence. The father is regarded as the head of the household. The nuclear families outnumber the extended families. The kinship plays vital role not only in their social life but also in economic life promoting mutual help and co-operation in various economic pursuits. There is no restriction for the remarriage of widows/widowers and divorcees, of course, with social approval. Inter-tribal marriage is neither tolerated nor encouraged, but in case of its occurrence, the man is ostracized and later readmitted to the community by the imposition of fine and offering of feast to their brethren.

After having a bird's eyeview or a threshold observation of the society, culture and the planned development experience among the Didayi it was felt necessary to organise Focus Group Discussion (FGD) units in study villages and employ other tools to elicit relevant data regarding people's prioritization for the achievement of development goals. Therefore, the study intended to analyze intensively as to how people's participation would be available in launching various development schemes and programmes for them. The field investigators were confronted with various questions. Do they think that there will be no problem if minimum needs for their food, clothing and shelter are fulfilled ? Are they concerned with reaping of fruits of development not for themselves alone but for their children, grand-children and great grand-children ? Do they consider education as not only beneficial for them but also for the future generation ? Do they feel that maintenance of their good health through medical care will ensure positive growth of their population, reduce the infant mortality rate, death rate and enhance their life expectancy? Are they prepared to undertake such programmes which will not cause the depletion of forests, soil erosion, disaster for wildlife, decrease of ground water level, mismanagement of water resources, etc. ? Do they realise that there will be no development unless they economize the use of locally available resources and preserve and go for value-addition ? Do they think that unless they and their women folk also participate in the development process they cannot achieve their goal ? The responses of leaders, elites and mass to the above questions and such other similar questions have been recorded, interpreted and analyzed. The documentation of such facts provided clues towards developing models for ensuring people's participation.

From the above discussion it transpires that an empirical model is to be evolved and established in order to ensure people's participation (women included) in their own development where optimum use of locally available resources-human as well as material, shall be made. Such models, to be functional, should ensure cultural as well as geophysical sustainability, be eco-friendly, fit into locally available resources (material, human as well as epistemological). Thus, the term 'strategy' should not be treated as a mere administrative jargon but be related to the organisational values of the community, environment and the community's resources.

Keeping in view the above objectives of the present study, the following hypotheses have emerged and they are to be tested from the data collected in the field:

1. No development is possible, if it is not culturally sustainable.
2. No development is possible, if it is not eco-friendly.
3. No development is possible, if it is not based upon locally available and exploitable resources.
4. No development is possible, if it does not ensure people's (women included) participation.

THE FIELD INVESTIGATION AND RESEARCH TECHNIQUE

Design of the Study

The research design is based on the principles of ethnographic case study (Merriam, 1988: 22-24). More than a simple case study, ethnographic techniques of data collection, e.g., observation, interview, documentary analysis, use of informants to study the cultural characteristics of subjects (Best and Khan, 1995:195-198), were extensively used. Further, socio-cultural analysis in studying different variables under study, e.g., income and savings, enrolment and dropouts at primary stage, women's participation, family planning, protection of natural environment, etc., sets the study apart from case study in other social sciences disciplines.

The study, therefore, may be categorized as empirical and synchronic ethnographic case study. The details of research design, the universe and sample, the tools and techniques of data collection, procedure of testing hypotheses and techniques of data analysis are discussed as follows:

The Area and the People

The Didayi constitutes an ethnocultural group/Scheduled Tribe of Odisha. They are unique in the sense that they are only found in

Odisha State and nowhere else in our country. Further, they are found only in Malkangiri district (a part of the erstwhile undivided Koraput District). Their habitat is within the Malkangiri uplands of the Sabari basin which constitutes one of the morphological units of the rolling uplands, developed to the west of the Eastern Ghats. These rolling uplands are characterised by lower elevations (150-300 metres), compared to high plateaus, which are flat in nature and contain good soil suitable for paddy cultivation in wet areas. Physiographically the area shows undulating topographical features. Two rivers, such as the Sileru and Sabari meet at Motu, the extreme south-west point of Odisha; the Sileru forming the south-eastern border and the Sabari the south-western border of Odisha State. The drainage pattern of Malkangiri district shows the direction from the north-north-east to the south-south-west. The Balimela reservoir has been created to generate hydro-electricity power from the river, Sileru. "The region forms the wettest part of Odisha after the onset of the south-west monsoon, and becomes the driest part during winter" (See Sinha, 1999:21, 41, 310-11).

"The Didayi" — a primitive tribal group of Malkangiri district constitutes the case or the focus of the present study. They are a little known Austro-Asiatic tribe in the hilly region of the Malkangiri district. The Didayi live in the immediate neighbourhood of another tribal community, i.e., the Bondo highlanders (*cf.*Guha *et al.*, 1970). Mr. R.C.S. Bells states in the Koraput District Gazetteer that the Didayi are confined to a stretch of twenty miles in Machhkund valley between Duduma and Kondakamberu and that they are more similar to the Gadaba than to the Bondo (Guha, *et al.*, 1970). The Didayi are described as a 'wild tribe' by Dr. Verrier Elwin (1950) and as the "Stratum of primitive, semi-nomadic shifting cultivators by Dr. C. Haimendorf, 1945 (see Chowdhury, 1990:97). In the past the Didayi were in the habit of shifting their settlements, from place to place for bringing suitable patches of forestland under shifting cultivation (see Chowdhury, 1990:98). But now they lead a settled life in the plains, in the hills and the cut-off area as well. However, temporary sheds are found in the shifting cultivation (*podu*) lands where they use to spend 2-3 months a year, particularly during harvesting.

The study area inhabited by the Didayi has been categorised into three distinctive sub-areas. The first sub-area, known as the Plains lying between the Bondo hills and the Jeypore-Chitrakonda Road is in fact partly plain and partly hilly and include 6 Didayi villages. The inhabitants of this sub-area mostly practise settled cultivation. The second sub-area, called the Hills area is characterised by rugged and mountainous terrains covering about 130 sq. km where the elevation of land varies from 3,000 feet to 4,000 feet and includes as many as 18 villages inhabited by the Didayi. The inhabitants of this sub-area depend, invariably, upon shifting cultivation. The third sub-area consisting of 15 villages lying on the left bank of the river Machhkund with an altitude ranging approximately from 1,500 feet to 2,000 feet is called the cut-off area. This sub-area is cut-off from the main land as a result of the Balimela reservoir consequent upon the construction of the Balimela hydro-electricity project. These villages, however, have been connected by motor launch and two motor launches ply once a day, one from Jantry to spill way (Chitrakonda) and the other from spillway to Jantry, covering around 70 km. The seclusion of these villages from the main land have tremendous impact on the socio-economic and cultural life of the inhabitants.

The Universe and Sample

The Didayi, a particularly vulnerable tribal group spread over 39 villages of Malkangiri District of Odisha constitute the universe of the study. The socio-economic status of the inhabitants of these sub-areas varies greatly due to a number of factors, e.g., communication facilities, agricultural practices, availability of resources exposure to the modern civilization and culture contact with other communities, etc. The Didayi, constitutes unit of analysis. Basic information was collected in respect of the universe through a comprehensive household survey schedule. Further, detailed information in respect of six villages, i.e., two villages from each sub-area were collected, using multiple data gathering devices, to make an in-depth analysis of the issues concerning people's participation and sustainable development of the target group. Purposive or criterion-based sampling technique (Chein, 1981; Goetz and Le Compte, 1984; In Merriam, 1988) was followed in the selection of the villages for the purpose of ensuring representation of typical characteristics, unique characteristics, extreme characteristics and ideal characteristics. The following table indicates the bases of selection of the sample villages, i.e., the sub-areas, size of the village in terms of number of households, association of the community with other people, i.e., the non-Didayi neighbours.

Table 1.1: Sample of the Didayi Villages

Sl. No.	*Name of the Village*	*Type of village location*	*No. of households*			*Ethnic characteristic feature*
			Didayi	*Others*	*Total*	
1.	Oringii	Plains	127	10	137	Multiethnic
2.	Purunagumma	Plains	42	31	73	Multiethnic
3.	Bayapada	Hills	33	0	33	Uniethnic
4.	Karkaguda	Hills	41	0	41	Uniethnic
5.	Orapadar	Cut-off	60	0	60	Uniethnic
6.	Jantry	Cut-Off	17	115	132	Multiethnic

The six Didayi villages selected for the in-depth analysis represented all the three sub-areas and 50 per cent of them are uniethnic and the rest 50 per cent are multiethnic.

Sample of Key Informants

The key informants for the study consist of (i) the members of the SHGs; (ii) beneficiaries of different poverty alleviation programmes; (iii) members of NGOs working in the area on different aspects of development; (iv) field functionaries of the micro project; (v) field functionaries, i.e., the government officials involved in the implementation of various developmental schemes; (vi) Heads of households, (vii) Opinion leaders including Naiks, Disharis, activists, ward members and Sarpanchas; (vii) members of women organisations; and above all the villagers.

The selection of key informants involved combination of both probability as well as non-probability sampling techniques, viz., Multi-phase and Accidental (Wilkinson and Bhandarkar, 1992: 287-288).

The use of multiple methods of collecting data, i.e., combining dissimilar methods to study the same unit contributed to building up a chain of evidences related to the sensitive research questions, e.g., women's participation in economic activities, contraceptive use, diseases, etc. The rationale for this strategy is that the flaws of one method are often the strengths of another (Denzin, 1970; In Merriam, 1988:69).

TOOLS AND TECHNIQUES OF DATA COLLECTION

The following tools and techniques were used in the collection of data:

(i) Household Survey Schedule

A comprehensive survey schedule inquiring about details of every household spreads over 37 Didayi villages under study was employed (see Appendix-II). The information in regard to family occupation, income and saving, family size, age and sex-wise literacy and marital status of members, status of health and sanitation, the movable and immovable property, etc., were collected.

(ii) Attitude Test Battery

This schedule (see Appendix-III) consists of four parts: Part-A seeks to study the attitude of the respondents towards various welfare activities being implemented by the D.D.A. and effectiveness of the project in terms of satisfaction and knowledge base of the beneficiaries about different schemes; Part-B seeks to ascertain, through a three point scale, the consequences of various developmental activites in terms of overall changes brought with reference to health, education, communication, drinking water, marketing, soil conservation, irrigation etc. and Part-C seeks to study the perception of the respondent about his personal gain/loss as a result of various developmental activities launched by the government from time to time. Further Part-D is devoted to study the values and ethos of the respondents pertaining to the basic aspects of their lifestyle with a view to assess the degree of transformation among them.

(iii) Observation

Data pertaining to various aspects of life of the Didayi were collected with the help of both participant as well as non-participants observation through observation schedule. The Village Observation Schedule (see Appendix- IV) is designed to have a pen picture of a village with reference to location, functioning of different institutions (e.g., health centre, school, dormitory), agricultural practices, natural resources (e.g., forest, water), common diseases, sanitation and livestock, etc. The technique of participant observation was followed during fieldwork wherever possible.

(iv) Interview

Interviews both individual and group were conducted with different categories of informants so as to explore facts pertaining to participation of women in economic activities, benefits of ongoing developmental programmes launched by the government from time to time, people's perception of development, etc. Individual/personal interviews were held with the beneficiaries of various poverty alleviation programmes through a semi-structured interview schedule (see Appendix-V) to explore facts pertaining to implementation of various developmental programmes. Informal interviews are held with the women folk, field functionaries including primary school teachers, health workers, VLWs, etc., on different aspects of development. Focus Group Discussions were conducted among the Didayi men and women; and the available field functionaries with special reference to the following issues:

- Income and Savings.
- Enrolment and dropouts.
- Common diseases and their methods of prevention and cure.
- Family planning.
- Protection of natural environment.
- Forest produce and their economic implications.
- Women's participation.
- Benefits of poverty allevation programmes.
- Economic needs/demands.
- Occupation and occupational hazards.
- Other Relevant Matters.

The Focus Group Discussion (FGD) provided the base for intimate interaction with the people in order to explore their perception attitude, aspiration, success and failure, planning for future, etc. The FGD was an effective technique where consensus or otherwise on particular issue could be arrived at and this could not have been possible through personal interview. The deliberation of one informant was validated by checks and balances and scrutiny provided by others present. An informant who could not have been vocal in personal interviews freely expressed his views in the FGDs.

The proceedings of selected Focus Group Discussion are given in Appendix VI to XVI.

(v) Documents

The term document has been chosen to refer to data collected from secondary sources other than those obtained through field work techniques, such as interview or observation (Holstic, 1969; in Merriam, 1988:104). Such data include what has been collected from printed materials, such as monographs, research reports, journals, revenue records, census hand books and still photographs (physical evidence).

Physical evidence as a part of methodological triangulation (Denzin, 1970; Mathison, 1988; In Merriam, 1988:69) was employed to illustrate interesting situations, typical situations ideal situations, and extreme situations pertaining to variables of the study. Photographs are given in the body of the report to supplement or substantiate data.

(vi) Field Notes

Field notes of interviews and discussions with people, interesting experiences and situations relevant to the variables under investigation were recorded in diaries of investigators on the spot and also at the end of each day during the field work.

RESEARCH PERSONNEL

The data were collected through field work by a team consisting of the Principal Investigator, one Co-Investigator, one Research Associate, four Associate Investigators and as many as twelve Field Investigators. (See Appendix-I). They visited the field, stayed there, established rapport and came in intimate contact with them for the collection of relevant data in the field situation and faced encounters which provided clues for understanding the crux of the problems. They had several rounds of discussion prior to the commencement of fieldwork and thereafter for effective collection of data and their processing, interpretation and analysis, keeping in view the objective of the study.

A small team of investigators made a pilot visit to the field including the office of the DDA at Kudumulgumma to gain primary knowledge about the study as well as for the pre-testing of schedules. The team then made separate visits to three different sub-areas, e.g., the Plains, Hills and Cut-off for the purpose of data collection. The duration of fieldwork in these sub-areas was five days, twenty days and one month, respectively. Besides, official data were collected as and when needed from different sources.

DATA ANALYSIS

Data collection processing and data analysis are indeed simultaneous process in qualitative research (Merriam, 1988: 123) the data obtained particularly through focus group discussion and field notes were analysed in the field itself to avoid any further distortion. These data were analyzed at the end of each day during fieldwork. However, the data collected through structured and semi-structured schedules, such as household information schedule, attitude schedule battery and observation schedule were put to qualitative techniques (e.g., describing attitude events behaviour or relationship) as well as simple quantitative techniques of frequency and percentage.

2

Socio : Demographic Profile

POPULATION

The Didayi tribe, which is sparsely populated, inhabit in 39 villages located in three distinctly marked sub-areas of the Malkangiri District. Its population numbered only 1,661 as per 1941 Census which increased to 1978 in 1961 and subsequently to 2,164 in 1971. It decreased to 1,971 in 1981 and again increased to 4,460 in 1991 and to 5,727 in 2001-02 (See Table 2.1).

DECENNIAL VARIATION

Table 2.1 presents the Didayi population from 1941 to 2001-02 and its decennial rate of growth, which may be positive or negative.

Table 2.1: Table showing the Population of the Didayi Tribe and its Decennial Variations in Growth Rate

Year	*Population*	*Decennial Growth (+)/ (-) rate (%)*
1941	1,661	—
1951	N.A.	N.A
1961	1,978	(+) 9.5
1971	2,164	(+) 9.4
1981	1,971	(–) 8.9
1991	4,460	(+) 126.3
2001-02	5,727	(+) 28.4

Source:
1. Census Reports of 1941, 1961, 1971 and 1981.
2. Annual Report on the Administration of Scheduled Areas in Odisha for 1997-98, S.C & S.T. Development Department, Government of Odisha.
3. As per Survey by COATS, Koraput (2001-02) which excludes 2 villages managed by the Bondo Development Agency, Mudulipada.

It may be understood from Table 2.1 that the decennial growth rate of the Didayi population does not show uniform positive growth trend.

For example, the growth rate maintained an increase of (+9.5) per cent in two decades, i.e., from 1941 to 1961 Census periods. In the next decade, (1961-1971) it increased to (+)9.4 per cent, but this growth rate again decreased to (–) 8.9 per cent in the decade 1971-1981. In the next decade, i.e., 1981-1991 it has a sharp increase of (+) 126.3 per cent which appears to be a favourable trend.

The field survey conducted by the COATS, Koraput arrived at the Didayi total population figure as 5,727 in 2001-02 and the decadal growth rate came to (+) 28.4 per cent.

AGE-SEX DISTRIBUTION

Population Distribution by Broad Age Groups

The following Tables 2.2.1 and 2.2.2 present the distribution of the Didayi population on the basis of three age-groups during the Census years 1961 and 1971 and also in three different age-groups in 1981 and 2001-02

Table 2.2.1: Table showing the Distribution of the Didayi Population by Broad Age Groups.

Census Years	*Total Population*	*Age-group-wise distribution of population*		
		0-14 years	15-44 years	45 years & above
1961	1978 (100.00)	658 (33.26)	770 (38.93)	550 (27.81)
1971	2164 (100.00)	977 (45.15)	788 (36.41)	399 (18.44)

Source: Census of India Reports, 1961 and 1971 (compiled) (Figures in parentheses indicate percentage).

From Table 2.2.1 it can be observed that as per 1961 Census 658 Didayis comprising 33.26 per cent or roughly one-third of their population, were in the age-group (0-14 years); 770 constituting 38.93 per cent were in the age group 15-44 years and 550 with 27.81 per cent in the age group of 45 years and above. As per 1971 census, 45.15 per cent of the Didayi were in the age group of 0-14 years,

36.41 per cent were in the age-group of 15 to 44 years and the rest of 18.44 per cent in the age group of 45 years and above.

From these discussions, we may say that their maximum concentration of population was in the age group 15-44 years and the minimum in the age group of 45 years and above.

Table 2.2.2: Table showing Distribution of the Didayi Population by Broad Age Groups.

Census Survey years	*Total Population*	*Age group-wise Distribution of Population*		
		0-14 years	15-59 years	60 years & above
1981	1971 (100.00)	837 (42.47)	1075 (54.54)	55 (2.79)
2001-02	5727 (100.00)	2349 (41.02)	3216 (56.16)	162 (2.82)

Source : 1. Census of India, 1981, Series - 16 Odisha, Part IX(IV) Special Table for Scheduled Tribes (Table ST-5 to Table ST-7)

2. Survey, 2001-02 by the Council of Analytical Tribal Studies (COATS), Koraput (Figures in parentheses indicate percentage)

Table 2.2.2 shows the distribution of the Didayi population by broad age-groups in 1981 Census and 2001-02 survey of the COATS, Koraput. The broad age-groups in the above census/survey includes three age-groups, such as 0-14 years, 15-59 years and 60 and above years which are different from those in 1961 and 1971 censuses. In both the above reference years there is maximum concentration of population in the age-group of 15-59 years, i.e. 54.54 per cent in 1981 and 56.15 per cent in 2001-02; followed by the broad age-group of 0-14 years, i.e., 42.47 per cent in 1981 and 41.02 per cent in 2001-02; and the least concentration of population in the age-group of 60 years and above, i.e., 2.79 per cent in 1981 and 2.82 per cent in 2001-02. The figures for the Census year 1991 are not available. The dependency ratio for 1981 came to 82.89 and subsequently reduced to 78.08 as per 2001-02 survey of the Didayi population.

Population Distribution by Broad Age-Group and by Sex Group

Now, the analysis of the age-sex distribution of the Didayi population can be attempted through Tables 2.3.1 and 2.3.2.

Table 2.3.1: Table sho[illegible]bution of the Didayi Population by Broad Age-Groups and by Sex-Groups.

…us	Population			Age Sex-wise Distribution								
				0-14 Years			15 - 44 years			45 years and above		
	Male	Female	Total	M	F	T	M	F	T	M	F	T
1961	962 (48.63)	1016 (51.37)	1978 (100.00)	258 (39.21)	400 (60.79)	658 (100.00)	393 (51.04)	377 (48.96)	770 (100.00)	311 (56.55)	239 (43.45)	550 (100.00)
1971	1131 (52.26)	1033 (47.74)	2164 (100.00)	502 (51.38)	475 (48.62)	977 (100.00)	398 (50.51)	390 (49.49)	788 (100.00)	231 (57.89)	168 (42.11)	399 (100.00)

Source : Population Censuses of 1961 and 1971 (compiled) (The figures in parentheses indicate percentage)

N.B : The sum total of Age Sex-wise break-up for male is 961 (2 less than the population total of male) and for female is 1006 (2 less than the population total of female)

Table 2.3.1 indicates varying degrees of relationship in the male-female population of the Didayi. The female population out-numbered the male in the year 1961 whereas it was nearly 5 per cent less than their male counterparts in 1971 Census. When the age-sex distribution of the Didayi population is analysed one can find the predominance of female population over that of the male population in 1961 Census in the age-group of 0-14 years. Their population, however, was more or less equally distributed between males and females in the age group of 15-44 years. One obvious reason of such equilibrium may be the women being married off to other villages after attaining youth. But, in the age-group of 45 years and above their sex-ratio becomes more inclined in favour of males. It can be found from Table 2.3.1 that in all the two Census years the male population of the Didayi is higher than the famale population in the age-group of more than 45 years. This leads to the conclusion that the Didayi males had a longer life span than their female counterparts.

Table 2.3.2 shows the distribution of the Didayi population by broad age-groups and by sex-groups in 1981 census and 2001-02 survey conducted by the COATS, Koraput. The 1991 census data in this respect are not available. The females have outnumbered the males in the total Didayi population in 1981 and in each of the broad age-groups. Similarly, in 2001-02 survey, there is preponderance of female population in the total population and broad age groups, except the age-group of 0-14 years in which the boys have outnumbered the girls.

SEX RATIO

The sex ratio of the Didayi, which may be stated as normal derived from the fore going tables is stated below:-

1961	–	1056
1971	–	913
1981	–	1046
2001-02	–	1033

N.B: As per Indian Standard, the sex-ratio is calculated as number of females per 1,000 males.

Table 2.3.2 : Table showing the Distribution of the Didayi by Broad Age-Groups and by Sex-Groups

Census Year	*Population*			*Age Sex-wise Distribution*								
				0-14 Years			15 to 59 years			More than 60 years		
	M	F	T	M	F	T	M	F	T	M	F	T
1981	963 (48.86)	1008 (51.14)	1971 (1000.00	404 (20.50)	433 (21.97)	837 (42.47)	534 (27.09)	541 (27.45)	1075 (54.54)	23 (1.17)	32 (1.62)	55 (2.79)
2001-2002	2817 (49.19)	2910 (50.81)	5727 (100.00)	1195 (20.87)	1154 (20.15)	2349 (41.02)	1549 (27.05)	1667 (29.11)	3216 (56.16)	73 (1.27)	89 (1.55)	162 (2.82)

MARITAL STATUS

Table 2.4 shows the marital status of the Didayi in 1961,1971 and 1981 census years and as per the survey conducted by COATS, Koraput in 2001-02.

Table 2.4 indicates that 35.69 per cent, 45.61 per cent, and 47.11 per cent of the population totals of the years of 1961, 1971 and 1981, respectively were estimated as unmarried. If the unmarried population on the basis of sex is interpreted it can be found that in the year 1961, the unmarried males (14.71%) were lesser than the unmarried females (20.98%). However, in the next two years, the unmarried males were found to be nearly equal to the unmarried females, i.e., 23.43 per cent and 22.18 per cent in 1971 and 24.06 per cent and 23.05 per cent in 1981. The percentages of the total married Didayis were the highest in all the years. On the contrary, the percentage of widowed population was low at 6.88 per cent in 1961, 2.40 per cent in 1971 and 4.47 per cent in 1981. Of them, the widows were more than the widowers were in 1961 and 1981. In the year 1971 the widowers (1.08%) outnumbered the widows (0.60%). The cases of divorced or separated Didayis were almost negligible, i.e., less than one per cent in all the years. This speaks of a very low rate of divorce or separation among the Didayi.

The analysis of the survey data 2001-02 shows that the unmarried males (51.46%) are more than their females (48.54%) counterparts, but the married females (50.66%) have outnumbered the married males (49.34%). Further, the percentage of widows (74.49%) is more than that of the widowers (25.51%). The divorced/separated males and females are very less in number, i.e., 3 (60.00 %) and 2 (40.00%), respectively.

LITERACY AND EDUCATIONAL STATUS

Education is said to be the key input of development. The areas having low literacy level are found to be socio-economically underdeveloped. Malkangiri, an underdeveloped district had as per 1991 census the literacy rate was only 16.3 per cent as compared to the State average of 48.55 per cent and from this one can easily infer about the literacy rate of the Didayi, which is a primitive tribe and leading a secluded life in the inaccessible tracts of the Eastern Ghats.

Table 2.5 presents the literacy and educational status of the Didayi from 1961 Census to 1981 Census and survey of COATS, Koraput, 2001-2002.

Table 2.4: Table showing Marital Status of the Didayi

[illegible]rital [illegible]tatus	1961			1971			1981			2001-02		
	Male	*Female*	*Total*	*Male*	*Female*	*Total*	*Male*	*Female*	*Total*	*Male*	*Female*	*Total*
Unmarried	291 (14.71)	415 (20.98)	706 (35.69)	507 (23.43)	480 (22.18)	987 (45.61)	474 (24.06)	454 (23.05)	928 (47.11)	1476 (51.46)	1392 (48.54)	2868 (100.00)
Married	622 (31.45)	502 (25.38)	1124 (56.83)	584 (26.99)	540 (24.95)	1124 (51.94)	461 (23.40)	488 (24.77)	949 (48.17)	1263 (49.34)	1297 (50.66)	2560 (100.00)
Widowed	43 (2.17)	93 (4.71)	136 (6.88)	39 (1.80)	13 (0.60)	52 (2.40)	27 (1.37)	61 (3.10)	88 (4.47)	75 (25.51)	219 (74.49)	294 (100.00)
Divorced Separated	06 (0.30)	06 (0.30)	12 (0.60)	01 (0.05)	00 (0.00)	01 (0.05)	01 (0.05)	04 (0.20)	05 (0.25)	03 (60.00)	02 (40.00)	05 (100.00)
Total Population	962 (48.63)	1016 (51.37)	1978 (100.00)	1131 (52.26)	1033 (47.74)	2164 (100.00)	963 (48.88)	1007 (51.12)	1970 (100.00)	2817 (49.19)	2910 (50.81)	5727 (100.00)

Source: Census data for 1961, 1971 and 1981 and the survey data collected by COATS, Koraput in 2001-02. (Figures in parentheses indicate percentage to total population).

N.B.: The break-up total of 1981 population is short by 1, whereas the actual total population is shown as 1971, (refer to Table 2.3.2). The female population is shown as 1,007 instead of 1,008.

Table 2.5 : Literacy and Educational Status of the Didayi as per 1961, 1971 and 1981 Census and Survey of 2001-02 by COATS, Koraput

Educational Status	*1961*			*1971*			*1981*			*2001-02*		
	Male	*Female*	*Total*	*Male*	*Female*	*Total*	*Male*	*Female*	*Total*	*Male*	*Female*	*Total*
Illiterate	916 (95.22)	1008 (99.21)	1924 (97.27)	1114 (98.5)	1033 (100.0)	2147 (99.21)	906 (94.08)	1002 (99.40)	1908 (96.81)	2463 (87.44)	2812 (96.64)	5275 (92.11)
Non-Formal Education	46 (4.78)	8 (0.79)	54 (2.73)	1 (0.09)	—	1 (0.05)	02 (0.21)	1 (0.10)	03 (0.15)	—	—	—
Primary	—	—	—	16 (1.41)	—	16 (0.74)	54 (5.61)	5 (0.5)	59 (2.9)	—	—	—
Middle School	—	—	—	—	—	—	1 (0.01)	—	1 (0.05)	—	—	—
Total	962 (100)	1016 (100.0)	1978 (100.0)	1131 (100.0)	1033 (100.0)	2164 (100.0)	963 (100.0)	1008 (100.0)	1971 (100.0)	2463 (87.44)	2812 (96.64)	5275 (92.11)

Source: Data of 1961, 1971, 1981 population census and data of survey of 2001-02 by COATS, Koraput.

N.B. : Includes 46 persons who were in schools, but discontinued before completing the primary level of education.

From Table 2.5 it can be observed that 97.27 per cent of the Didayis were illiterate in 1961, which increased to 99.21 per cent in 1971 census and showed a marginal improvement with 96.81 per cent in 1981 census. The literacy in the year 1961 was 2.73 per cent, 0.79 per cent in 1971 and 3.19 per cent in 1981. If the educational status of males and females is compared, it can be seen that 99.21 per cent of the females were illiterate against that of 95.22 per cent of the males in 1961. In 1971, 100.0 per cent females were found illiterate against 98.50 per cent of the males and in the year 1981, 99.40 per cent females were illiterate against 94.08 per cent of males.

Among the literate, 2.73 per cent had informal education in 1961 and in other years, it was almost nil. Not a single person had primary or middle school education in 1961. In 1971 census only 16 persons (1.41%) had primary education and nobody could complete middle school. In 1981, 59 persons (2.99%) had primary education and only one male had middle school education.

There has been no improvement in the literacy and educational status of the Didayi from 1961 to 1981, a period of three decades.

The survey conducted by COATS, Koraput, 2001-02 reveals that the illiteracy among the females (96.64) was more than that of the males (87.44). As the total illiteracy comes to 92.11 per cent the rest 7.89 per cent are literate. The literacy rate, which was 2.73 per cent in 1961, decreased to 0.79 per cent in 1971 and subsequently increased to 3.19 per cent in 1981. Thus as per the survey 2001-02 there is an increasing trend in literacy rate (7.89%).

DISTRIBUTION OF POPULATION

It has earlier been discussed that the Didayi population lives in 39 villages located in three distinctly marked sub-areas. These sub-areas are (1) Plains sub-area, (2) Hills sub-area and (3) Cut-off sub-area. The plain sub-area consists of 6 villages given in Table 2.6. The Hills sub-area has maximum of 18 numbers of villages, which are widely scattered without having any road connection and devoid of minimum basic infrastructure. One has to climb hills for hours together to go to any village in the hills area. The cut-off sub-area consists of 15 villages lying within the fertile valleys of Kondakamberu plateau and Machhkund River, all of which are cut-off from the main land because of the reservoir of the Balimela Hydro-Electricity project. One can only be able to reach such villages with the available motor launch or country boats.

The distribution of the households and population in these the Didayi inhabited villages are given in Table 2.6.

Table 2.6: Table showing Number of Households and Population by Sex in Didayi villages located in 3 Sub-areas

Name of the Village	*No. of Households*	*Population*		
		Male	Female	Total
I. PLAINS SUB-AREA				
1. Purunagumma	42	87	95	182
2. Tikarpada(A)	45	96	101	197
3. Chelipadar	17	33	34	67
4. Oringi	127	281	290	571
5. Muduliguda (A)	93	182	197	379
6. Kudumulugumma	2	8	7	15
Total	326	687	724	1411
Average (Per village)	54.33	114.50	120.67	235.17
II. HILLS SUB-AREA				
1. Bayapada	33	70	90	160
2. Suripada	22	46	49	95
3. Gangapada	74	165	151	316
4. Bataguda	24	43	53	96
5. Badankiguda	68	131	134	265
6. Ghisingibeda	62	128	129	257
7. Anguruguda	15	27	39	66
8. Ambilibeda	61	131	153	284
9. Tikarpada(B)	32	74	75	149
10. Naringijhola	29	65	61	126
11. Khajuriguda	31	58	74	132
12. Bamaring	19	44	40	84
13. Burlubandha	23	46	40	86
14. Karkaguda	41	76	82	158
15. Kaning	26	62	55	117
16. Nilapari	30	61	76	137
17. Damodarbeda	97	227	237	464
18. Muduliguda(B)	04	9	9	18
Total	691	1463	1547	3010
Average (per village)	38.39	81.28	85.94	167.22
III. CUT-OFF SUB-AREA				
1. Orapadar	60	139	140	279
2. Kodigandhi	03	6	9	15
3. Sanyasiguda and Bhojaguda Hamlet	4+2	10+2	13+3	23+5
4. Totaguda	20	46	35	81
5. Disariguda	15	37	33	70
6. Jantry	17	40	38	78
7. Dhakadpadar	40	105	92	197
8. Dabuguda	28	68	77	145

(Contd.)

TABLE 2.6: (*Contd.*)

Name of the Village	No. of Households	Population		
		Male	Female	Total
9. Arlinguda	10	19	15	34
10. Taber	41	83	79	162
11. Nadimanjari	16	33	28	61
12. Kantamanjari	12	25	24	49
13. Ramguda	04	8	9	17
14. Maribeda	21	36	35	71
15. Andirapalli	3	10	9	19
Total	296	667	639	1306
Average (per village)	19.73	44.47	42.60	87.07
Grand Total	1313	2817	2910	5727
Average (per village)	33.67	72.23	74.62	146.85

Source: Census Survey by COATS, Koraput, 2001-2002

Table 2.6 indicates that the Plains sub-area consists of 326 Didayi households having a total population of 1411, the average household per village being 54.33 and the average population comes to 235.17 per village. There are two villages, namely Oringi and Muduliguda(A) which have the largest number households, i.e., 127 and 93 with population of 571 and 379 respectively.

The Hills sub-area, which has the largest number of 18 villages has, however, an average of 38.39 households and a population of 167.22 per village. The largest village is Damodarbeda which has 97 households and a population of 464 souls. It is followed by Gangapada village having 74 households and population of 316 Didayis.

The Cut-off sub- area includes 15 villages, each accommodating an average number of 19.73 households and average 87.07 persons per village. The biggest village is Orapadar, which has 60 households and 279 people. On the contrary, Kodigandhi and Andirapalli villages have only 3 households each and population of 15 and 19 numbers respectively.

3

Persistence and Change

Culture is the sum total of a nation's thinking and living, capable of influencing the society. It is the way of life based on common traditions and environment. Culture has two main aspects, i.e., material and non-material. The non-material aspects of the culture include the values, goals, world views, thoughts and belief processes, languages and symbols, statuses and roles, etc. On the other hand, its material aspects are technology, habits of clothing and eating, etc. Hence, culture is a broad concept which includes belief, idea and attitude, religious, social, political and economic organisations along with science and technology.

Viewed from the connotations of culture given above, every tribal community has its own cultural values, which guide their socio-economic life. The tribal culture is cognated to tribal economics. The economic system of tribals can be understood in the purview of cultural factors. In the conventional economic science, non-economic factors, like social and cultural relations may be considered non-essential; but they are the tribal reality for the organization of their economic process. The implementation of various economic development schemes in tribal areas without taking into account the cultural background of the particular tribe, has mostly resulted in failure, and hence, frustration. The case of the Didayi tribe is no exception to it. It is, therefore, necessary to understand the socio-economic organisation of the Didayi before suggesting any alternative strategy for their sustainable development.

SOCIAL LIFE

The Didayi social organisation consists of a number of clans, each with a totem. All members of a particular *Gta* pay reverence to their totemic animal or object. Any harm or disrespect to it is strictly prohibited.

Each clan is further subdivided into several lineage groups, called *Biria* — formed by close relatives in a village under the joint leadership of the *Manag* (the eldest member of the group) and *Dhanang* (the second elder member of the group). Both of them discharge important social functions, like regulating the conduct of marriage negotiations of its members and in representing and protecting the interests of the group in traditional village panchayat.

From the general picture of the entire tribal organisation, the dual organisation or moiety does not appear to be present in its perfect form. Its existence in the past, however, cannot be ruled out. The passage of time and expansion of the tribal fold as well as their dispersioin and contact with other groups has led to the partial break up of dual organisation (Guha, *et al.*, 1970: 60).

The Family

The family is the primary social institution and the unit of primary production and consumption.

Among the Didayi, a simple family consists of a man, his wife (or wives), unmarried sons and daughters. Generally, a son has to leave his parental home and hearth soon after his marriage. Therefore, a Didayi family is normally nuclear and monogamous. Most of the extended families are, therefore, transitional in nature, But in few cases married sons live with their parents or two married brothers live jointly.

In hill areas the frequency of the nuclear type of family is higher than those in plains villages. Comparatively large areas of cultivable land and the nature of economic pursuit with greater necessity as well as scope for joint and corporate work in the field, is most probably responsible for a comparatively high frequency of joint families in the plains villages (Guha, *et al.*, 1970).

Monogamy is the common practice among the Didayi but polygamy is also not unknown. A man is free to take two wives when he feels like doing so.

The duties and responsibilities of each member of the family is clearly defined and demarcated. Certain activities, like fetching of firewood and water, keeping the house clean, cooking, and collecting certain roots and tubers are entrusted to women. Men plough field, cut bamboo and timber, and go for hunting, etc.

The succession and inheritance of property are always made in the male line. If a man dies without a son the property is inherited by his brother.

In spite of the fact that Didayis are patriarchal, the status of women is not low. She is considered as the dominant partner. Household management with money or paddy is the responsibility of women. A man cannot hold any post in the traditional panchayat, such as Naik or Chalan without the consent of his wife.

Children are looked after with extreme care and affection by the parents, and when the children grow up they lend helping hands to their parents.

Marriage

Boys and girls exercise their choice in selecting their mates only with the condition that they must not choose anyone from their own clan.

Various forms of marriage are prevalent among the Didayi, such as marriage by negotiation (*toso*), marriage by ceremonial capture (*udulia*), marriage by service (*garjya*), marriage by intrusion (*gaisamuddi*), etc. The negotiation marriage is prestigious but cost effective because of the payment of bride-price, observation of rituals and arrangement of feast. The marriage by mutual consent and elopement are common among them. Bride price is given to bride's parents after proper negotiation in terms of cash and/or kind, such as liquor, rice, clothes etc. In case of inability for payment of bride price as determined by the community the boy is required to serve the girl's father for a period of three years or so as decided in lieu of bride price. This form of marriage is called marriage by service (*garjya*).

The widow remarriage and junior leviration are permitted in their community. The consent of the deceased elder brother's widow is a decisive factor in finalising the junior leviration. Divorce on grounds, like adultery, laziness and maladjustments, etc., is allowed. The marital status of the Didayi based on the present study may be discussed hereunder as per Table 3.1

From Table 3.1 it is evident that the unmarried males have outnumbered their females counterparts in the age-group of 15-59 years, the percentage being 19.04 and 17.17 respectively. The married females (98.07%) in the said age group are more than the married

Table 3.1: Table showing the Marital Status of the Didayi by Sex and Age-groups

Marital status	*Male*				*Female*				*Total*			
	0-14	*15-59*	*60 & above*	*Total*	*0-14*	*15-59*	*60 & above*	*Total*	*0-14*	*15-59*	*60 & above*	*Total*
Unmarried	1195 (80.96)	281 (19.04)	—	1476 (100.00)	1153 (82.83)	239 (17.17)	—	1392 (100.00)	2348 (81.87)	520 (18.13)	—	2868 (100.00)
Married	—	1219 (96.52)	44 (3.48)	1263 (100.00)	1 (0.08)	1272 (98.07)	24 (1.85)	1297(100.00)	1 (0.04)	2491 (97.30)	68 (2.66)	2560 (100.00)
Widowed	—	46 (61.33)	29 (38.67)	75 (100.00)	—	154 (70.32)	65 (29.68)	219 (100.00)	—	200 (68.03)	94 (31.97)	294 (100.00)
Divorced or Separated	—	03 (100.00)	—	03 (100.00)	—	02 (100.00)	—	02 (100.00)	—	05 (100.00)	—	05 (100.00)
Total	1195 (42.42)	1549 (54.99)	73 (2.59)	2817 (100.00)	1154 (39.66)	1667 (57.29)	89 (3.06)	2910 (100.00)	2349 (41.02)	3216 (56.16)	162 (2.83)	5727 (100.00)

Source : Survey conducted by the COATS, Koraput, 2001-02.

Note : Figures in parentheses indicate percentage.

males (96.52%). The widows (219) are more than the widowers (75) in two broad age-groups of 15-59 years and 60 years and above. The cases of divorced/separated are very rare.

Status of Women

A Didayi woman has passion and emotion, love and jealousy, possessiveness and devotion to her husband and children. The Didayi community has accorded to her an elevated position and granted a lot of freedom. Although men can only inherit ancestral property, women have greater liberty, more mobility and enviable role in household decision making process. A woman can choose her husband and can change him at her will. She can go to forest and market alone. She plays major role in the management of the household.

Currently, in the changing canvas, the role performance of the Didayi women is worth noting. Besides the traditional roles, the emerging roles have resulted in making them more vibrant, dynamic and outward-looking. In this context, the participatory roles of the Didayi women, which provide clues to explore their potentialities for involvement in the planned development intervention may be discussed below:

Participatory Role of the Didayi Women

I. Traditional Roles

1.1 Hearth and Home
- 1.1.1 Husking of paddy and other cereals
- 1.1.2 Grinding of pulses and spices
- 1.1.3 Cutting of vegetables, fruits and green leaves
- 1.1.4 Cutting and processing of non-vegetarian items
- 1.1.5 Cooking of edibles including baking
- 1.1.6 Distribution of edibles among family members
- 1.1.7 Storage of edibles for future consumption
- 1.1.8 Fetching of drinking water
- 1.1.9 Storage of drinking water and water for other uses.
- 1.1.10 Cleaning of household utensils and appliances

1.2 Management
- 1.2.1 Participatioin in house building
- 1.2.2 House cleaning and maintenance

...ng of house premises

1.2.4 Nourishing and caring of children

1.2.5 Caring of other family members and guests

1.2.6 Participation in household decision making process

1.2.7 Taking decision in choosing life partner

1.2.8 Taking decision in the dissolution of marriage

1.2.9 Taking decision in remarriage

1.3 Participation as Economic Partner

1.3.1 Food gathering including collection of food, fodder, fuel and non-timber forest produce.

1.3.2 Participation in shifting cultivation

1.3.2.1 Clearing of shifting (*biri*) land by cutting and uprooting small plants, grass and shrubs.

1.3.2.2 Hoeing

1.3.2.3 Weeding

1.3.2.4 Reaping or harvesting

1.3.2.5 Threshing

1.3.2.6 Carrying cereals home through head load

1.3.2.7 Storage and preservation of produce

1.3.2.8 Carrying food and drinks to the field

1.3.3 Participation in settled cultivation

1.3.3.1 Ploughing of low and wet land (*khal*)

1.3.3.2 Weeding

1.3.3.3 Transplantation

1.3.3.4 Reaping or harvesting

1.3.3.5 Threshing

1.3.3.6 Carrying cereals home through head-load

1.3.3.7 Storage and preservation of produce

1.3.4 Participation in Kitchen gardening

1.3.4.1 Hoeing

1.3.4.2 Weeding

1.3.4.3 Collection of vegetables and fruits

1.3.4.4 Storage

1.3.4.5 Marketing

1.3.5 Participation in Domestication of animals and birds

1.3.5.1 Regular cleaning of animal sheds

1.3.5.2 Feeding animals and birds

1.3.6 Working as wage-earner in agricultural sector

1.3.7 Working as wage-earner in non-agricultural sector
1.3.8 Participation in barter and market exchange
1.3.9 Participation in extra-economic exchange
1.3.10 Contributing to the family income pool (cash and/or kind)
1.3.11 Saving (cash and/or kind) for future contingencies
1.3.12 Participation in other income generating activities.
1.4 Participation in rituals (including rites de passage)
1.5 Participation in youth Dormitories
1.6 Participation in recreational activities
1.7 Participation in fairs and festivals

II. Emerging Roles

2.1 Participation in election to the officer under Panchayati Raj Institutions (PRIs)
2.2 Participation in Self Help Groups (SHGs)
2.3 Participation in entrepreneurial activities through SHGs for the diversification of their existing economic base.
2.4 Participation in the immunisation programmes for children

ECONOMIC LIFE

The economic life of the Didayi is essentially that of a tribe of cultivators, and forest produce collectors (food gathering), with hunting and fishing. Agriculture is the main source of their livelihood and it is mainly forest based, as overwhelming majority of them live in the hills and forests of the Kondakamberu Range of Malkangiri district. An important characteristic of the Didayi economic life is their coordinated efforts and concerted action — particularly in case of reclamation of lands, field preparation, hunting and house building, etc.

A study of the Didayi conducted by a team of researchers of the Anthropological Survey of India (1966) under the leadership of Smt. U. Guha, classify the Didayi under three economic groups (Guha *et al.*, 1970:26):

(i) Permanent agriculturist who own fertile lands and who have a surplus domestic economy (Lokanathan, p.s. 1962:16);
(ii) Cultivators who have a hand to mouth existence either because of the land they possess is quite insufficient or of inferior quality; and

(iii) Landless labourers who work on the land of other rich farmers mostly of their own group or engage themselves as wage earners in forests.

The Didayi of the first sub-area live in the multiethnic village in the plains sub-area and mainly depend upon settled cultivation in whatever quantity of wet land they possess. The forest collection and wage-earning are their subsidiary sources of income. Average areas of cultivated land per family in these villages are 1.39 acres of low lying paddy, land, and 1.28 acres of *Dongar* and shifting land as revealed from the present field investigation. They have adopted agricultural implements similar to that of the caste Hindu cultivators in their paddy lands.

The Didayi living in the Hills sub-area villages belong to the second category and they practise *biri* or shifting cultivation. They possess less fertile land, use old method of cultivation with primitive tools and inferior quality of seeds. They carry on shifting cultivation in hill slopes adjacent to their villages. In the upland they grow few varieties of millets, oil seeds and grams while in the low land they grow paddy. Bullocks driven ploughs are used in the low lands in comparatively plains land.

The people of cut-off sub-area consists of landless labourers, who work, as agricultural or non-agricultural workers where and when such works are available. Wages are paid mostly in kind and cash payment is usually uncommon. Those who work under forest contractors or in construction works wages are usually paid in cash. Now with the submergence some 14 Didayi villages in Chitrokonda reservoir, the Didayi habitat country may be divided into three divisions, *viz*., (a) Hills sub-area, (b) Plains sub-area, and (c) Cut-off sub-area and study of the Didayi economy may be analysed under these three sub-areas.

CULTIVATION

Cultivation, which is the principal source of living among the Didayi can be divided into two categories, *viz*. (a) Shifting cultivation; and (b) Settled agriculture. It is interesting to find that most of the Didayi families have kitchen gardens adjacent to their houses in which tobacco, pumpkins and some other vegetables are grown.

Shifting Cultivation

Shifting Cultivation on hill slopes of the Didayi areas is the principal source of subsistence to a large majority of the Didayi people. It is described as *bri* or *biri*, a term which is synonymous with the term *podu*, prevalent in Koraput region.

Method of Shifting Cultivation

It is a primitive type of agricultural practice with very few agricultural implements, like axe for cutting trees and other vegetations and the sickle for clearing grass. Spades are used for preparation of fields and dibble sticks for putting seeds inside soil. The only manure used is the ash from burnt trees and bushes which is spread on *podu* lands. A *bri* (*podu*) land is used by them for three years, after which they shift to another plot where fertility of the soil has not been exhausted. Earlier they were returning to the old plots for cultivation only after 10 to 15 years, now due to forest restrictions this period, i.e., shifting recuperation has come down to 5 to 6 years.

In olden days, they had full freedom to slash and burn any forest tract for shifting cultivation. But nowadays they have to take permission from the forest officials who allot a particular plot of land in the vicinity of forest villages. They always choose *podu* land near their villages. Generally a plot with a dense growth is preferred as its vegetation can last for two to three burnings and its fertility is not exhausted. Apart from the consideration of distance, a Didayi generally selects his plot for cultivation where weeds are scarce. Disputes regarding distribution of *bri* lands are unknown as they have mutual understanding and cooperation in the process of shifting cultivation.

During January and February when forest is dry, they select a hill slope and start clearing and felling the trees. The felling period lasts for about a month. Fruit bearing trees, like mango and jackfruit are not destroyed. The felled trees and bushes are left for drying and they are set on fire in April and May. Within four to five days the ashes cool down. The ashes are spread over the plot just before sowing.

In June, when the monsoon sets in the preparation of field for sowing starts. Mixed cropping in *podu* field is the usual practice among the tribals, so also with the Didayi. They grow minor millets like *ragi*, *suan*, *jawar*, and *kandul* (redgram) etc. in the first year and *biri* (black gram), niger, brinjal and tomato in the subsequent years. A few of them also grow chilly and tobacco in the shifting land. After the third year the plot is abandoned and they go to a new patch of forest land for cultivation.

Weeding is required for some pulses and grams and vegetables, such as tomato and brinjal. Both men and women take part in weeding operation. It continues till August-September.

Harvesting of various crops starts periodically from September - October in which men, women and children take part. As various crops ripe at different times the harvesting is done accordingly.

Threshing is done [illegible]ng with stick or by letting men and animal tread on the seeds on a hardened threshing floor. The threshing floor is prepared and plastered with mud before harvesting by Didayi women.

Economics of Shifting Cultivation in the Didayi Area

As it is evident from the types of work involved in shifting cultivation, it is a labour intensive type of agricultural practice in which tribal men, women and even children take active part. It involves cutting of trees and bushes, drying and burning, preparation of field with spreading of ashes, sowing, weeding, watching the field against wild animals and birds, and harvesting are the activities in which almost all members of a family take part. Our field study in these villages reveals that the average annual income per household from hill areas where mostly shifting cultivation is adopted comes to Rs. 3684.52 only.

This of course includes shifting land, *Dongar* (upland) low foothills and kitchen garden land. The value of the yield per acre of shifting land in hill areas comes to Rs. 1291.49; as against Rs. 1622.74 in low foothills settled land, and Rs. 2093.97 in kitchen garden land. Even in the *donger* land (upland) where crop is grown, per acre yield is Rs. 1413.16 which is again higher than that of *bri* land (*podu* land). It may be mentioned here that in hills area situation where shifting cultivation is the major source of agriculture 1250 acres of *dongar* (upland) cultivation is carried on in 554 acres, low foothills land (settled) cultivation in 171.50 acres and kitchen garden land cultivation is carried on in 288.25 acres.

Plough Cultivation

The Didayi living in lower slopes and foothills have adopted plough (plains land) cultivation. But many parts of the Didayi area is entirely unsuitable for plough cultivation/settled cultivation.

Plough cultivation is gaining popularity among the Didayi of the plains. Adoption of the plough has not made plains Didayi to abandon their *bri* (*podu*) cultivation entirely. Most of them practise shifting cultivation in the nearby hill slopes along with plough cultivation. The field investigation in the Didayi villages situated in the plains revealed that settled cultivation was carried on in 455.25 acres of land whereas 152 acres were put to shifting cultivation in the nearby hills by these villagers. They also put 264 acres of *dongar* (upland) and 120.50 acres *bari* (garden) land under cultivation. The average per household income from agriculture in plains area where mostly plough cultivation is adopted and shifting cultivation is not totally abandoned, comes to Rs. 3951.25. This is comparatively better than that of the hills area where average income per household from cultivation comes to Rs. 3084.52 only. But it is interesting to note that average per acre income from settled paddy land comes to Rs. 2279.10 as against Rs. 1066.49 from shifting land and Rs. 1194.77 from *dongar* land under the same situation. As against this the *bari* land (garden) gave an average per acre income of Rs. 1352.82.

The use of plough resulted in a socio-cultural change among the Didayi as many of the agricultural activities are transferred from men to women (Guha *et al.*, 1970:42). The yield under plough cultivation is generally more than that of shifting cultivation and also *dongar* cultivation. The average yield per acre under plough cultivation was estimated to be 10 *puttis** while that of shifting cultivation it was 5 *puttis* of paddy (Guha *et al.*, 1970:42).

The Didayi under plough cultivation mainly raise rice. Apart from rice, jawari-millet and ragi are also cultivated in the permanent fields mainly in *dongar* lands. There is not much difference in the method of cultivation, size of holdings, and related problems in plains land cultivation here in this tribal area with that of other areas inhabited by settled agriculturists in Koraput region.

But out of three sub-areas, the average per household annual

---

* A putti' is equivalent to 20 manas. One Mana contains 2.5 kgs of paddy, 3 kgs of rice & 3.5 kgs of Ragi.

return from agriculture in cut-off sub-area is better (i.e., Rs. 4316.69). It is Rs. 3684.52 in hills sub- area and Rs. 3951.25 in plains sub-area. This is mostly a better performance of the *bari* (kitchen gaden) land where a total of Rs. 4,03,518 was the income in 168.50 acres the average value of returns coming to Rs. 2394.76. As against the average value of per acre yield came to Rs. 1182.68 in settled, Rs. 1165.25 in *dongar* and Rs. 1007.48 in shifting cultivation in the villages of cut-off area. The Didayi villagers in cut-off sub-area had put 205.55 acres of settled, 544.40 acres of *dongar*, 412 acres of shifting and 168.50 acres of kitchen garden land under cultivation during last agricultural year.

Food Gathering and Forest Collection

Although agriculture is the main source of living of the Didayi, food gathering is still an important and supplementary source of livelihood. They collect edible fruits, roots, leaves, etc., in various seasons. They consume at the spot most of what they collect and bring home the remaining quantities.

Items of such food collection include caryota urns, a sago-like palm, flower of *Mahua tree* (out of which they distil country liquor and also cook as curry). *Mahua* seed (out of it oil is extracted), Mango (fruit is eaten and mango kernels are dried, processed and crushed into powder for preparing gruel for consumption), and Kendu fruit, etc.

They collect bamboo shoots, which forms a part of their diet. The other roots and tubers existing in the area are *gbu* (*bara Kanda*), *tamo* (*darkonda*), *torla* (*toraj Konda*), *kondala* (*pet konda*), *saraila* (*sarangi konda*), and *kirla* (*pota konda*).

Of all the edible leaves *gudiali* is the most important. *Bhaji* is also another kind of leaf collected during the rainy season. *Saroo* (arum calocasia) leaves and *saroo* are also collected, cooked and eaten.

The palm-wine is drawn and used as a favourable drink. The fresh wine is very sweet but in a few hours it is fermented and becomes intoxicant. The Didayi women boil it at times to reduce the alcoholic content.

Tamarind is collected, consumed at home and the surplus is sold in weekly markets.

The Didayi gather *hiona* (tapenga), a kind red ant throughout the year. They make it into a paste with salt and chillies and eat.

Kendu leaves (*Diospyros melanoxylon*) are the most important non-edible leaves collected by the Didayi. They are used in the manufacturing of *biris*, the country made cheerut with tobacco.

The Didayi collect fuelwood to be mostly used at home as small logs of timber for house construction, bamboo for roofing and fencing, thatching grass, *siali* ropes and leaves, etc. Both men and women take part in forest collection. Reserved, protected as well as village forests found near the Didayi villages help them in food gathering and collection.

Although the forest area is gradually declining due to several factors, the dependence of the Didayi on forest is still a significant factor. The field investigation in these villages shows that 27.35 per cent of the average annual income of the Didayi comes from forest collection and food gathering, taken together.

Hunting

It has now become a past time due to depletion of forest and imposition of regulations in recent times. But importance of hunting has not disappeared from their life altogether. Some of them are skilled hunters who never miss any opportunity to hunt.

Bow and arrow are still used for shooting squirrel, hare and birds. A few guns have recently come to their hands. Animals like deer, sambar, kutra, etc., are hunted particularly in the annual hunting ceremony, called *goesendia hia* observed in the month of *Chaitra* (March-April) and also during the first eating ceremony, called *ghia panda* observed in *Baisakh* (April - May).

The Didayi hunt only in those forests in which they have rights. They do not dare to violate the boundary rule in respect of hunting and gathering.

Fishing

The Didayi who live on the banks of the Machakund river were spending a considerable time in catching fish. Presently about 14 Didayi villages have been submerged in water due to Balimela dam project and in the cut-off sub-area of the Chitrokonda reservoir. It has opened an avenue for fishing as a supplementary source of livelihood. The Didayi Development Agency (D.D.A.) at Kudumulugumma is encouraging the Didayis in cut-off sub-area and people by the side of reservoir to undertake fishing as an occupation by providing boats and nets for the purpose.

Didayis living in the interior hills seldom have the opportunity of coming down to the rivers, streams of the plains and bank of the reservoir for fishing. The Didayi of the plains go for fishing in the neighbouring perennial streams.

The annual average income from fishing has been calculated to be only Rs. 85.84 and for Cut-off sub-area it is Rs. 194.86.

Fishing as a source of livelihood has so far not gained much importance among them. It contributes on an average less than one per cent (0.81%) of their total income. Only in cut-off sub-area, its contribution is little higher, i.e., nearly 2 per cent (Survey COATS, 2002). The Didayis living in cut-off sub-areas and also by the side of the reservoir generally demand boats and nets to fish in the reservoir. The Didayi development project authorities in recent times have started providing boats and nets for the purpose to these villagers.

ANIMAL HUSBANDRY

Formerly the Didayi had no domesticated animals except pigs and dogs. Pig was one of the earliest domestic animals to be reared by them; mostly by the Hill Didayi. In the plains villages there are many households who own cows, buffaloes, oxen, goats, sheep, fowl and geese. Now in hill villages, Didayis have started keeping domestic animals, like cows, goats, sheep, fowl, etc. "It is worthwhile to mention, therefore, that the transition from hunting and collecting to cattle breeding is easier than from hunting and collecting to agriculture (Guha *et al.*, 1970:44).

The cattle are reared by them for ploughing and also as a source of meat Cows are not milched. They are also used in payment of bride price at the time of marriage. They are gradually leaving the habit of eating beef. At night cows and oxen are not tethered to wooden posts near the house but left free in the cattleshed. Recently only a few households in the plains have been reported milching cows. They supply milk mainly to local tea shops of Kudumulugumma (Guha, *et al.*, 1970:45). But majority of them neither milch their cows nor drink milk.

Contribution of livestock to the total annual income of the Didayi comes to be 11.83 per cent. Coming to its sub-area-wise break-up, in cut-off sub-areas it contributes 10.73 per cent, in hills sub-area 13.86

per cent and in plains sub-areas 8.71 per cent to the total annual income on an average (Survey by COATS, Koraput 2001-2002). The annual average income from livestock has been calculated to be Rs. 1,250 (Rs. 1060.94, Rs. 1457.60 and Rs. 981.70 in cut-off, hill and plain areas respectively). Availability of grass land in hills and cut off areas and still the existing forest area give an opportunity for livestock rearing in these areas.

Poultry

Almost all Didayi households have kept fowl, which is of considerable economic importance for them. Eggs are eaten sometimes by the Didayi children. Chickens are generally sold in the neighbouring markets. Sometimes they exchange fowls for clothes, ornaments and other commodities. Fowls are also used for sacrificial purposes.

Wage-earning

Landless families in the off season when agricultural activities are comparatively less, engage themselves in wage work. Wage labour has contributed 17.24 per cent to the total annual income of the Didayis. Its importance as a source of income is more prominent in plains sub-area as one-fourth (25.45%) of the total income of the people come from wage earning, as against 12.58 per cent and 14.95 per cent in cut-off sub-areas and hills sub-areas respectively (Table 3.2).

Table 3.2: Percentage Break-up of Annual Income of the Didayi in 3 Sub-areas by Economic Pursuits

Economic Activities	*Cut-off (296 households) sub-area*	*Hills (691 households) sub-area*	*Plains (326 households) sub-area*	*Total*
Agriculture	43.67	35.00	35.00	36.87
Livestock	10.73	13.86	8.71	11.83
Wage earning	12.58	14.97	25.45	17.24
Forest collection and Food gathering	28.53	29.00	22.93	27.35
Fishing	2.00	0.78	0.10	0.81
Services	0.34		2.72	0.80
Business	1.43	0.17	1.25	0.69
Others	0.72	6.22	3.84	4.41
Total	100.00	100.00	100.00	100.00

Source: Survey by COATS, Koraput, 2001-02

Table 3.3: Average Annual Income Per Hosuehold from Different Economic Activities and the Total Income of the Didayi Households in Different Sub-areas during 2001-2002 (in Rs.)

Economic Activities	*Cut-off (296 sub-area households)*	*Hills sub-area (691 households)*	*Plains sub-area (326 households)*	*Total*
Agriculture	4316.69	3684.52	3951.25	3893.26
Livestock	1060.94	1457.60	981.71	1250.00
Wage earning	1244.11	1574.67	2865.64	1820.68
Forest collection of Food gathering	2819.77	3060.63	2584.82	2888.20
Fishing	194.86	77.17	5.20	85.84
Services	33.78		306.74	83.84
Business	141.95	7.67	141.68	83.77
Others	71.40	651.25	432.00	71.22
Total	9883.50	10513.51	11269.04	10,176,91

Source: Survey COATS, Koraput 2001-02

By analysing the foregoing table it is evident that agriculture followed by forest produce collection (including food-gathering) are the two principal sources of livelihood of the Didayi. They have received 36.87 per cent of their total household income form agriculture, followed by forest produce collection (i.e. 27.35%). Hence agriculture and forest activities taken together have contributed as high as 64.22 per cent of the total income of the Didayi. Agriculture on an average has given Rs. 3893.26 as annual income per family, followed by forest produce collection, i.e., Rs. 2888.20. Hill people's dependence on forest is the highest as 29 per cent of their earnings have come from this source closely practised by them in the cut-off sub-area (28.53%) and plains sub-area (22.93%). Next to agriculture and forest activities comes the wage earning, which has contributed 17.24 per cent of the total annual income of the Didayi. Out of the three sub-areas, the contribution of wage work to their total income is the highest in plains (25.45%), followed by Hills (14.97%) and cut-off sub-area (12.58%) (Table 3.2).

There seems to be a good scope for livestock rearing in the Didayi country. On an average 11.83 per cent of the total income of Didayi households comes from livestock activities with an average of Rs. 1250 per annum. Other economic pursuits are of minor importance in these sub-areas (Table 3.3).

PRODUCTIVE FACTORS AND PRODUCTION DECISION

Over and above, a brief analysis of the nature and performance of factors of production and production decision may make the picture of the Didayi economy more clear and comprehensive. First of all, let us take the case of Land, the most important and the primary factor of production. The available land in the Didayi area may be classified under four broad heads, i.e., (a) Shifting or *podu* land, (b) *Dongar* (hill slope dry) land, (c) settled (low-lying paddy) land, and homestead (including *bari* or *kitchen* garden) land. In addition to these, there are forests on the hills adjacent to the villages, which include reserved, protected and unreserved categories. Didayis exploit these land resources both for cultivation and forest collection including food-gathering. The nature of the soil is rocky and red in most parts of the region. It is mostly porous having low water retaining capacity. The surface consists of undulating beds of laterite resting on rock beds.

Forests of the area contain deciduous species, like *sahaj*, *bije*, *simuli, dharua, kendu*, bamboo, etc., in the hilly region and *sal* and teak in the comparatively plains area.

Next to land, labour is the most important factor in tribal economy. The Didayi are found to be hard-working; and able-bodied persons Both men and women as well as children above six years of age are found to be engaged in various economic pursuits in the hills, forests and fields. Co-operative labour and exchange labour are the marked features in their socio-economic life. Cooperation and combination of efforts have been observed in the house-building, preparation of agricultural fields, and in ritual functions connected with hunting, sowing and harvesting.

The division of labour between sexes among the Didayi is more marked. The food-gathering is done by both men and women and also by children. In certain agricultural operations women help their male partners. Certain other activities, however, such as, hunting, ploughing and basket-making are exclusively done by males.

In a subsistence economy as that of the Didayi, there is little scope for saving out of the surplus income. The capital formation is at the rudimentary stage. Most of the Didayi farmers are unable to possess a set of required agricultural implements and pair of plough bullocks, particularly, those who have taken to settled cultivation. In the hill areas, the Didayi farmers, adopting shifting cultivation, have their indigenous tools which include axe, hoe, spade, and dibling stick, etc. Seeds are stored or purchased by the Didayi farmers for sowing in the fields. The Didayi Development Agency (D.D.A.) at Kudumulugumma has started providing help in the shape of agricultural implements and fishing aids, etc.

The Agency has started to supply agricultural implements, like plough, spade, crowbar, sickle, improved variety of seeds of paddy, ragi, maize, *biri*, *arhar*, *moong*, groundnut, soyabeen, turmeric, ginger, niger, mustard, wheat, horticultural seedlings of jack-fruit, pineapple, mango, coconut, lemon, papeya, cashew, guava, vegetable seeds ginger, lady's finger (*bheindi*), pumpkin, potato, tomato, brinjal, Onion, cauliflower, cabbage, chilly and cucumber and chemical fertilisers and pesticides. In addition to these nets and boats are provided for fishing to Didayis living in cut-off area and on the bank of river and reservoir.

The Didayi economy basically being a self-sufficient one is at the subsistence level organisation of economic activities centre around the family, the basic unit of production and consumption. Economic performances with an intention to earn profit and engaging labour and capital in the enterprises to that end is not very much found among them. They mostly attend the weekly markets not with an intention of doing business and trade but to exchange their goods against their essential requirements or to purchase these with cash.

The family being the basic unit of production, the production decision is mainly taken by the family members and the head of the family plays an important role.

AN ANALYSIS OF THE CONSUMPTION EXPENDITURE

From the COATS survey conducted for the purpose (see Table 3.4) it is found that average annual expenditure of a Didayi family comes to Rs. 10038.28, its monthly expenditure being Rs. 836.45. Of the total expenditure, food expenditure only consists of 54.78 per cent. About 10 per cent of the total household expenditure is estimated as expenditure on fuel. Although Didayi families collect fuel wood from the neighbouring forests without involving any expenditure except the labour imputed in it, the cost of fuel wood used by them has been estimated for the purpose of analysis. Little above 6 per cent of the expenditure is made on clothing and almost the same percentage of total expenditure is made on houses repairing including construction of new houses. It is interesting to note that about 6 per cent of the

Table 3.4: Table showing Annual and Monthly Average Expenditure per Household on Various Items and its Percentage (1,313 households), 2001-02

Sl. No.	*Items of Expenditure*	*Annual expenditure per H.H.*	*Monthly expenditure per H.H.*	*% to total expenditure*
1.	Food	5498.60	458.21	54.78
2.	Clothing	689.00	57.42	6.86
3.	Fuel	1000.59	83.38	9.97
4.	Kerosene Oil	282.24	23.52	2.81
5.	Medicine	106.00	8.83	1.06
6.	Festivals	459.18	38.24	4.57
7.	Agricultural Implements	80.56	6.71	0.80
8.	Marriage	70.65	5.88	0.70
9.	Birth/ Death	105.55	8.80	1.05
10.	House repairing	624.12	52.00	6.22
11.	Construction of new house	17.15	1.42	0.17
12.	Match box	51.64	4.30	0.51
13.	Drinking	226.65	18.88	2.26
14.	Tobacco	373.22	31.10	3.72
15.	Radio, cycle, watch	57.60	4.80	0.57
16.	Others.	395.53	32.96	3.95
	Total	10038.28	836.45	100.00

Source: Survey — COATS, Koraput, 2001-2002

total expenditure is made on both alcohol and tobacco, but the expenditure on tobacco is higher (Rs. 373.22, i.e., 3.72 %) than that of drinking (Rs. 226.65, i.e., 2.26%). Of the Didayi total expenditure (Rs. 459.18, i.e., 4.57%) covers the cost on festivals.

INCOME AND EXPENDITURE — AN ANALYSIS

From table 3.5 it is evident that on an average the Didayi have a self-sufficient economy, though at a subsistence level. The average annual income and expenditure nicely tallies with each other, with a marginal surplus of income Rs. 520.69 over expenditure. The surplus of income over expenditure is the highest in cut off sub-area (Rs. 583.18), followed by Hills sub-area (Rs. 520.02) and plains sub-area (Rs. 465.13).

As it was found during the survey that in 18 villages consisting of some families 7 in cut-off sub-area, 1 in Hills sub-area and 10 in plains sub-area have incurred loans amounting to Rs. 77,775 in total. This shows that of all the Didayi households, 1.37 per cent have reported to have incurred loans.

Table 3.5: Table showing Sub-area-wise Annual Per Household (H.H.) Average Income and Expenditure (1313 Didayi Households), 2001-02 (in Rs.)

Sl. No.	*Sub-areas*	*Annual Average Income*	*Annual average Expenditure*	*Surplus (+)/ or Deficit (–)*
1.	Cut-off (296 hh)	9883.50	9300.32	(+) 58318
2.	Hills (691 hh)	10513.51	9993.49	(+) 520.02
3.	Plains (326 hh)	11269.04	10803.91	(+) 465.13
4.	Average Grand Total	10558.97	10038.28	(+) 520.69

Source: Survey, COATS, Koraput 2001-2002.

CONSUMPTION

The Didayis have a subsistence economy and their major activities centre round the quest for food. Even in the villages where plough cultivation is found to exist, the majority of them still depend on food-gathering.

Ragi is the staple food of Diḍayis. They supplement their diet with rice, edible roots, fruits, tubers of various creepers and plants. Ragi is prepared as gruel and then taken. The Didayi of the plains take rice along with Ragi. There is no segregation of sexes in respect of taking their meals. Husband, wife, and children take their meals together. Generally, they do not waste their food.

The Didayis generally do not drink non-alchoholic beverages like milk, tea and coffee. The younger generation have started taking tea and coffee from tea shops of the neighbouring villages when they go out for marketing. *Salap*, the palm juice of caryota tree is drunk.

POVERTY IN THE DIDAYI AREA

On the basis of the measurement by the district and Block authorities to find out the households below the poverty line (BPL), i.e., Rs. 250

Table 3.6: Sub-area-wise Number of households (H.H.) living below the Poverty Line

Sl. No.	*Sub Areas*	*No. of H.H*	*No. of H.H. Below Poverty (BPL)*
1.	Plains	326 (100.00)	196 (60.12)
2.	Hills	691 (100.00)	496 (71.78)
3.	Cut-off	296 (100.00)	227 (76.69)
	Total	1313 (100.00)	919 (70.00)

Source: Calculated on the basis of the survey by (COATS), Koraput. 2001-02 (Figures in the brackets indicate percentages)

per capita expenditure per month, an attempt has been made to find out the number of Didayi households living below poverty line. Table 3.6 shows that 70 per cent of the total Didayi households still live below the poverty line (BPL) as per survey of COATS, Koraput, 2001-02.

Out of the sub-areas, it is in the cut-off area that maximum number of people found to be poor, i.e., 227 out of 296 which is estimated to be 76.69 per cent, followed by Hills sub-area (71.78%) and plains sub-area (60.12%). In this connection, it is relevant to state that the B.P.L. for the Malkangiri district and Kudumulugumma Block was 82 per cent and 90 per cent respectively as per 1997 survey. The B.P.L. position for Odisha State in 1999-2000 was estimated as 47.15 per cent of which the rural and urban percentage came to 48.01 per cent and 42.83 per cent respectively (Govt. of Odisha, 2002:12).

EXCHANGE AND DISTRIBUTION

In the recent past, the Didayi possessed a self-sufficient economy, though at the subsistence level. They derived major share of their requirements from their surrounding land hills and forests. They constructed house with the materials collected from neighbouring jungles without taking prior permission from officials of the Forest Department, and with the co-operation of members of his family, relatives and friends within a couple of days. For food each household was self-sufficient. They raised various kinds of pulses and millets in the hill slopes. There was the provision of the direct exchange of goods and services among themselves. All the families were raising same crops or the other and the surrounding forests offered equal opportunities to the food collectors. Pigs, goats and chicken were reared by them but they were never exchanged on barter. Fines for violating social customs were imposed in terms of these animals.

Didayis were buying tools and implements used in food gathering, hunting, shifting cultivation and preparation of food, etc., mainly from the neighbouring weekly markets. The men made their gourd containers, bows and arrows, prepared baskets and mats, etc., while the women could weave clothes and were engaged in domestic works and in looking after pigs, goats and chickens, etc.

Still there were many tools, which the Didayi could not produce by themselves, *viz.*, the arrow head, the iron hoe blades, the iron part of digging stick, iron axe to fell trees and clear forests and knife for basketry. All these iron implements were procured from outside. In exchange of forest produce, baskets and ragi, etc., pots have been bartered from the potters of the plains. In course of time, the Didayi left their traditional bark clothes. No Didayi woman now weaves bark clothes. Now the cotton clothes have been bartered. Ornaments have been bought in exchange, chillies, salt, grains, pulses, oil seeds, vegetables, fish, rice and tamarind are still bartered in the villages and neighbouring markets. Sometimes outsiders come with commodities, like salt, match box, dry fish, potato, tomato, etc., to exchange pulses and grains with them. Cash payment to buy dress, iron implements, pots and cattle are comparatively recent happenings.

In addition, there are extra-economic exchanges in their community by way of gifts and presentations.

MONETIZATION OF ECONOMY

Money has now become the medium of exchange among the Didayi. The self-sufficient economy of the Didayi has now been disrupted. The extension of effective political administration to the hill areas and the growing contacts of the Didayi with the caste Hindu people of the plains are the major reasons for this. When the hill villages were brought under the revenue administration, the Didayi were asked to make money payments for the use of land and forest produce.

In order to pay their dues to revenue and forest authorities, the Didayi have to dispose of their produce and animals for cash in the neighbouring markets instead of bartering them. Their contact with the plains people gradually increased. Articles, such as salt, spices, clothes, metals, aluminium utensils and ornaments which were once luxuries to them have now become necessaries. Comparatively better off Didayi families are now in possession of radio, watch and torch, etc. Gradually new wants have been stimulated among them. Above all the shift to new economy brought the Didayi into close contact with the advanced methods of agricultrue. The Didayi of the plains have adopted plough cultivation using cows and bullocks, whereas the Didayi of hills still practise shifting cultivation. For plough cultivation in the plains, the Didayi need cattle. Most of them do not have sufficient money to buy cattle. Hence, they have to buy them on credit or borrow a pair of cows or bullocks against a share of crop.

Formerly, the Didayi were passing rent partly in cash and partly in kind but now they have to pay only in terms of cash. They feel it as a great burden. The Revenue Inspector collects land revenue from them in cash. As requirement for cash payment have increased, they are now forced to sell rice, ragi, and other forest produce for deriving cash.

DISTRIBUTION

The crops produced in the fields (Shifting *dongar*, settled and garden) and items collected from forests are mostly meant for self consumption; and a small portion of it is meant for exchange in the market. Land areas mostly are self-owned, and there is not much evidence of hiring land on rent for cultivation. Labour used in agricultural and forest operations are family labour to a great extent, and hired labour is used mainly settled agriculture, construction works and forest operations. To a great extent the system of exchange labour is prevailing in these areas. Hired labours are paid mostly in kind and sometimes in cash. There are some cases of interest payment on loans incurred for purchase of agricultural implements and plough bullocks etc. The DDA, at Kudumukugumma is now supplying seeds and plants with a marginal payment of cost. Of course, economic benefit schemes where a loan content is there, the interest is to be paid and capital to be repaid. There is prevalence of the system of mutual ceremonial exchange of goods among clan members and relations including exchange of labour.

POLITICAL LIFE

In the recent past, the Didayi had well organised socio-political organisations at different levels. Their traditional territorial organisation could be classified into three categories (i) The central organisation of the entire tribe embracing all their villages; (ii) regional organisations and (iii) the village organisations (Guha *et al.*, 1970)

The central political organisation with its headquarters at Kudumulugumma is now defunct. A number of problems relating to the tribe were discussed and settled. The meeting was attended by most of the office bearers of the Didayi villages such as the *Naik*, the *Chalan* and other responsible memebrs (Guha *et al.*, 1970:85). Inter-village and inter-clan problems which could not be solved by smaller political organisations were placed for consideration by the central political organisation.

The regional organisations comprised only a few contiguous or neighbouring villages having more or less similar geographical situation. These regional organisations consisted of villages having common forest territories. The villages coming under one regional group had the right to exploit the fauna and flora of the forest and select patches of land for shifting cultivation. The non-Didayi living in these villages such, as *Doms, Komars* and others also have similar rights regarding exploitation of land and forest on account of their domicile in any of the villages in the group.

Solidarity to a limited extent is found among the villages in a group. Sometimes joint hunting explorations are arranged, they remained in readiness to come to each other's help in the event of any threat from outside. This also found a substantial mutual dependence for acquisition of spouses in these villages.

Of all the territorial organisations the village known as *hini* in their language is the most important. It is more or less economically self-sufficient. It has also substantial control and access to most of the economic resources. It regulates the annual cycle of their activities and is politically independent. Certain clans in the village have specific functions in regard to the entire community.

The traditional Village Panchayat or the village council (*lepar*) is the old and most powerful socio-political organisation at the village level. Every head of the household and in fact every adult male has the right to participate in the meetings of the Village Council. The Village Council is a well-organized and powerful organisation. Its function embrace all corporate activities in social, political, economic and religious spheres of the village.

The headman of the village is called the *Naik*, who is assisted by the *Chalan and Barik*. They along with adult male members from each family constitute the Village Council. It decides cases brought before it relating to such matters as theft, quarrel, divorce, desertion, and offences of sex, etc. It imposes punishment according to nature of the case mostly in terms of fine.

The council, in consultation with the village *Palasi*, the priest, decides about the dates of sacrifices and offerings to various deities and celebration of the annual festivals it collects funds from villagers for the offerings and sacrifices and for performance of ritual.

The council functions through its office bearers particularly the headman (*Naik*) and his executive assistant, the *Chalan* and these posts are hereditary.

Panchayati Raj System, Panchayats (Extension to Scheduled Areas) Act, 1996 and After

In the post-independence period, statutory panchayats were created and later the Panchayati Raj was extended to the scheduled areas. The elected leaders then came forward to lead and manage the village affairs. Any villager can now seek the election for the purpose. He becomes the elected member of his village to represent in Gram Panchayat comprising of a number of contiguous villages. Because of his contacts with the Panchayat and other officials in the Block level, the elected Panchayat member has considerable influence in the village.

Now, the functioning of statutory Panchayats and Panchayati Raj system in the tribal areas of Odisha is gradually being shaped according to the provisions of the Panchayats (Extension to the Scheduled Areas) Act, 1996 which was meant to extend the provisions of the 73rd Constitutional Amendment Act of 1992 to the Scheduled V areas in the country. The Central Act No. 40 of 1996 is very significant in the sense that it accords statutory status to the "Gram Sabhas" with wide ranging powers and authority. The Act says, "A State legislation on the Panchayats shall be in consonance with the customary law, social and religious practices and traditional management practices of community resources." These provisions aimed at strengthening the community way of living in the tribal areas and also ushering them in a new era of self-governance, based on basic premises of participative democracy.

The provisions of the Central Act were adopted in Odisha, by amending the Odisha Gram Panchayats Act, 1964; Odisha Panchayat Samiti Act, 1959, and Odisha Zilla Parishad Act, 1961. The amendments to those acts were passed by the State Legislature in 1997. The Principal Act of Odisha states that there shall be a Gram Sasan (local version of Gram Sabha) for every *gram* (village).

The Principal Act of Odisha amended in accordance with the Panchayats (Extension to Scheduled Areas) Act, 1996 has demarcated the scope of important activities in all tiers for the Gram Sabha, Gram Panchayat, Panchayat Samiti and Zilla Parishad in the following manner:

(i) The Zilla Parishad has been entrusted with the activities, like grant of licence or mining lease and grant of concession for exploitation of minor minerals.

(ii) As regards enforcement of prohibition or to regulate and restrict the consumption of any intoxicant, ownership of minor forest produce, prevention of alienation of land and restoration, management of village markets, and money lending in scheduled areas the Gram Sabha (Gram Sasan) is to control and the Gram Panchayat is to execute.

(iii) The Panchayat Samiti will exercise control over institutions in social sectors.

(iv) Regarding control over local plans and resources including the Tribal Sub-Plans — the Gram Sabha is to be consulted while preparing plans and the Panchayat Samiti is to prepare the Plan and exercise control over it.

In order to get an indepth idea as stipulated by the Planning Commissioin, about the present status of traditional Panchayats in the Didayi area after the introduction and functioning of statutory Panchayats, a sample opinion survey in some Didayi villages was undertaken. As many as 150 persons from 6 different Didayi villages were interviewed which included villagers of different age-groups and also traditional village functionaries (i.e., *Nayak, Pujari* and *Chalan*, etc.) and Statutory Panchayat leaders, like Ward Members, Samiti Members and Sarpanchs, etc. The important findings of the survey are discussed hereunder:

(a) Traditional village councils exist in each Didayi village with their office bearers, like the *Naik* (headman), *Pujari* (priest), *Dissari* (medicine man-cum-magician) and *Chalan* (village messenger). People have faithes and respect for the traditional leaders of the village council.

(b) The traditional Village Council sits on an average 10 to 12 times a year to decide matters, like observance of festivals, marriage related problems, litigations and quarrels of minor nature, and disputes on land, etc. Cases of serious nature, like murder are referred to police stations and major types of quarrels, disputes and litigations, which cannot be decided at village level are referred to leaders, like Sarpanchs and Chairman of Panchayat Samiti, etc., or, in few cases, (of very serious nature) to the courts.

(c) In accordance with the Amended Panchayat Act passed in Odisha Legislature (1997) Palli Sabhas have been constituted at village level and Gram Sabhas at the Panchayat level in the tribal villages. All the persons in a village whose names appear in the voter's list are also members of Palli Sabha.

(d) In the Palli Sabhas of the Didayi villages the office bearers of the traditional village councils automatically become members (as their names are there in the village voters list). The villagers admitted that in the meetings of the Palli Sabha the opinion of traditional village leaders, like *Naik* and *Pujari*, etc., is taken into account and given due weightage.

(e) It was revealed by the villagers interviewed that they have so far avoided contests in case of election to the post of village Ward members. All the villagers generally meet in a sitting of the village council and unanimously select one person as Ward Member. This shows the unity that exists among the villagers in a Didayi village. It was found that young persons are preferred to be elected for the post of Ward Members. However, there have been contests so far as elections to the posts, like Samiti Members, Sarpanch and Chairman of Panchayat Samiti, etc., are concerned. At least one-third of the seats have been reserved for women candidates, in these Didayi villages. The present chairperson of Kudumulugumma Block is a Didayi woman.

(f) Another fact which came to light during the discussion in these villages is that the villagers of a particular village were not so far divided on the basis of party politics in the sense that all the villagers cast their votes in favour of a single person, to whichever party he might belonged to. However, about 40 per cent of persons interviewed confessed that political party functionaries try to convince the voters, but the Didayi people are not very much influenced.

(g) Functionaries of statutory Panchayats including Ward Members, Samiti Members, Sarpanchs, etc., take decisions on developmental activities in the area. Such activities include construction of roads, minor irrigation projects, functioning of schools, *Anganwadis* and health centres, etc. These matters and also selection of beneficiaries, e.g., for *Indira Awas*, and BPL, etc., are first decided at the village level in the Palli Sabhas and again taken at the Gram Sabha for final decision. In such matters decisions taken by the Statutory Panchayats are never contradicted by traditional leaders.

From the above analysis, we may infer that in spite of new Panchayat System, the Didayis are still found to preserve their traditional socio-political institutions. The status of the traditional Panchayat system has not been completely undermined due to the introduction of the statutory Panchayats in the Didayi villages. It is good thing that the traditional functionaries are taken into confidence and involved in the meetings of the Palli Sabha. Both the institutions, i.e., the traditional political organisation and Statutory Panchayats, are complementary and neither competitive nor contradictory to each other in the Didayi area. If this spirit is maintained, then there is a good future for successful functioning of statutory panchayats in the tribal areas in general and the Didayi area in particular.

Consequent upon the opinion survey conducted by COATS for in-depth study the roles of the traditional socio-political organisation among the Didayi *vis-à-vis* the new Panchayat System, it transpires that the people have accepted the new system in spite of their respect for the traditional organisation. Since the tradition and modernity do not conflict and clash with each other, rather show cooperation, it would be better not to go back at this critical phase. The new Panchayat System has cherished hopes and aspirations and gained confidence in the Didayi area at the micro context. Keeping in view the Pan-Indian context of Panchayat System and its philosophy and policy frame, the Didayi people have already welcomed it. It is also noticed that the vitality and vigour of traditional political organisations are more devoted for looking into social aspects for the maintenance of social order. The young and enthusiastic Didayi people are in favour of Statutory Panchayat System and it is hoped that the onus lies in them to march ahead with the ongoing socio-economic development interventions and it would, no doubt, bring a better future for them.

RELIGIOUS LIFE

The religious life of the Didayi centres round the worship of Mother Earth represented in a big stone, called *Bribu*. Though Mother Earth is regarded as the supreme being, the name *Mahapru* identifies as the creator which is uttered at the time of each worship. Their pantheon includes several gods and goddesses. They are *Bhirubhairo* and *Nahnangri, Bangur* and *Raskurka, Goa* and *Sendia, Rau* and *Aksia, Goud* and *Suni, Thakrani* and *Burima, Bok* and *pa*, as their gods and goddesses respectively.

Deities are propitiated at regular intervals through a series of religious ceremonies round the year. The festival *Lendi Pande* signifies beginning of the agricultural cycle observed in the month of *Magha* (January-February). It is observed very elaborately in honour of Mother Earth. In the month of *Chaita* (March - April), ceremonial sowing of seeds is done by village priest. The ceremony is called *Sibo Love Hia* in honour of *Iswar* and *Parvati*. It is followed by annual hunting ceremony in the same month called *Goesendia Hia*. *Ghia Pande* is another important festival observed in April-May which makes the first eating of new fruits like *sal* seeds, mango, *mahua* flower, etc., followed by ceremonial hunting. *Dihir Hia* and *Gonghir Hia* mark the beginning of ceremonial harvesting of the main crop rice in the month of *Pond* (November- December). The *Pusarke Pande* is the closing religious ceremony of the year celebrated in the month of *Pus* (December-January).

On the occasion of each of the ceremonies sacrifice of animals like fowl, goat and pig is common. These are celebrated with dancing and singing continuously for several days.

The post of *Palasi* or village priest requires some amount of specialisation. It is not a hereditary post. But it generally remains in the hands of the descendants of the outgoing *Palasi* as they have better opportunities for acquiring the knowledge required for the job. It thus remains practically in the same lineage for generations. Even the village council has the power to elect any one for the post of *Palasi* without any regard to hereditary principles.

The Palasi is responsible for conducting all rituals in connection with collective offerings on behalf of the village. He propitiates the ancestral spirits to prevent them from doing harms to the village. He performs special functions on the occasion of festivals, before villages start for hunting, etc. He advises the Naik and other village elders in regard to fixation of date for celebration of annual festivals in the village.

In addition, there are magico-religious practitioners (*gunias*) and shahman in the Didayi community.

SOCIALISATION ENCULTURATION AND EDUCATION

Socialisation is a process by which an individual acquires values, ethos and skills required to live in a society meaningfully. In this process a number of social agencies, e.g., home, school, group, cult, temple and shrine, churches, State, print media, and radio and television, etc., are involved. It, therefore, is a life long process and varies from society to society depending upon the socio-cultural environment, resources available or social setting to which an individual is exposed. In the process of socialisation of the Didayi two agencies, namely, family or home and immediate social environment, play vital role. A Didayi child, during the early years of his life, is exposed a little to the outer modern world. He is mostly confined to his home and village, i.e., the immediate social environment. Many Didayi habitations are found unserved or ill served by formal schools due to various reasons including poor communication facilities, size of habitations being small, and teacher absenteeism. In such situations majorities of the school-aged population fail to pursue formal education and are, therefore, exposed only to family and other social institutions. It was observed that the children, particularly aged 6-11 years are found either at home/village or at cultivated field (*Dongar* and Wet Land). The girl child at home is normally engaged in taking care of younger siblings and performing household activities whereas the male children at *Dongar*/wet land help their parents in cultivation, e.g., cleaning lands, fetching water, harvesting, etc. It was futher learnt that some Didayi couple, during sowing as well as harvesting, proceed usually to their *podu* field along with wards of all ages and prepared food, in the morning and return home in the evening. In such situation, the male children above 10 years age assist their parents in physical work.

It can be noted from the usual performance of the Didayi children that they acquire basic life skills, such as earning livelihood and undertaking responsibilities in future informally. Presentation of the following case study makes the issues concerning the process of socialisation more transparent.

CASE STUDY OF A DIDAYI FAMILY

Two associate investigators during their fieldwork in hills sub-area along with a team of five field investigators, met a Didayi family on their way from Samanathpur (G.P. headquarters) to Karkaguda through steep ghats. The family consists of five members, namely, K. Muduli (Husband) aged about 38 years; B. Muduli (wife) aged about 30 years; and three children; A. Muduli (son), L. Muduli (son), P. Muduli (daughter) aged about 13 years, 10 years and 1 year respectively. It was 12 noon, all the five memebrs of the family were in their shifting cultivation land around 2 kms away from village. Wife and husband were busy in harvesting of *niger* (a kind of oil seed), while the eldest son was fetching drinking water from the nearby stream in a plastic container and the second son was caring his one year old daughter in a hut built almost at the centre of the *podu* land. They have occupied nearly three acres of land and growing ragi, *alsi* and cumin, etc. Both wife and husband are illiterate and their sons aged 13 years and 10 years are not enrolled in primary school. To our question as to why A. Muduli and L. Muduli are not enrolled in primary school, the father replied at once and smartly that his village does not have a school and the nearest primary school is at a distance of about.12 kms from their village Karkaguda. The wife was shy and not able to communicate clearly. K. Muduli (husband) reported that they spend around 5 months a year, particularly during sowing and harvesting seasons, in their temporary hut in shifting cultivation land. They usually leave home in the morning with cooked food, stay in the field for the whole day and return back home in the afternoon everyday.

The situation narrated in the above case study implies that family plays a vital role in the process of socialization of a Didayi child.

The process of socialization during adolescence and youth was found to be regulated by the youth dormitory. Dormitory is a non-kinship association found in almost every Didayi village separately for boys and girls. A dormitory is normally a small hut located at the centre of the village, where adolescent and young boys /girls make merry and sleep together at night. Dormitory provides ample scope for interaction and exchange of skills among the members, which have immense implications for their adult life. The two associate investigators had a night halt in the male dormitory of the village Karkaguda. Their experiences recorded in the filed notes revealed that dormitory is not simply a resting place rather a seat of training, recreation, amusement, learning and living together, through mutual help and cooperation and exchange of skills, knowledge and ideas.

The area inhabited by the Didayi is an educationally priority area. The educational profile of the area and the people with reference to access (enrolment) and retention, rate of literacy and infrastructural facilities are discussed as follows (Table 3.7):

The data presented in Table 3.7 indicated that the rate of dropout among the Didayi children at Primary stage is as high as 90.31 per cent. The corresponding figures for the boys and girls are 87.27 per cent and 94.19 per cent respectively.

Table 3.7: Enrolment of the Didayi Children at Primary School Stage from 1997-98 to 2001-02 by Sex

Year	I			II			III			IV			V		
	Enrolment in Classes I - V														
	B	G	T	B	G	T	B	G	T	B	G	T	B	G	T
1997-98	110	86	196	54	37	91	65	43	108	28	32	60	34	19	53
1998-99	119	85	204	59	39	98	70	55	125	49	40	89	37	24	61
1999-2000	54	33	87	57	43	100	42	28	70	25	22	47	28	11	39
2000-2001	79	61	140	66	57	123	39	26	65	26	19	45	19	16	35
2001-2002	92	67	159	71	55	126	62	46	108	24	15	39	14	5	19

Source: Office of the Block Education, Officer, Kudumulugumma Block, Malkangiri. 2001-2002 (B-Boys, G-Girls, T-Total)

Table 3.8: Didayi Villages of Malkangiri District by Population, access to Primary Education, Number of Teachers and the existence of School Building.

Name of the village	*Total Population*	*Pop. Aged 06-11 yrs*	*Primary School*	*Nearest Primary School*	*No. of Teachers*	*School Building*	*Literacy rate*		
							M	*F*	*T*
Hills Sub-Area									
Karkaguda	158	23	No	8 km	—	—	0.0	0.0	0.0
Nilapari	137	16	Yes	—	4	Yes	29.85	13.16	21.90
Ambilibeda	284	34	Yes	—	3	Yes	12.21	0.0	5.63
Bataguda	96	12	No	—	—	No	0.0	0.0	0.0
Ghisingbeda	257	43	No	6 km	—	—	3.91	0.0	1.95
Gangapoda	316	46	Yes	—	1	Yes	1.21	0.66	0.95
Suripoda	95	16	No	3 km		—	8.70	0.0	4.21
Badankiguda	265	30	Yes	—	1	Yes	0.0	0.0	0.0
Angurguda	66	17	No	5 km	—	—	0.0	0.0	0.0
Muduliguda(B)	18	5	No	4 km	—	—	0.0	0.0	0.0
Khajariguda	132	22	No	3 km	—	—	0.0	0.0	0.0
Naringijhola	126	20	Yes	—	2	Yes	1.54	0.0	0.79
Bayapada	160	38	Yes	—	2	No	10.0	2.22	5.63
Tikarpada(B)	149	30	No	12 km	—	—	0.0	0.0	0.0
Barulbandh	86	13	No	8 km	—	—	0.0	0.0	0.0

(*Contd.*)

Table 3.8 (*Contd.*)

Name of the village	*Total Population*	*Pop. Aged 06-11 yrs*	*Primary School*	*Nearest Primary School*	*No. of Teachers*	*School Building*	*Literacy rate*		
							M	*F*	*T*
Hills Sub-Area									
Bamaring	84	18	No	10 km			0.0	0.0	0.0
Kaning	117	18	Yes				27.42	7.27	17.95
Damodarbeda	464	70	Yes		1	Yes	11.01	0.0	5.39
Cut-Off Sub-Area									
Orapadar	279	41	Yes		2	Yes	6.47	0.0	3.23
Totaguda	81	15	No		1	Yes	21.74	0.0	12.35
Dhakadpadar	197	43	No	3 km			11.43	0.0	6.09
Dabuguda	145	25	Yes		1	Yes	8.82	0.0	4.14
Jantry	78	14	Yes		1	No	37.50	7.89	23.08
Taberu	162	20	No		1	No	0.0	0.0	0.0
Maribeda	71	9	No	4 km			0.0	0.0	0.0
Disariguda	70	10	No	2 km			29.63	3.33	12.86
Arlingpada	34	2	No	5 km			0.0	0.0	0.0
Nadimanjri	61	11	No	6 km			0.0	0.0	0.0
Kantamanjri	49	8	No	5 km			0.0	0.0	0.0
Bhojaguda	5		No	4 km			50.0	0.0	20.0
Sanyasiguda	23	8	Yes		1	Yes	20.0	0.0	8.70
Andirapalli	19	7	Yes		2	Yes	20.0	11.11	15.79
Ramguda	17	1	No	5 km			25.0	0.0	11.76
Plains Sub-Area									
Muduliguda (A)	379	45	Yes		2	Yes	51.65	16.75	33.51
Tikarpada(A)	197	35	No	9 km			3.13	0.0	1.52
Purunaguma	182	34	Yes		2	Yes	50.57	24.21	36.81
Oringi	571	90	Yes		3	Yes	30.96	8.62	19.61
Chelipadar	67	06	Yes		2	Yes	24.24	8.82	16.42
Kudumuluguma	15	04	Yes		5	Yes	50.0	28.57	40.0

Source: Survey of COATS, Koraput, 2001-2002

The finding of Table 3.8 indicates that out of 39 Didayi inhabited villages as many as 19 villages do not have primary schools within the habitations nor within a distance of one kilometre. The children of these villages, therefore, do not have access to primary education. The village, namely, Ghisingbeda (see Sl. No. 5 Table No. 3.8) with a population of 257 has neither a primary school within the village nor within a distance of one kilometre. It can further be seen that out of 20 primary schools in Didayi inhabited villages eight are single teacher schools and four are without building of their own. The percentage of literacy among the Didayi was calculated to be as low as 7.89 per cent. The corresponding percentage for males and females are 12.56 and 3.36 respectively. In view of the natural barriers, like hills, forest and streams; and distance between school less habitations and the nearest primary schools, it is imperative on the part of the respective authorities of the government to establish primary schools/ NFE centres in all the 19 villages which are currently without school. It is further necessary to appoint additional teachers in eight single teacher schools; and construct building for four schools run without building.

HEALTH AND SANITATION

The Didayi men and women are well-built with slim body. They have smiling face and friendly look. Although the houses are kept clean by plastering the floors and walls with cowdung, the inside rooms remain mostly dark, as there is no provision of window in the rooms. There is no provisioin of drainage of waste water or rainwater from the house site. Naturally paths and lanes of the village remain mostly muddy in rainy season and dirty in other seasons.

People still suffer from malaria. They also suffer from hookworms, dysentery and conjunctivitis. They have still faith in supernatural beings, and offer sacrifices and take the help of traditional magico religious functionaries to be cured from serious diseases.

After the working of the Didayi Development Agency, Multipurpose Workers (MPWs) have been imparted with training by the local medical authority. The MPWs are supplied with medicines by the DDA, like Lariago, Paracitamol, Flagilf, Metron and Dependal tablets for malarial fevers and diarrhoea, etc. The serious patients are brought to the nearest hospital for their treatment. At Nakamamudi G.P. in the hill sub-area and Andirapalli in cut-off area medical facilities are available where one doctor, one ANM and one attendant each are posted. There is a PHC at Kudumulugumma. However, long distance of the villages from these centres and lack of communication pose serious hurdles for carrying patients to available medical centres.

VALUE ORIENTATIONS

The Didayi is a small community where each member is a valuable asset for the community. There is mutual love and cooperation among them. They are more receptive and more open minded people. In honour and cheerfulness, few tribal people can surpass the Didayi.

The Didayi is frank and honest. Petty thefts and non-payment of debts are almost unknown. There is no beggary among them. Greedy persons are disliked by them. They are very much hospitable in nature.

The Didayi are free, independent and open-minded people. They do not consider themselves inferior to anyone. They seem not to nourish hatred or anger much. There are very few instances of taking vengeance. In this respect we find a uniqueness among Didayi. Their tolerance helps in conflict resolution in a reasonable way.

The Didayi passionately love to their children and their land. Tolerance forms the core of their personality. They give importance and prominence to their women counterparts. In the management of hosuehold affairs women has the upper hand. Woman is the virtual power inside and outside home.

Live and let live is the underlying philosophy of the Didayi life. Deep sympathy, and delicate understanding guide them in their actions (Guha *et al.*, 1970: 239). Cooperative spirit and mutual help is marked in the spheres of socio-economic activities among them.

There are many such growth-positive traits in the Didayi value-orientation, which may be properly utilised, while implementing schemes for their development. As for example, they have learnt from their forefathers to exploit and utilise natural resources without causing damage to the natural environment, which may be regarded as a growth positive trait. They adhere to the pernicious practice of shifting cultivation under compulsions.

EPISTEMOLOGICAL ISSUES

Like many other tribes, the Didayi are the men of hills and forests who have the intimate relationship with the natural and supernatural elements. Since time immemorial they have developed their knowledge and expertise in the construction of their houses, preparation of agricultural fields, use of available water resources both for drinking and irrigation, crop rotation, and exploitation of forest resources, etc., suiting to the ecology or environment in which they live. Although they are mostly illiterate, they possess working knowledge about their environment. They have their own indigenous skills inherited from their forefathers, which they timely utilise to sustain their economy, though at a subsistence level. Living in the interior hills and forests, having less contact with the outside world, they could satisfy their limited needs of life by exploiting the available land, forest and water resources. Their self-sufficient life system has been disturbed in recent years, like that of many other tribes, with the degradation of natural resources including forests.

When the children in the Didayi society grow up, they acquire knowledge regarding physical cleanliness, food gathering, cultivation and hunting, etc., and also behavioural patterns, like respecting elders welcoming and treating guests mostly through socialization and verbal instructions. Their oral literature is very rich in folktales, myths, songs, riddles, and proverbs. They have plenty of games, both indoor and outdoor.

4

Planned Development Intervention

The concept of National Extension Service Block later on converted as Community Development Blocks was started as a, "means to initiate in the villages certain process of growth that would progressively raise the level of rural life economically and socially" (Government of Odisha, 1957: 79). It aimed at helping the rural communities to help themselves in all matters of rural development. In order to take additional care for the development of tribal areas, Special Multipurpose Tribal Development Blocks (S.M.P.T.) were started in the second Five Year Plan. These S.M.P.T. Blocks were renamed as Tribal Development Blocks (T.D.B.) during the Third Plan when the programme was further intensified on the recommendations of Elwin Committee.

BLOCK DEVELOPMENT EFFORT

Kudumulugumma and Govindapalli (presently known as Khairaput) Blocks were converted as Tribal Development Blocks during the Third Plan period, i.e., 1965-66. The main objective of the conversion was to bring about rapid improvement in the socio-economic status of the tribal people by supplementing the provisions available under the normal Community Development budget in especially under-developed but compact areas.

The development efforts made by the Block authorities was negligible till the end of the Fourth Plan period. The available data for the year 1970-71 reveals that out of 250 hectares of land irrigated from different sources in the erstwhile Malkangiri Sub-Division, only 5 hectares were irrigated in Kudumulugumma Block (Government of India, Ministry of Works and Housing; 1974: 30). Out of 33 Service

Co-operative Societies in the sub-division only three service co-operative societies were existing in the Block (Project Report for Malkangiri Integrated Tribal Development Project, 1976: 16). The service co-operative societies were opened at Kudumulugumma, Somnathpur and Panasput, which were either in the Block Headquarters or nearer the Block Headquarters. Out of 19 weekly markets in the project area only two weekly markets, i.e., Kudumulugumma and Mundaguda were functioning in the Block. Out of 12 sale sub-centres of the Malkangiri Branch of Tribal Development Co-operative Corporation (TDCC) in the area only one was functioning at Kudumulugumma. The communication facilities were extremely inadequate. As against 7 kms and 4 kms of road length for 100 square miles for the State and the district respectively, it was as low as 0.27 kms in the project area. Only 26 kms of Panchayat Samiti and Gram Panchayat Road existed in 1974-75 in Kudumulugumma Block (Ihud 1976:p.178). The facilities for providing health services were extremely poor. Only one P.H.C., three sub-centres and provision of indoor facilities for six persons existed in the Block.

The educational opportunities created in the Kudumulugumma Block was very poor as compared to the needs of the people. There were only 47 L.P.and U.P. schools and one middle school available in the Block during 1974-75 to meet the needs of 3,050 children in the age group of 6-14. The literacy rate of the Didayi, declined from 2.72 per cent in 1961 Census to 0.78 per cent in 1971 Census due to non-availability and non-functioning of schools in the Block.

Educational Institutions

The following socio-economic infrastructures have been created through the efforts made by the Block authorities in the Didayi Development Agency Project area. One residential Girls High School has been established at Purunagumma and one UGME School at Nakamamudi, 18 Primary Schools have been established by the Education Department for providing educational facilities in the project area. Five of them are located in the cut-off sub-area, eight in the hills sub-area and five in the plains sub-area in the villages detailed below. In addition three more primary schools with hostel have been established by H & TW Department at Nakamamudi, Rasobeda and Andirapalli.

Cut- off sub-area	*Hills Sub-Area*	*Plain Sub-Area*
1. Orapadar	1. Bayapada	1. Oringi
2. Sanyasiguda	2. Badankiguda	2. Muduliguda (A)
3. Jantry	3. Damodarbeda	3. Purunagumma
4. Andirapalli	4. Amblibeda	4. Chelipadar
5. Dabuguda	5. Kaning	5. Kudumulugumma
	6. Nilapari	
	7. Naring Jhola	
	8. Gangapada	

Health Facilities

There is only one Primary Health Centre located at the Block headquarters, Kudumulugumma, on the main road connecting Jeypore-Balimela-Chitrokonda. There are only two A.N.M. centres in the project area. In the absence of a Medical Aid Centre nearer the cut-off sub-area and hills sub-area villages they mainly depend on the *Disari* (the local medicine man) for their health care.

Veterinary Service

The Veterinary Dispensary at Kudumulugumma and one Livestock Inspector Centre at Jantry are the only service centres in the entire project area for treating the domesticated animals.

Electrification

No village in the project area has been electrified till today. In few villages, like Totaguda, Jantry, Orapadar, and Solar photovoltaic lights have been supplied.

Communication

Only five villages in the project area, namely Oringi, Muduliguda, Purunagumma, Chilipadar and Nilapari are approachable by jeep. The fifteen villages situated in the cut-off sub-area located across river Machhkund are negotiable by boat/launch on the Balimela reservoir. The Hills sub-area villages and the villages in the cut-off sub-area are approached by foot only.

Co-operative Institutions

The LAMPS at Kudumulugumma Block Headquarters has been established to meet the credit-cum-marketing requirements of the 'Didayi' project area. However, due to absence of sub-centres, it is not able to play an effective role in providing services in the project area.

Indira Awas Yojana (IAY)

Sixty-eight poor households have been provided with housing facilities under Indira Awas Yojana by the Block authorities as a measure of poverty alleviation programme.

Self-Help Groups (SHGs)

In order to empower the women thirtythree Self Help Groups have been formed in 21 Didayi villages during the period from June 2000 to September 2000. These SHGs will enable the women to generate additional income. Only 3 out of the 33 S.H.Gs. have received incentive grant of Rs. 10,000 recently. The members in these S.H.Gs. vary from 11 to 20 and there are 494 women members in these 33 S.H.Gs.

DIDAYI DEVELOPMENT AGENCY EFFORTS

It has been mentioned earlier that the Didayi Development Agency (DDA) was created in August 1986, *vide* Government Resolution No. 23449, dated 5-8-1986. The Agency was registered under the Society Registration Act, 1860 on 17-10-86 with the main objective of alround development of the 'Didayi'. The jurisdiction of DDA covers two villages of Rasabeda Gram Panchayat of Khairaput Block and 37 villages of Kudumulugumma, Nakamamudi and Andirapalli Gram Panchayats of Kudumulugumma Block.

The action programme for 1986-87 and 1987-88 was discussed in the Governing Body in its first meeting held on 3-3-87. The programme was approved after suitable modifications for implementation at the field level. Initially, it was decided to cover seven villages, i.e., Oringi, Muduliguda, Chelipadar, and Purunagumma (the plain sub-area villages) and Bayapada, Suripada and Tikarpada (the Hills sub-area villages).

During these two years, 310 Didayi households covered under different agriculture and horticulture programmes as against the target of 200 households. In the second phase, ten more Didayi, villages were included in 1989-90 and it is understood that during 1993-94 all Didayi villages were covered up under the development programme.

Table 4.1 shows the funds received and utilised from 1986-87 to 2001-02 (up to May 2001) by the D.D.A.

Important Programmes Implemented

Development of Agriculture Sector

Agriculture is the mainstay of the Didayi economy. As per the survey conducted by the Council of Analytical Tribal Studies (COATS), Koraput during 2001-02, 96.95 per cent of the Didayi households (1273 out of 1313 households) depend either on settled cultivation or on shifting cultivation or on both the types of cultivations. They were using old and outdated agricultural implements, traditional variety of seeds and primitive methods of cultivation before the establishment of D.D.A. in 1986. It was rightly decided by the DDA authorities to lay more emphasis on the development of settled agricultural practices and make gradual efforts to wean the tribals away from the shifting cultivation. The various important programmes implemented for the development of agricultural practices are the following:

(i) Supply of agricultural implements, like spade, pick-axe, crowbar and M.B. plough were made to raise the productive efficiency and acquaint the tribals with such new tools and implements so as to introduce comparatively new and improved production technology in the area. During the year 1987-88, 300 households of seven villages were provided with pick-axe and spade, 96 households with crowbar and 197 households with M.B. plough. During the year 1989-90 and 1990-91, these implements were provided to 395 households. Ten more villages were included in the second phase, Again duirng the year 1995-96, 617 agricultural implements were provided to 617 cultivators.

(ii) Introduction and popularisation of improved and high-yielding varieties of crops, i.e., cereals like *paddy, maize, ragi*, wheat; pulses, like *arhar* green gram (*mung*), black gram (*Biri*); Oil seeds, like niger, mustard and groundnut; cash crops, like ginger, turmeric, chilly and vegetables like soyabeen Lady's finger, bittergourd, etc., were undertaken for better return per unit area in place of low yielding traditional crops.

(iii) Most of the Didayi huoseholds are in the habit of maintaining a kitchen garden at the backyard of their houses. They usually grow tobacco, mustard, some root and tuber crops. The D.D.A. has taken advantage of this practice among the Didayi households and have introduced cultivation of chilly, ginger, turmeric and vegetables, like brinjal, Lady's finger, bitter Gourd, potato, tomato, onion, cauliflower and cabbages, etc. The study made by COATS reveals that the per acre average yield of backyard kitchen garden is the highest in the Didayi area (i.e., Rs. 2027 as against Rs.1873 in case of settled cultivation).

(iv) Gradual and systematic introduction and supply of chemical fertilizers and pesticides have been made to ensure more and assured returns to the cultivation. Simultaneously the farmers have been encouraged to continue compost manuring in a more scientific way. During the year 1991-92, 114 qtls of *Syamali*, 40 qtls of DAP and 165 qtls of urea were distributed to 357, 185 and 335 beneficiaries respectively. During the year 1992-93 and 1993-94 pesticides like Demicran, Endotaf, Bavisthin and Dethen 45 were distributed to the farmers.

(v) *Horticulture*: Development of horticulture in the backyard of the households as well as in the suitable sites can provide a continuous source of income and sustainable development of the beneficiaries. Grafted mango, pineapple, banana, lemon, papeya, coconut and pomegranate saplings were planted in the project area. Since the establishment of DDA, efforts have been made for plantation of cashew and tamarind on the hill slopes where shifting cultivation practices have resulted in severe soil erosion. When pineapple cultivation on a demonstration basis was taken up inMuduliguda village it did not succeed due to various factors. Banana plantation, lemon and papeya plantation have succeeded in many of the villages in the cut-off and the hills sub-area. The cashew plantation taken up on the hill slopes in the hills sub-area villages have shown good results. Greater interest was shown by the beneficiaries of cut off sub-area for plantation of coconut, to meet with their religious rites and festivals. Around 2000 banana suckers, 1670 mango plants, 470 coconut plants and 150 papeya saplings were distributed among beneficiaries during the initial three year-period. The DDA has been distributing these species from time to time among the beneficiaries of the entire project area.

(vi) *Irrigation Facilities*: In order to provide irrigation facilities and to check soil erosion during rainy season from the perennial streams, two check dams were constructed at Oringi and Purunagumma. Two diversion weirs were provided in Bayapada and three Water Harvesting structures were built in Muduliguda and Nilapari villages during the period from 1993-94 to 1995-96. In the cut-off sub-area also a Water Harvesting Structure has been provided in Jantry village which provides assured irrigation to the lands below the structure. The hilly terrains and the large number of streams in each and every village of the cut-off and hills area villages provide enough opportunities for construction of water harvesing structures, Check Dams and Diversion weirs.

(vii) *Fishing*: There is a vast stretch of water surface on the Balimela reservoir offering plenty of scope for fishing with the help of boats and nets. A number of Didayi, villagers living close to both the banks of the reservoir are expert in fishing. The DDA has taken advantage of this situation to provide boats and nets to two beneficiaries. The fish collected is sold in the Chitrokonda, Ankadally and Kudumulugumma markets regularly. More and more Didayi households started demanding the benefits under the scheme.

During the years from 1993-94 to 1995-96, 30 units of boats and nets were supplied to 60 beneficiaries of the cut-off sub-area and the villages located in the bank of the reservoir. The beneficiaries were imparted training on the use of net and boat in the reservoir by the staff of fisheries department.

(viii) (A) *Supply of Bullocks*: The poor Didayi households were unable to purchase a pair of bullock to cultivate their lands. They were borrowing a pair of bullocks from their neighbour Bondo at a cost of Rs. 500 to Rs. 600 per annum. In addition, it is the practice in the area to entertain the Bondo with chicken and wine whenever they come to see the conditions of the pair of bullocks loaned by them. In order to make the 'Didayi' self-sufficient in the matter, bullocks have been supplied to 90 beneficiaries during the period from 1992-93 to 1995-96. However, in many cases it was found that one pair of bullocks have been supplied to two beneficiaries at the rate of one bullock per beneficiaries. Most of the beneficiaries came with the complaint that each needy household including landless labourers need to be provided with a pair of bullocks, so that in addition to their work, they can go on hire basis to well-to-do cultivators and supplement their meagre income.

(B) *Supply of Smaller Animals and Birds*: The goat and sheep units have been supplied to the beneficiaries. The goat-rearing units have yielded good results in the 'Didayi' area. The poultry units supplied to them have not yielded good results due to spread of epidemic.

(ix) *Drinking Water Facilities*: Thirty-two tube wells have been constructed in the project area to meet the requirement of drinking water, i.e., 7 tube wells in the plains sub-area villages, 11 in the hills sub-area villages, and 14 tube wells in the cut-off sub-area villages. In the recent past open wells and cisterns have been provided in the villages of the plains and hills sub-area of the project area.

(x) *Communication Facilities*: It has been already noted that the communication facilities are inadequate in the cut-off sub-area and hills sub-area villages. In order to improve the situation and provide better communication facilities, village path and link roads have been constructed in the Didayi villages. Oringi and Bayapada Road, Bayapada and Damodarbeda Road, Bayapada and Naringjhola Road, Dhakadpadar and Dabuguda Road and Dabuguda and Taberu Road have been constructed during the years 1994-95 and 1995-96 by the DDA project.

(xi) *Health Programmes*: Under health programme, health check up camps have been organised by the D.D.A. in the Didayi villages with the co-operation of the medical officers of Khairaput and Kudumulugumma.Medicines have been supplied to the Didayi patients as per the medical advice. However, the absence of a Medical aid centre in the project area is creating a lot of difficulties to the Didayi people inhabited in the cut off sub-area and hills sub-area villages.

(xii) *Education*: Adult education centres were introduced in the Didayi villages for promotion of educational opportunities in the hills sub-area and cut-off sub-area villages. Under this programme slates, books, pencils, erasers, lamps and dresses have been provided to attract the illiterate Didayi people to come to the centre. During the year 1994-95 the TLC programme was also introduced in the project area. The education programmes in the project area have not come up to the expectation mainly due to teacher absenteeism in the schools run by education and H & TW departments.

The Anganwadi centres run under the I.C.D.S. programme have also failed to come up to the expectation of the people on the area due to irregular supply of foód by the *Anganwadi* workers.

(xiii) In addition to these programmes, different skill promotion activities, i.e., training in basket making, mat making and other bamboo produce needed in the area were provided during the initial years of the establishment of D.D.A. Training in woollen carpet weaving for Didayi women was organised during the year 1991-92.

ONGOING DEVELOPMENT PROCESS

The Didayi Development Agency has continued to take interest in the development of various sectors of economy in the project area. Under the agricultural development programme, input assistance of Paddy, Ragi and Groundnut seeds during the *Khariff* and vegetable seeds during the *Rabi* season were provided to 848 Didayi beneficiaries by collecting 10 per cent of the cost of the seeds during the year 2000-2001. As per the decisioin of the 15th Governing Body meeting of the D.D.A., H.Y.V. short and medium duration paddy have been provided to around 1000 beneficiaries covering about 500 acres of land during the year 2001-02. Efforts have also been made for promotion of ginger and groundnut cultivation in limited areas during the year. Green Gram seed at 4 kgs per beneficiary have been provided to willing cultivators.

The vegetable seeds, like radish, cabbage, tomato, brinjal, bittergourd, lady's finger (Bhindi) and beans have been distributed among 448 beneficiaries covering 28 villages. 1000 mango grafts and 4000 banana suckers have been distributed among willing beneficiaires at a subsidised rate during the year 2000-2001.

Twenty more beneficiaries falling below poverty line were provided with nets and boats after collecting 10 per cent of the cost during the year 2000-2001. It has been planned to provide ten boats and nets during the current year.

Nine Didayi boys are continuing as teachers in the non-formal schools run by the DDA in inaccesible pockets. During the year 2001-2002, 142 Didayi boys and girls have been admitted in 9 residential schools of Kudumuluguma and Khairput Block. The DDA have provided to these students reading and writing material as well as school uniforms.

During the year 2000-2001, Didayi people from different areas selected as Multipurpose Health Workers (MPHW) were imparted training at the Ashakiran Hospital. These health workers are supplied with different medicines for distribution to the Didayis who suffer from malaria, diarrhoea, cold fever and viral fever, etc.

As goat-rearing scheme has become successful in the area, a sum of Rs. 50,000 has been earmarked for supply of goat-rearing unit in the cut-off and other areas. The responsibility of selection of beneficiaries has been entrusted to "Palli Sabha" during the current year.

During the previous years, tiles have been supplied to the needy Didayis to construct roof of their houses. The tribal representatives requested for providing tiles this year also. But keeping in view the durability and transport convenience, it has been decided to provide 12 numbers of G.C.I. sheets per beneficiary to 15 beneficiaries in the cut-off sub-area. The G.C.I. sheets will be distributed before the rainy season to the beneficiaries to be selected in the village meetings. We may discuss hereunder the findings of case studies undertaken in the field during the present study:

Implementation of Poverty Alleviation Programme in the Study Area: Case Study of 51 Households

In order to assess the impact of various poverty alleviation programmes which were implemented in the study area, as many as 51 beneficiary households were selected following the incidental random sampling techniques. The data were collected with the help of a Schedule (see Appendix- III) enquiring about the nature of assistance, the sources of assistance and the basis of selection of beneficiaries, etc. Analysis of the results revealed indicating success or failure of these schemes is stated below:

1. Out of the sample of 51 beneficiary households, 41 were assisted through Block and the rest 10 through D.D.A.
2. Majority of the beneficiaries (62.75 %) have been assisted in terms of cash. The amount of assistance vary between Rs. 5000 and Rs. 22,000. Out of the rest 37.25 per cent who have been assisted in the form of kind, 17.65 per cent have been provided with bullocks, 11.76 per cent with nets and boats and 7.84 per cent with tiles for roofing.
3. The maximum number of the beneficiaries (86.27 %) were selected through the *Palli Sabha*.
4. Most of the beneficiaries (92.16 %) have reported that they had undertaken the schemes out of their own interest. In other words, these beneficiaries are not compelled to undertake the activities connected with the schemes.
5. As high as 84.31 per cent of beneficiaries reported that they did never spend any money to get the scheme sanctioned in their favour.

The above facts indicate that various poverty alleviation schemes have successfully been implemented in the study area.

DIDAYI PERCEPTION OF DEVELOPMENT

The Didayi are very mild, docile, law-abiding, sincere and receptive people. That they can absorb the shocks of life is evident from the way the cultivators of both the banks of river Machkund settled down on the hill slopes when they were displaced due to the construction of the Balimela Project. They respect their traditions and customs, obey the village eleders and follow the norms and mores of society even today. It is because of their cultural apparatus they eke out their livelihood in spite of ecological, geophysical and other odds.

Agriculture is the primary source of livelihood. Scarcity of plains and valley lands and absence of other economically viable alternative sources of livelihood force them to take up shifting cultivation practices. The Didayi of cut-off and hills sub-areas cannot think of

Table 4.1: Statement showing Funds received and utilisation Certificates submitted to Government (Annual of Didayi Development Agency Kudumuluguma) since inception.

Sl. No.	Year	Opening Balance as on 1st April	Amount received directly from H&TW Dept.	Total funds available for expenditure	Amount utilised during the year	Utilisation certificates sent	Balance for expenditure
1.	1986-87	—	475000.00	475000.00	447385.00	—	27615.00
2.	1987-88	27615.00	2400000.00	2427615.00	148729.00	—	2278886.00
3.	1988-89	2278886.00	680000.00	2958886.00	615809.00	—	2343077.00
4.	1989-90	2343077.00	550000.00	2893077.00	2324467.00	311654.00	568610.00
5.	1990-91	568610.00	1300000.00	1868610.00	1094305.00	767534.00	774305.00
6.	1991-92	774305.00	1067000.00	1841305.00	1553905.00	615070.00	287400.00
7.	1992-93	287400.00	1507000.00	1794400.00	1440592.00	2596511.00	353808.00
8.	1993-94	353808.00	1121000.00	1474808.00	1246046.00	3292546.00	228762.00
9.	1994-95	228762.00	1160000.00	1388762.00	1161415.00	1434941.00	227347.00
10.	1995-96	227347.00	1796000.00	2023347.00	1099097.00	1021178.00	924250.00
11.	1996-97	924250.00	587000.00	1511250.00	1454030.00	2347608.00	57220.00
12.	1997-98	57220.00	1372000.00	1429220.00	1052686.00	1057326.00	376534.00
13.	1998-99	376534.00	1369000.00	1745534.00	1459456.00	1459456.00	286078.00
14.	1999-2000	286078.00	1243000.00	1529078.00	1107464.00	815305.00	421614.00
15.	2000-2001	421614.00	1656000.00	2077614.00	1016979.00	1180192.00	1060635.00
16.	2001-2002	1060635.00	6403000.00	7463635.00	1289987.00	1358748.00	6104887.00
	Total	—	24686000.00	34902141.00	18512352.00	18258069.00	16321028.00

stopping the Podu cultivation. They think that only Podu cultivation is providing them food for their sustenance. Next to agriculture, which provides them 36.67 per cent of their total income, 27.70 per cent of their income is dervied from the collection and sale of forest produce. The timber, non-timber, grass and minor forest produce besides meeting with their essential consumption needs fetch some cash when small part of it is sold in the market. They worship forest gods, collect their requirement from it and depend upon it day in and day out.

Most of the Didayi households work as a daily wage earner at least for 30 to 40 days in a year. The survey of COATS 2001-02 reveals that 86.67 per cent of the households depend on wage earning activities to maintain the subsistence level and earn around 17.15 per cent of their income.

They are also experts in fishing in the reservoir with the help of nets and boats. Around 8.38 per cent of Didayi households depend on fishing and earn around Rs. 1024 per annum. Those who fish in the reservoir have also acquired the skill of knitting fishing nets of different patterns and sizes out of nylon wires or mill made yarn purchased from the nearby weekly markets.

The basket making skill of Didayi is also very much encouraging. They collect bamboo from the nearby hills and forests, make different types of baskets and mats for their own use and for selling them to get cash.

Most of them are illiterates and due to lack of outside exposure, their awareness is very much limited. They are very often cheated by the unscrupulous traders and middlemen in weights and measures at the time of selling their produces for cash or exchanging their produce for daily necessities.

They love singing and dancing in groups consisting of young men and women during the days following harvesting of crops. They lead a corporate life and share their pleasure and pain together. Their limited size of population helps them in emerging as a socially cohesive unit for perpetuation of their social identity and for maintenance of their social boundary.

The Didayis were satisfied with the crops they grew, the forest produce they collected and were maintaining a hard life. The intervention of Didayi Development Project has brought a considerable change in their perception of development. They have now started feeling the need of agricultural implements, like pickaxe, crowbar, spade, a plough with a plough share, improved variety of seeds and a pair of bullocks. Even the landless labourers need the agricultural implements and a pair of bullocks to work in other farms to get higher wages. They have now started thinking of saving in terms of cash as well as in kind to meet with their future contingencies. The COATS Survey, 2001-02 reveals that a little more than 92 per cent of the households have some amount of saving in cash and kind.

The animal husbandry support extended by D.D.A. has also helped to some extent for improvement in the standard of living of the Didayi. At present, 85.22 per cent of the households have some animals or birds with them. The goat-rearing scheme implemented by the D.D.A. has become successful in the area. Many Didayi households came forward to express their need for a goat-rearing unit to supplement their meagre income.

The Didayi perception of development is now quite favourable for the D.D.A. authorities to inject further development inputs. They now further need better housing facilities, a little education for their children, essential medical services facilities in their own area.

The formation of 33 Self Help Groups in 21 villages with 494 ladies have laid the foundation for the empowerment of women. The women group have started thinking about the type of business they will take up after receiving the incentive fund of Rs.10,000 from the D.R.D.A. It has really started developing entrepreneurial skill in a modest way especially among the Secretaries and Presidents of SHGs. A spirit of competition is gradually developing among the S.H.G.s developed in the same village. The introduction of SHGs has really made an attempt among women to perceive development with a new look.

Felt Needs

In order to ascertain the felt needs of the people, Focus Group Discussions (FGDs) were organised in ten villages of the study area covering the plains sub-area, hills sub-area and cut-off sub-area villages. The cultivators of most of the villages needed a comprehensive agricultural development programme. Most of them wanted the D.D.A. authorities to provide a pair of bullocks to each cultivator, who do not have it, provide cereals, pulses, oil and vegetable seeds in such quantities as each cultivator needs for taking up cultivation and agricultural implements like crowbar, spade, pickaxe, and a plough share.

The watershed projects, water harvesting structures, Diversion weirs and Check dams constructed by D.D.A. authorities have provided benefit to few villages in terms of reducing soil erosion and increasing productivity of crops. Therefore, the people have started demanding further such facilities in villages where these facilities have not been provided.

The villagers are aware of the evils of shifting cultivation practices, but they follow this method of cultivation due to scarcity of low lands and absence of viable alternative employment opportunities. During the course of discussion when they were explained about the indigenous practices followed in parts of NEFA and Nagaland (i.e., placing of the cut-off tree trunks across the slope to arrest soil erosion and to form a rudimentary terrace) they accepted our suggestions. However, this practice instead of stopping shifting cultivation will encourage it and will lead to further deforestation. Therefore, they were suggested to follow the method of stone terracing to reduce the evil effects of soil erosion, to which also they readily agreed. They requested for demonstration of the process in one or two villages, so that they can follow the practice.

A great interest has been shown by the inhabitants for plantation of economic species, like mango, tamarind, *kusum*, guava, lichi, coconut, cashew, lemon and pomogranate. Hence, the Didayi Development Authority has to make adequate provisions for these plantations on the hill slopes and hill tops to wean the tribals away from shifting cultivation as a loss run programme.

In order to make double crop cultivation, the villagers in the bank of the Balimela reservoir requested for provision of pump sets to irrigate the lands nearer the reservoir.

Cash crop cultivation, like Ginger, Chilly, Tobacco and Tomato are well accepted whereas the proposals for leaf plate making, rearing of buffaloes and installation of *Gobar Gas* plant are resented.

Many of the inhabitants of hills sub-area and cut-off sub-area came forward with the view that a P.H.C. should come up through the Government efforts in a central village, so that they can avail the benefit at the time of their need.

The teacher absenteeism in schools is the main obstacle for educating their children. In many places, villagers came forward with a proposal to post a teacher who can stay in the village and teach the students regularly.

The absence of communication facilities was pointed out as one of their major problems by many villagers. They needed better communication facilities for marketing their surplus produce and to purchase their common necessities easily from the nearby market. Another interesting point raised by them in one of the study villages was that they needed narrow roads instead of wide ones apprehending the syphoning of their material resources, derived from the existing natural resources, by outsiders through truck loads.

5

Participatory and Sustainable Development : Inventory of Resources and Resource Utilisation

LAND RESOURCES

The Didayi Development Project area is endowed with vast natural resources, like land, water and forest. However, the extent of low land available for cultivation is very much limited. Except in the plains villages, the entire project area is covered up with hilly terrain lands. The study conducted by COATS reveals that only 832.80 acres of low land is owned by 384 households. Out of this only 76 households in the cut-off area and 79 households in the hill area own 205.55 acres and 179.50 acres of low land respectively. Again 455.75 acres of low land, i.e., 54.73 per cent of the total low land in the project area is owned by 229 households inhabited in the plains villages. The extent of upland owned by 601, i.e., 44.75 per cent of the total households is 1362.40 acres. A major part of these uplands is owned by the inhabitants of the cut-off area and hill area villages. Further, 220 households in the cut-off area own 540.40 acres of upland and 252 households in the hills area own 554.00 acres of upland. A major part of these uplands are undulating in nature having 10 degree to 20 degree slope and covered up with stones here and there.

The R.O.R. abstract made available to the investigators at the Chitrokonda Tahsil Office for 30 villages in the project area reveals that 6,320 acres of Government land is available. A study made by the Ministry of Works and Housing, Government of India, 1974 reveals that the percentage of areas potential for extension of cultivation is only 661 hectares, i.e., 11.59 per cent in

Kudumulugumma Block. Hence, the percentage of areas potential for extension of cultivation in fallow land and cultivable waste in the project area is very much limited.

On the other hand 97.64 per cent of the people of the Project area are dependent on cultivation and a major part of the income, i.e., 36.67 per cent is derived from agriculture. Due to scarcity of plains land and absence of viable employment opportunity, 759 households are forced to follow the pernicious practice of shifting cultivation.

The existence of a number of hills at a higher altitude of 2000 feet to 3000 feet altitude offer enough scope for extensive plantations of fruit bearing trees as well as other trees having economic value. In addition, the agro-climatic conditions of these hill ranges offer a large agro-climatic scope for cultivation of cash crops, like vegetables, spices and the like. The slopy highland having 10^0 to 20^0 slope is unsuitable for crop cultivation. As these lands are unbounded they lead to soil erosion and become unsuitable for cultivation after raising two to three crops.

During the rainy season when the water level rises on both the banks of Balimela reservoir rich alluvial soil deposits are made. The banks of the reservoir offer good scope for cultivation of tobacco, vegetables and other cash crops. There are a large number of natural springs with perennial flow in the project area.

FOREST RESOURCES

It has already been pointed out earlier that the economy of the local tribals is largely forest based. Forests provide them their prime necessities, such as food, fuel, materials to build their houses, edible leaves, roots, wild game, etc. Forest supports not only the Didayi's self-needs but also their cattle and livestock population, with fodder, shady shelter and water. Besides, they collect a number of minor forest produce for their own consumption as well as for sale in the nearby weekly markets. Bamboos, fibres and leaves are utilised in cottage crafts like basketry, rope making and roof thatching.

There is approximately 5000 hectares of reserved land known as Kondakamberu reserved land in the cut-off area, around 2000 hectares of protected reserve forest known as Balimela P.R.F. in the hill area and approximately 1000 hectares of unreserved land in the plains area villages.

A number of medicinal plants and herbs are available in the forest and collected from time to time.

WATER RESOURCES

In addition to a large number of perennial streams in the hilly and mountainous region, the Balimela reservoir covers deep waterbody of around 1000 sq. kms. The water provides ample opportunities for pisciculture.

HUMAN RESOURCES

It has been already pointed out earlier that the Didayi are very mild, docile, law abiding disciplined and receptive people. They have learnt from their experience to exploit natural resources to maintain their livelihood. However, without formal education, they lack the knowledge and skill of scientific use of land, forest and water resources.

Health facilities are almost absent in the project area. They suffer from a number of diseases and normally depend upon the local medicineman, known as *Disari*. Educational opportunities provided in the area are not adequate. Teacher absenteeism have made almost all the schools non-functional. Due to large-scale illiteracy in the project area the general level of awareness is very low as a result of which they are exploited by middlemen/businessmen in the weekly markets while exchanging or selling their produce.

RESOURCES MOBILISATION

Natural resources, including material resources and human resources need to be properly mobilised for the socio-economic development of the Didayi. Since the inception of the Micro-project, the Government has concentrated on an integrated approach-mainly having two broad components. The first component is family oriented core programme for economic development and the second one is infrastructure development and social services support.

The family-oriented core programme of economic development consisted of supply of agricultural implements, seeds, fertilisers and pesticides for the development of agriculture sector. Supply of fruit tree of different variety was the main thrust given for horticulture development. Supply of bullocks, goat-rearing unit, poultry unit, etc., were made for the development of animal husbandry sector in the area. Supply of boats and nets aimed at fishery development.

An examination of distribution of these benefits among the beneficiaries reveals that they were not fairly distributed in all villages. Plain area villagers have derived more benefit than villagers of cut-off area. The beneficiaries of the hill villages in inaccessible area have received lesser benefit.

Similar is the case with infrastructure development and social service support. For example, check dams and diversion weirs have been provided in plain area villages, like Oringi, Purunagumma, Nilapari and Muduliguda whereas in the cut-off area and Hill area villages only Jantry and Bayapada have been provided with such facilities. This way of implementation of programme may be justified by the D.D.A. on the ground that they have done it on a systematic and phased manner. But it has created a sense of dissatisfaction and discontentment among the inhabitants of the hill area and cut-off area villages where such facilities were not provided.

The participation of the people in any such programmes will yield more benefits of such utilisation of resources. Hence, before implementation of any programme in future, resources may be mobilised in a more systematic and equitable manner rather than on an *ad hoc* basis.

While planning for resource mobilisation, emphasis may be paid on few programmes on an extensive basis to a larger number of villages. This way of dealing with the problem will create better awareness on the programme of resources utilisation. For example, agricultural implements have been distributed in three to four phases, i.e., during 1987-88, 1989-90 and 1990-91. After proper identification of needy benificiaries in the 'Palli Sabha' such assistance can be given in one year. Similarly, while providing infrastructure development, there needs to be a more or less equal distribution of the benefit to all the three sub-areas. The fair distribution of limited material resource will ensure better participation of the people as a whole, by minimising discontentment arising out of sub-area disparity.

The financial resources provided by the Government varied between Rs. 4.75 lakhs during 1986-87 to Rs. 24.00 lakhs during 1987-88. The financial resource flow should take into account the need of the people, the preparedness of the project authorities to implement such programmes and existence of adequate staff to shoulder such burden of implementation. It was found that the post of Welfare Extension Officer is vacant in the project since February

1997. The vacancy of such an important post in the project has caused a lot of dislocation in the implementation of programmes.

THE CHALLENGE AND THE RESPONSE

The Micro Projects have been constituted around the country in particularly vulnerable tribal pockets, with the main objective of alround development of the tribe on a sustainable basis. The micro projects are expected to continue for a definite period of time till the socio-economic and skill development of the people is enhanced to such an extent when they will no more need any external agency to work for their upliftment. This does not mean that a micro project will function for an indefinite period of time. The project officials may agree to bear this in mind and to earmark their limited resources in such a way that people's participation is ensured at all phases, i.e., formulation, implementation and evaluation of projects to enable them to face future challenges.

There is need to create awareness among the beneficiaries of the project that in case of the discontinuance of the micro project, they must be prepared to perpetuate their attempts to maintain the *status quo* and go ahead for improving their lifestyle.

The world is fast changing on account of globalisation and liberalisation of trade policies. Promotion of efficiency in all fields is one of the prime necessities to face the new market competition. The Didayi must be made aware of this aspect in simple and intelligible terms. The concept of patent right may be explained to them so that they will be wiser to protect the valuable medicinal plants in the forests of their own area.

The Didayi shall be made aware of the future challenges and respond accordingly.

PEOPLE'S SUSTAINABLE DEVELOPMENT

The Didayi (erstwhile, Gntre) constituting an ethno-cultural group with the constitutional status of a Scheduled Tribe and subsequently identified as a particularly Vulnerable Tribal Group, having small population represents a simple society with rich cultural heritage. Over a period of six decades (1941 to 2001-02) their average decennial population growth is estimated at (+) 6.81 per cent which is far below the standard decennial growth rate. The concentration of population in the most active and dynamic age group (15-59 years) shows 56.16 per cent of the total population as per 2001-02 survey. The literacy rate is extremely low, i.e., 12.56 per cent for males and 3.36 per cent for females and total comes to 7.89 per cent only. A single Didayi household consists of 4.36 members on an average in the study area. The per household and per capita monthly income are estimated at Rs. 884.86 and Rs. 202.95 respectively. The per household and per capita monthly expenditure comes to Rs.836.54 and Rs.191.87, respectively. Therefore, on an average the per household and per capita monthly income surplus may be estimated at Rs.48.32 and Rs.11.08, respectively. They earn the maximum annual income from the economic pursuit of forest collection, the per household and per capita income being Rs. 2888.20 and Rs. 662.16 respectively. It is followed by the income derived from the practice of shifting cultivation with Rs.1669.53 and Rs. 382.76 as per household and per capita income, respectively. It is further followed by the income from the Upland (*dongar*) cultivation with Rs.1319.63 and Rs. 302.55 as per household and per capita income, respectively. Next comes the income from the settled low land cultivation with per household and per capita income of Rs.1188.19 and Rs. 272.41, respectively. Out of the total expenditure more than a half, i.e., 54.78 per cent goes towards food and only 1.06 per cent for medicine and less than one per cent for education. Roughly 70.00 per cent of the Didayi households are below poverty line, applying the norm of per capita monthly expenditure of Rs. 250.

With the preliminary observation, as stated above, on the Didayi people we may proceed for discussion of their sustainable development. We need to combine natural resources, including material resources derived out of the former and human resources for the socio-economic development of the community in its ecological setting, or in other words, the development *in situ* (see Chart-1). Accoding to Professor W.A. Lewis, the resources put limit on the amount and the type of development and States, "They usually have to begin with and concentrate on the development of locally available natural resources as an initial condition for lifting local levels of living......." [quoted in Devi, Laxmi (eds): 2, 1996: 360]. Further, Devi states, ". . . . natural resources are passive by nature and as such are incapable of initiating economic growth. This passivity of natural resources necessitates their exploitation and use by scientific techniques and human effort" (*Ibid.*: 2: 996; 360-361). For the attainment of sustainability in the development process, an integrated planning would ensure the optimum use of resources, strike a balance between under utilisation and over utilisation and the conservation of renewable resources. The external development inputs, in cash and/or kind, for a community cannot be guaranteed for all times to come. The people have to stand on their own promote self-dignity, free themselves from servitude and enhance their quality of life, simultaneously enriching the quality of environment (both physical and socio-cultural) through the only apparatus available with them, i.e., culture (see Fig. 5.1). In the context of development the human resource is considered both a means and an end. Since the Didayi connot be kept separated from other humans and the nation at large, their human resource is likely to change. The socio-structural and techno economic changes around their micro-world will require upgradation of skills and abilities to foster coping mechanisms for future living for themselves and their descendants.

ATTITUDE TOWARDS DEVELOPMENT

Attitude of the Didayi towards development was studied through an attitude test battery (see Appendix- III) administered over a sample of 87 heads of household. The test battery consisting of four parts sought to ascertain the attitudes of the respondents towards the ongoing programmes of D.D.A. as well as the government in bringing personal development and development of the community as a whole.

Table 5.1 shows the response of beneficiaries on development programme undertaken by the D.D.A. in different villages.

Table 5.1: Showing the response of Beneficiaries on Developmental Programmes undertaken by the D.D.A. in different villages.

(N-87)

Name of schemes/ programmes	*Percentage of Response*
1. Supply of house building materials	62.07
2. Supply of agricultural implements	58.62
3. Supply of plough and bullocks	56.32
4. Supply of seedlings	26.44
5. Supply of household utensils	26.44
6. Supply of nets and boats	5.75
7. Supply of seeds	52.87
8. Construction/repair of road	45.98
9. Construction of M.I.P.	20.69
10. Installation of Tube-well	28.74

Chart-5.1: Classification of Resources

Natural Resources	*Meterial Resources*	*Human Resources*
I. Land 1. Upland 1.1 Hill Top 1.2 Hill Slope 1.3 Foothill 1.4 Plateau Land 1.5 Waste Land 1.6 Forest Land 1.7 Degraded Forest Land 1.8 Grass/ Pasture Land 1.9 Co, unity Land 1.10 Kitchen Garden Land 1.11 Homestead Land 2. Low Land 2.1 Irrigation 2.2 Non-irrigated 2.3 Cultivable/ Arable land 2.4 Cultivated Land 2.5 Uncultivated Land 3. Mines & Quarries 3.1 Limestone 4. Soil Types 5. Flora & Fauna II. Water 1. Surface (Rain) Water 1.1 River 1.2 Hill Stream 1.3 Ditch/Unprotected Well 1.4 Protected Well 1.5 Tank 2. Ground Water 2.1 Tube Well	I. Wood 1. Timber 2. Non-timber 2.1 Fuel 2.2 Fencing II. Bamboo 1. House Building 2. Thatching 3. Basketry 4. Edible Shoots 5. Fencing III. Grass 1. Fodder 2. Thatching IV. Reeda 1. Broom 2. Mat-making V. Edible Roots & Tubers VI. Twigs & Creepers VII. Leaves 1. Edible Green Leaves 2. Tendu Leaves (*biri*) 3. For Plate & container VIII. Tree Bark IX. Resin X. Gum/Catechu XI. nuts XII. Fruits XIII. Mushrooms XIV. Games animals XV. Wild Birds XVI. Fish XVII. Honey XVIII. Insects XIX. Hide & Other animal remnanats	1. Men & Women in age groups 0-5, 6-14, 15-59 & 60 Years and above 1. Knowledge Base (Ethnoscience) 2. Ability and Competence 3. Work Experience 4. Skill (Indigenous) 5. Skill (acquired through training) 6. Literacy 7. Education 8. Health & Sanitation 9. Work force participation (men) 10. Work force participation (Women) 11. Potentiality

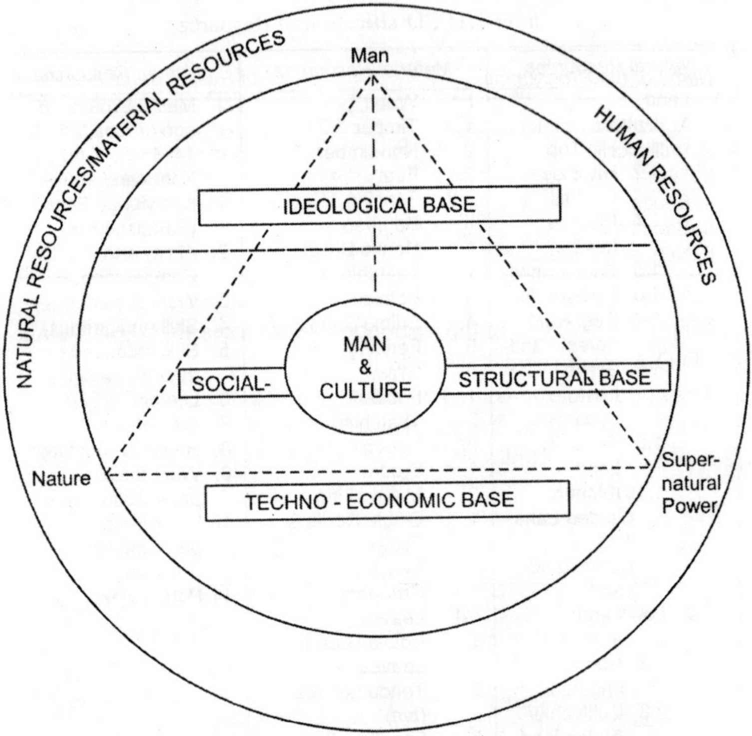

Fig. 5.1: A sociogram showing the bases of sustainable Development

The maximum number of respondents supported the implementation of scheme in serial No. 1, followed by serial No. 2, 3 and 7 presented in table 5.2.

The distribution of respondents based on assistance their families have received from the D.D.A. can be seen from Table 5.2

Table 5.2 shows that the majority of the Didayi interviewed have received seeds (81.61%) followed by agricultural implements (74.71%).

It was learnt that some materials are provided by the D.D.A. free of cost whereas some other at subsidised rates, 28.69 per cent of respondents have reported to have paid 10 per cent of the cost for the materials, whereas 79.31 per cent of the beneficiaries reported to have received them free of cost.

Table 5.2: Distribution of Respondents by Assistance received from the D.D.A.

Name of the Programme	*% of Respondents benefited*
1. Agricultural Implements	74.71
2. Bullocks	49.43
3. Tiles for roofing	26.44
4. Seeds	81.61
5. Seedlings	6.90
6. Nets and Boats	16.09

Majority (63.23%) of the respondents expressed that the officials from D.D.A. paid regular visits to their villages.

The opinion of the Didayi on the impact of various developmental activities, launched by the government on different aspects of their life is presented in Table 5.3.

Table 5.3: Impact of Development Programmes on Different Aspects

N=87

Aspects of Development	*Percentage of Response*		
	Yes	*No*	*Uncertain*
1. Children's Education	63.22	36.78	—
2. Medical/Health facilities	57.47	42.53	—
3. Roads	74.71	25.29	—
4. Electricity	20.69	79.31	—
5. Drinking Water	66.67	33.33	—
6. Anganwadi	68.97	25.29	5.75
7. Marketing	12.64	86.21	1.15
8. Savings Facilities	45.98	49.42	4.60
9. Loan Facilities	57.47	37.93	4.60
10. Communication	10.34	85.06	4.60
11. Irrigation	36.78	59.77	3.45
12. Soil Conservation	1.15	31.03	67.82

It can be seen from Table 5.3 that government programmes launched from time to time have shown positive response in the fields of road facilities (74.71%), drinking water facilities (66.67%), Anganwadi (68.97%), children's education (63.22%), medical/health facilities (57.47%) and loan facilities (57.47%). The result of Table 5.3 further indicates that government programmes have failed to provide adequate marketing, communication, electricity and irrigation facilities.

Table 5.4 presents the attitude of respondents pertaining to their value-orientations.

Table 5.4: Showing the attitudes towards value-orientations

N-87

Value-Orientations	*Response (In percentage)*		
	Yes	*No*	*Uncertain*
1. Children need to know our traditional customs and manners	90.80	2.30	6.90
2. Children should learn new facts and new customs	90.80	1.15	8.05
3. Hard labour is only the key to success	65.52	—	34.48
4. Blessings of deities is only the key to success	71.26	11.50	17.24
5. Our old lifestyle was good and we should retain it.	57.47	16.09	26.44
6. We cannot live better unless we accept new ideas	86.21	—	13.79

The results of the Table 5.4 show that majority of the respondents have shown a balanced attitude towards their tradition (90.80%) and change (90.80%).

The question in Serial No. 4 indicate their adherance to traditional values relating to their core-culture, i.e., religious beliefs in deities and positive response in this regard (71.26%) surpasses the mundanity of life in stating about the hard labour (65.52%) in Serial No. 3. In response to serial Nos. 5 and 6, there is more tilt towards change (86.21%) than the retention of traditions (57.47%).

Keeping in view the above considerations and people's prioritisation in selecting development inputs which would positively contribute for their overall development and also side by side ensure people's participation at all phases, an empirical model has been designed from the present study. The model is an operational design or rather a field model and not an ideal theoretical construct. It needs experimentation at different stages of operationalisation and suitable modifications, if any, would help in the emergence of a better one with generalisations for its application in development efforts for such other similar ethno-cultural groups.

FURTHER DEVELOPMENT INPUTS

We may hereunder state the development inputs as has been envisaged by the Didayi people themselves in broadly 3 sub-areas or thrust areas identified through the present study, such as the plains, the hills and the cut-off sub-areas.

Plains Sub-Area

1. Education

Since the literacy and educational status is very low among the Didayi people have laid emphasis on priority basis for the promotion of literacy and education through provision of necessary infrastructural and personnel components. As in the past lack of school buildings and teacher absenteeism stood on the way of educational development, they have come forward to participate in the construction of school buildings in their locality and provide necessary support for teacher's accommodation in their village.

2. Health, Nutrition and Sanitation

In addition to the existing ethnomedicinal practices among them, they need the help of modern medicines for the prevention and cure of various diseases. They need at least an additional Primary Health Centre at Oringi, the nodal village of this Sub-area. In the context of medical pluralism, there is need for the promotion of tribal medicine, by way of extending support for the growth of herbaria of tribal medicinal plants and herbs. The aged, expectant mothers in their pre-natal and post-natal stages and children require nutritional diets. They require good houses to live safe and sanitary toilets to prevent some infectious diseases.

3. Safe Drinking Water

They need safe drinking water supply, as water collected from hill streams is not free from contaminations. The tube wells, often defunct, do not provide potable water as it contains some minerals.

4. Communication and Electrification

They have clearly realised that the inadequacy of roads stands on the way of their socio-economic development. They need roads for transportation of men and materials to weekly market places and nearby urban centres. They require street lighting at the initial stage with supply of electricity in their villages.

5. Cultural Centre

In each village they need a cultural centre in the shape of a community hall to provide facilities for the promotion of their histrionic talents through dance, song, performing art, etc. Such a community hall will also provide space for village meetings, accommodation of guests, storing of musical instruments, etc.

6. Forests

They need afforestation through social-forestry programme with joint forest management for its optimum utilisation coupled with its conservation for future generation. They realise the ill-effects of *podu* ravaged hill slopes and agree to go for terracing in order to prevent soil-erosion by adopting suitable measures.

7. Horticulture

In the context of horticulture, they have already experienced with growing of fruits, vegetables and cash crops and they need massive plantation in *podu* ravaged areas so that their food stock is supplemented with additional income generation opportunities. They agree to take care of such plantations, which are not only beneficial for the present generation, but also for the generations to come. They also agree to participate actively in raising plants and vegetable seedlings if a nursery is set up in their areas. They need to promote the backyard cultivation, as it is felt lucrative economic pursuit for them.

8. Agriculture and Soil Conservation

They need the upgradation of their land resource which includes low land, upland and shifting land, by the provision of agricultural implements, plough bullocks, improved variety of seeds, fertilisers and pesticides, irrigation facilities and soil conservation measures, etc.

9. Animal Husbandry

They need supply of bullocks, cows for dairy farming, goat-rearing units and poultry units to supplement their income.

10. Co-operation and Marketing

They need establishment of co-operative societies at the village level involving primary producers and it will go a long way in promoting the marketing nexus.

11. Handicrafts and Cottage Industry

They need training for developing various handicrafts and cottage industries, such as bamboo craft, wood craft, mat making, brooms making, food crafts and semi-processing of other consumable goods, provided they are assisted to run such units with funding.

12. Service Sector

In the service sector, they have shown interests in such services as tailoring, cycle repairing, hair cutting, etc.

Cut-off Sub-Area

The cut-off sub-area of the Didayi people pose similar felt needs as their counterparts in the plains sub-area in the sectors, such as education, health, nutrition and sanitation, safe drinking water, cultural centre, forest, horticulture, agriculture and soil conservation, co-operative and marketing, handicrafts and cottage industry and service sector. In cases of communication and electrification and fishing and pisciculture, the Didayi people of cut-off sub-area have posed their needs which may be treated as unique and area-specific.

1. Communication and Electrification

They need road from Jantry to Ambilibeda, connected by a bridge and then from Ambilibeda to Oringi by *ghat* road as Oringi village is connected by road with Kudumulugumma, the headquarters of the block and the D.D.A. as well. Thereafter, electrification of remote villages may be taken up.

1. Fishing and Pisciculture:

They need more boats and nets, especially for young and ablebodied male youths who intend to earn their livelihood through fishing in the reservoir. They have also shown interests for pisciculture through demonstration and necessary training.

Hills Sub-Area

In the hills sub-area, the Didayi have come up with similar felt needs as expressed by their counterparts in the plains sub-area and the unique area-specific need is discussed below:

1. Animal Husbandry

In addition to supply of bullocks, goat-rearing units and poultry units, they need piggery units as they had originally domesticated pigs since the recent past.

AN EMPIRICAL MODEL

The general objective in building an empirical model or a field model, in the present study, is to attain the goal of sustainable development among the Didayi people in general and the Didayi women in particular, in consonance with their felt needs by ensuring people's participation in the development process (ref. Fig. 5.2)

The specific objectives of the model may be stated as follows:

1. To take up such schemes/programmes which have in-built elements for ensuring people's participation as has been envisaged in their own perceptions of and approaches to development.
2. To provide administrative and technical support in implementing such schemes and programmes which are considered by themselves as culturally sustainable, eco-friendly and based primarily upon available as well as exploitable resources material, human and epistemological.

The basic tenets of the model for providing development inputs are based on the following assumptions:

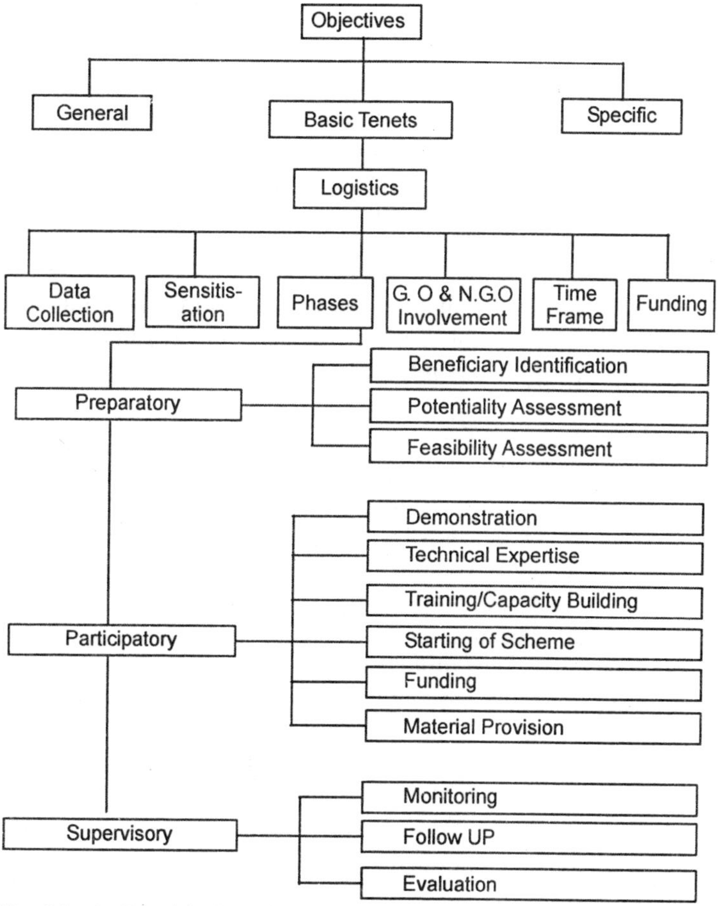

Fig. 5.2: An Empirical Model for Sustainable Development by Ensuring People's Participation among the Didayi of Malkangiri District (Odisha)

Assumptions

I. The Didayi people living in uniethnic or multiethnic villages are not secluded, isolated and encysted in absolute terms; rather they show interactions with the neighbouring ethno-cultural groups because of living together for generations.

II. In the multiethnic, multilevel and multi-dimensional interactions, the Didayi in their micro region develop cooperation, mutual interdependence and harmony, rather than conflict, mutual distrust and contradictions, despite differences among the neighbouring ethno cultural groups, for crises management through peaceful co-existence.

III. The Didayi's have their own perception of and approach to development, based on epistemological considerations. Although illiterate and uneducated, they have their indigenous skills, knowledge, ethical judgements and value orientations which enable them to discriminate between the right and the wrong to exercise choice for the best out of the available alternatives, and to better the existing lifestyle which they have inherited from the historically created designs for living.

IV. The Didayis have during the post-independence period experienced the planned development intervention, especially since a decade and a half through the Didayi Development Agency (DDA) and also through Block Development effort.

V. The literacy and education in their community are having an alarmingly low status.

VI. Despite masculine dominance in a patriarchal society like theirs, the status of the Didayi women is not low. They play their vital role not only in the hearth and home but also in outdoor income generating activities. Given opportunity, they will with their perseverance and potentiality, participate better in the development process than their male counterparts.

VII. The Didayis possess basic knowledge regarding locally available and exploitable resources, their consumption and protection; but lack technical and scientific knowledge which they intend to get from outside experts for capacity building and utilisation.

VIII. Didayis have their own basics regarding prioritisation of development efforts, based on primary needs and cultural responses and the realisation of imperatives.

IX. Like other simple tribal communities with limited aspirations they have no appreciation for such development inputs which envisage prolonged gestation period. They prefer such a scheme, which assures them benefits within a reasonably short period, and this is because of their economic organisation.

The model logistic may be briefly discussed below:

Prior to starting of a scheme/programme for implementation among the people it is necessary to collect the basic data which would enable the development practitioner in doing the preparatory phase of work.

The intended beneficiaries are to be sensitised by building awareness to enable them to understand all relevent facts connected with a scheme unambiguously.

The operationalisation of schemes/programmes would require the involvement of Government Organisation (G.O.) and Non-Governmental Organisation (NGO).

The implementation of any scheme would require the explicit pronouncement of a time frame, without which the goal attainment strategy is jeopardised.

The most vital aspect is funding which is synchronous with the starting of the scheme.

Further, the model logistics include broadly three operational phases, such as the Preparatory, Participatory and Supervisory.

The Preparatory phase would proceed for beneficiary identification basing on the basic data already collected. The next step, i.e., potentiality assessment would examine the potentiality of the beneficiary identified for the scheme. Further, the feasibility assessment would indicate the suitability, congeniality and viability of implementing the scheme.

The participatory phase would go for the demonstration of various aspects of the scheme and provide the technical expertise necessary for the scheme. Further a scheme may require training for capacity ehancing in order to implement it. The starting of scheme with funding and necessary material provision would be undertaken with people's participation.

The supervisory phase would involve both the beneficiaries and development practitioners jointly for concurrent evaluation or monitoring for idenitfying the bottlenecks or shortcomings in the way of the implementation of the scheme; and follow-up action would be taken immediately for the eradication of the defects. Finally, the evaluation (*ex post*) which would be taken up after the completion of scheme would also be a joint venture (*cf* Gengaje and Setty, 1992:545-571 and Mahapatra, 1986-87:1-23.).

As an overview of the present chapter, it is apt to state that keeping in veiw the theoretical frame and juxtaposing the methodological perspective with it, there was need to verify the propositions of the study by way of empirical observations to arrive at the findings to tell us whether such propositions hold good. In the words of Pelot, (1970:12) "Theoretical systems are the general sources for researchable propositions (hypotheses), and it can be argued that every hypothesis (and the concepts of which it is composed) is derived from some sort of theoretical system, even when the person presenting the hypothesis is unable to state the nature of his theoretical assumptions". The structural inquiry of the present study includes four hypotheses, each pinpointing its own dimension and uniqueness. In consonance with the tenet of each hypothesis facts were presented before the informants lucidly, unambiguously and in a simple style, so as to be intelligible to them. As a prelude to Focus Group Discussions, hypotheses were explained repeatedly in order to collect their responses and assess their validity and reliability. Such Focus Group Discussions were conducted in a number of villages in all the three sub-areas of the Didayi habitations, so that the findings were subject to comparision and verification. Moreover, the tenability of such hypotheses was verified by the investigators through personal interviews with the informants. The outcome of these exercises showed that there was no disagreement or dissonance in the responses of informants regarding the hypotheses and thus, they may be regarded as tenable. Further, after the completion of fieldwork the investigators of all categories met and discussed about their basic findings, encounters and experiences and merits and shortcomings before proceeding for report writing and the entire process connected with the study could be streamlined. After the interaction among the investigators it was possible to understand certain events, occurrences and phenomena in the field situation in their right perspective. The investigations conducted by employment of the techniques of Focus Group Discussion and personal interviews were replicated or recycled in other villages in order to evolve and locate consistencies to proceed for generalisation.

To conclude, it may be reiterated that sustainability is yet to be achieved in the Didayi development process and hence the present exercise.

Photographs

Plate 1: Ploughing land at Purunagumma

Plate 2: Preparing land for sowing seeds at Purunagumma

Plate 3: A watch hut with indigenous device to protect crops from wild animals

Plate 4: A temporary hut near Podu land at Karkaguda

Plate 5: The shrine of Bhirubhairo at Purunagumma

Plate 6: Didayi woman bringing cereal from field to home at Jantry

Plate 7: Focus Group discussion at Orapadar

Plate 8: Investigators collecting data at Oringi

Plate 9: Investigators on their way to Taber

Plate 10: Head of the Household with his children

Plate 11: Old woman husking *suan* at Badankiguda

Plate 12: Grinding cereal by wooden grinder at Sanyasiguda

Plate 13: Children at Orapadar

Plate 14: Investigators with dance party at Orapadar

Plate 15: Investigators greeted by dance party at Orapadar

Plate 16: Discussion of Investigators at Orapadar

Plate 17: Didayi woman with her children at Orapadar

Plate 18: Didayi woman cleaning utensils at Orapadar

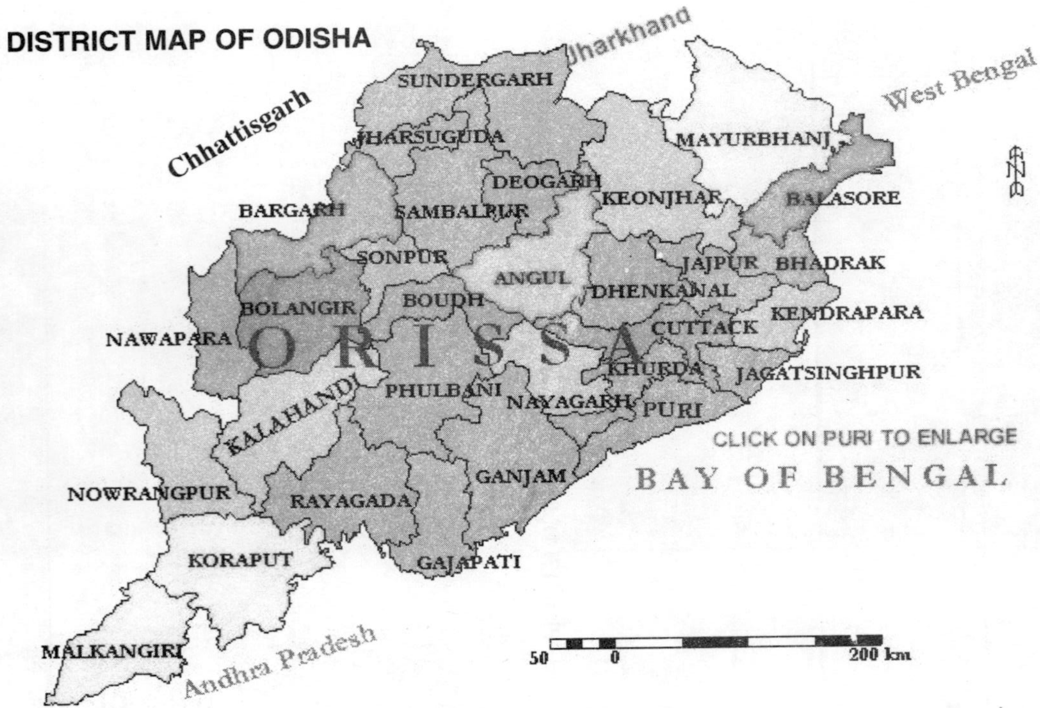

Map 1: District Map of Odisha

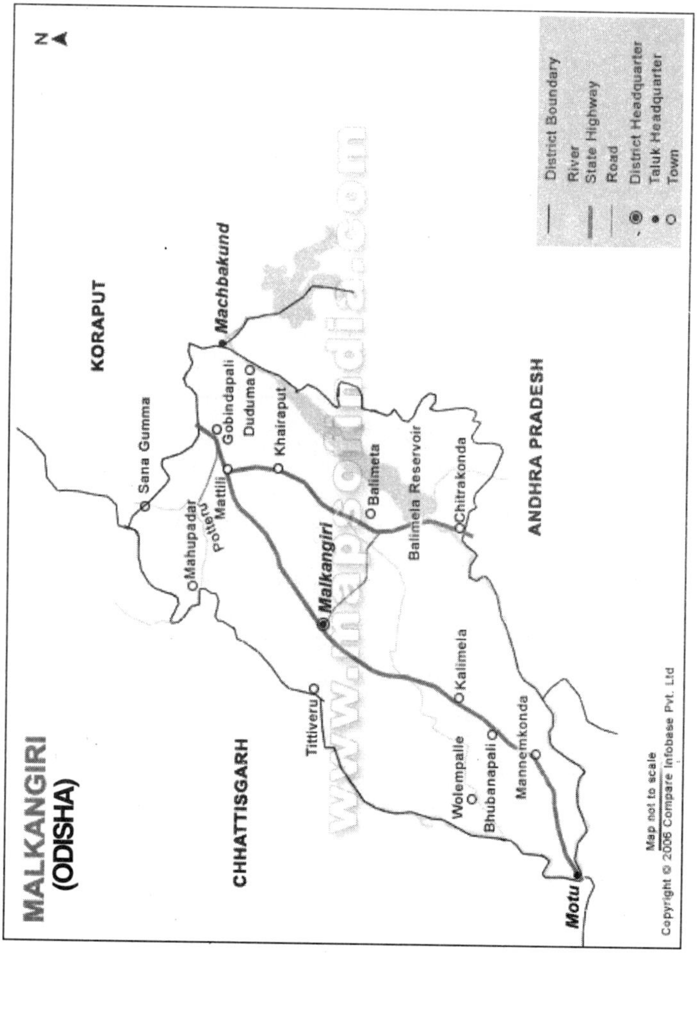

Map 2: Malkangiri (Odisha)

MUZUMULI MAP OF KUDUMULUGUMA BLOCK
DISTRICT KORAPUT
Scale-1″ = 2 Miles

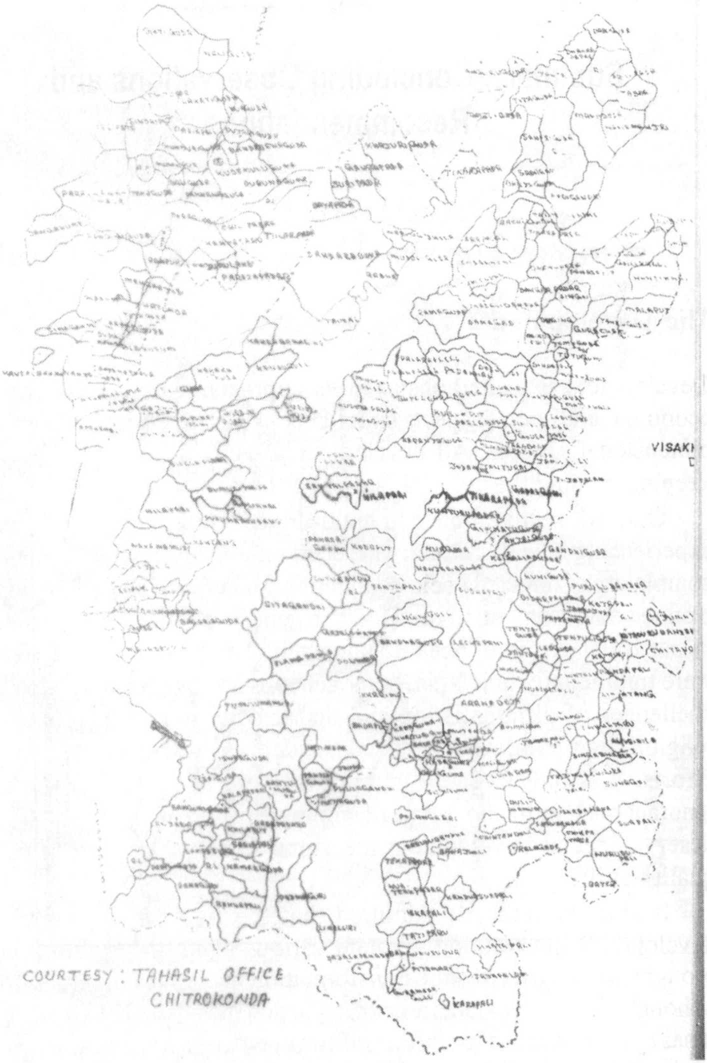

Map 3: Muzumuli Map of Kudumuluguma Block District Koraput

6

Summary, Concluding Observations and Recommendations

SUMMARY AND CONCLUDING OBSERVATIONS

The Development

Development is to be holistic in its approach, and it must include economic and social aspects simultaneously. Therefore, it is a multi-dimensional process. All developmental activities must be framed keeping in mind the cultural fabrics of the particular society.

Ours is a multi-ethnic and multi-lingual country which has been experiencing social, cultural and economic changes over time. The complexity of directed socio-economic changes, during half a century planned development, in rural India in general and tribal communities in particular has now been documented. The tribal villages, which were traditionally uniethnic, homogeneous and simple are facing the challenges of differentiation and disharmony in social, economic, religious and political spheres consequent upon these development efforts. It is only because of high incident of poverty, illiteracy, ignorance and indigenous type of employment, the tribal communities deserve special development measures for enhancement of their quality of life.

It must be honestly admitted that the five decades of tribal development intervention, through various plans and schemes, has brought out socio-economic transformation in the tribal micro-world, although the achievements are not in consonance with the aspirations. It has opened avenues for further efforts in order to attain sustainability in the field of participatory development, so that the tribal people became self-reliant, free from exploitation, and enrich their quality of life *vis-à-vis* the enrichment of the quality of environment.

Participatory Development

Now, the time has come to rethink human development through active participation of the people. It was found that a top-down approach in development planning could not deliver the desired goods. Hence, it was rightly thought that implementation of development programmes cannot realise their targets without peoples' participation at all levels, i.e., programme formulation, implementation, and evaluation.

Especially, in the field of tribal development, the pertinent question arises as to how peoples' participation in the development process could be ensured. The problems encountered here are, that the tribal world is relatively isolated, and encapsulated and tribal people are relatively shy, inward looking and less modernised. If properly thought and done, the participatory development will certainly bridge the hiatus between the intended tribal beneficiaries and the development practitioners by ensuring mutual confidence among them.

Sustainable Development

While coming to sustainable development, it is to be emphasised that immediate needs of the present population is to be fulfilled without hampering the requirements of the future generations as well as safeguarding the ecology and environment as such through the development process. While ensuring compatibility between ecology and economy a striking balance is maintained between mankind as consumer and natural system as producer. More precisely, the sustainable development processes are to continue in such a way that the socio-economic order is maintained and long term carrying capacity of the land in the region is assured. Since human beings are the cause and consequences of development, sustainability is the prime need in the socio-economic development process.

The Present Study : "The Didayi"

The present study is undertaken on the "Didayi", a particularly Vulnerable Tribal Group of Malkangiri District of Odisha. Its primary aim is to build a field model to ensure peoples' participation for sustainable development. A micro-project named the Didayi Development Agency (DDA) has been functioning with its headquarters at Kudumulugumma, the Block Headquarters, since 1986-87. The DDA includes a total number of 39 villages mainly inhabited by the Didayi people. Out of these 6 villages are located in the foothills, mostly in plain sub-area, 18 villages in the hills or mountainous areas and the rest 15 villages in the cut-off areas of Chitrokonda reservoir consequent upon the construction of Balimela Hydro-Electricity Project.

The plains Didayis are comparatively more advanced than their counterparts in the hills and cut-off areas because of their culture contact, accessibility and in-road of modernisation process. The plains Didayis have now accepted settled agriculture, whereas the hills and cut-off area Didayis are in the pre-agricultural stage mainly pursuing shifting cultivation; food gathering and hunting. Fishing has also become a subsidiary occupation among the Didayi living in cut-off areas of Chitrokonda reservoir.

But, on the whole, because of their pre-agricultural level of economy and technology, low level of literacy, and declining or near stagnant population, they have been rightly identified as one of the Particularly Vulnerable Tribal Groups (PTGs) as per the Government of India criteria.

Although, Didayis have already experienced planned development intervention for a period of one and a half decade; the programmes launched and the investments made for the purpose of their development have not yielded the desired result, i.e., the benefits in real terms have not reached the Didayi people.

Main Objective

The main objective of this study is to evolve an appropriate mechanism to arrest differential flow of development opportunities and promote accrual of benefits to the poorest of the poor Didayi, so that the basic survival is assured. One word of caution that is to be kept in mind here is that, in spite of their low techno-economic base they possess the repository of traditional knowledge and the cultural apparatus, and unless the development approach is compatible with their culture, attempts towards the attainment of sustainability will prove to be futile.

The Didayi Culture : Human Values

The Didayi are peace-loving, hospitable, rational and gentle. They are also innovative, indigenous, industrious and sincere. They maintain inter-ethnic amity among themselves. It is quite natural to observe that like many other tribals their value orientations have undergone transformation due to various factors such as modernisation, peasantisation, of economy, introduction of schooling, literacy intervention, implementation of development schemes and programmes, etc. They need to develop their coping mechanism for better integration with the changing environment both physical and human and it would require capacity enhancement througth training.

The Didayis are, no doubt, marginalised, due to lack of education, and literacy, but they are not less knowledgeable in life situations and about the micro-world around them. They are also able to forecast, foresee and visualise, if not far, the near future and take care of life sustenance for human beings, animals and plants.

The Didayi women folk play a vital role not only in the household sphere but also assume responsibility in supplementing household income. They have liberty and freedom in the social life. The marriage for a woman cannot be performed without her consent. Their men folk take their (women's) advice while taking any socio-political responsibility in their society. Their latent leadership quality has been manifested in the assumption of roles under Panchayati Raj institutions and they have become reasonably vocal to express their ideas for betterment of the community as a whole. The Didayi women to be brief, are hard working, sincere and capable of shouldering responsibilities and given appropriate scope they would participate actively and equally as their male counterparts.

Health Management

So far as the health management is concerned, the Didayi still cling to their indigenous ethnomedicinal practices often coupled with magical performances with the help of their own medicinemen. It is not a fact that they are not aware of modern medical facilities but it is not available in their proximity and their income does not allow them to go for it. However, the multipurpose village level workers (MPWs) are distributing medicines among ailing persons for very common ailments. At times chances of cure are rare as there is no health check up, proper diagnosis and follow-up action.

Economy

The Didayi economy is mainly based on agriculture and forest collections inclduing food gathering. In the plains area the Didayi households, which are in possession of low lying land, practise settled cultivation as their primary occupation and in addition, they grow seasonal vegetables and tobacco in their kitchen gardens. In the cut-off area, the Didayis practise shifting cultivation and in addition, they pursue food gathering and fishing. In the hill area, the Didayi practise shifting cultivation and pursue minor forest collections for their livelihood. The hunting as an economic pursuit has become rare due to depletion of forests. Currently they are utilising boats and nets for fishing in the reservoir and selling fish in the local markets to earn their living. There is a future scope for pisciculture in this area. Further, there is need for boosting animal husbandry practices as they possess the indigenous skills for rearing and caring animals. The nearby natural forests and grass land provide a positive opportunity in this field. The development of dairy project will take time in the Didayi area as they do not milch their cows. Like other tribal people, the Didayi lack entrepreneurial skill and motive of capital formation. All these need careful probing at the field level.

The Political Organisation

Their traditional political organisation was very simple and useful in the maintenance of their internal and external affairs. They were never lawless. The headman of the village, the Naik, was considered as the secular chief of the village and was assisted by the *chalan*, the messenger. The inroad of Panchayati Raj System recently has given rise to the emergence of new leaders, elected representatives instead of hereditary ones and the traditional politico-jural organisation is fast weaning. However, the traditional village Panchayats still carry weightage in the Didayi areas.

The Religion

The Didayi are polytheists, believers in a number of deities —

benevolent, malevolent and ambivalent. They worship the Sun as the supreme deity, the Earth Goddess, forest deity and a host of gods and goddesses for their blessings. The deities are appeased with offerings and sacrifices on specific occasions. They also worship ancestral cults. The Palasi is the saçerdotal chief of the Didayi community.

The Social Organisation

The Didayi society is divided into a number of clans and lineages under the unilineal principle. The clans are totemistic, and besides other functions, play a vital role in regulating marriage in their community. Didayis are partriarchal, partrilineal and patrilocal. They have various ways of acquiring mates, but the marriage by negotiation appears to be prestigious and significant. After marriage, the married couple generally, lives in a separate house. The kinship plays a vital role not only in their social life but also in economic life promoting mutual help and cooperation in various economic pursuits. There is prevalence of remarriage of widows/widowers, and divorces, of course with social approval.

Focus Group Discussions

After eliciting information on society, economy, culture and planned development experience among the Didayi, it was felt necessary to organise Focus Group Discussion units and employment of other tools to elicit relevant data regarding people's prioritization for achievement of development goal. The study is, therefore, intended to analyse intensively as to how peoples' participation would be available in launching various development schemes and programmes for them. The documentation of such facts would provide clues towards developing models for ensuring peoples' participation for a sustainable development.

The Hypotheses

From the discussions made above, the following hypotheses have emerged to be tested from the information collected in the field.

1. No development is possible, if it is not culturally sustainable.
2. No development is possible, if it is not eco-friendly.

3. No development is possible, if it is not based on locally available and exploitable resources.
4. No development is possible, if it does not ensure people's (women included) participation.

Objectives

The principal objectives of the study are (a) to explore and establish empirical models to ensure active participation of the people (women included) in their own development, (b) to make optimum use of locally available resources, human as well as physical including material, and (c) to find out such models which will be eco-friendly and fit into locally available resources (material, human as well as epistemological).

The Research Design

The research design is based on the principle of ethnographic case study which include observation, interview, documentary analysis and use of informants to study the socio-cultural characteristics of subjects. Further, socio-cultural analysis in studying different variables under study, e.g., income and savings, enrolment and dropouts at primary stage, women's participation, family planning, protection of natural environment, etc., sets the study apart from case study.

The Didayi — a particularly vulnerable tribal group of Malkangiri district constitutes the case or focus of the present study. The study area inhabited by the Didayi has been categorised into three distinct sub-areas i.e., (a) the plains sub-area, the inhabitants of which are mainly settled cultivators, (b) the hills sub-area which is characterised by rugged and mountainous terrains, and (c) the cut-off sub-area the villages have been submerged in the Chitrokonda reservoir of Balimela Dam Project.

The socio-economic status of the inhabitants of these sub-areas varies due to a number of factors, e.g., communication, agricultural practices, availability of resources, exposure to modern methods of cultivation and cultural contact with other communities, etc.

Data Collection : Methodology

The basic information was collected in respect of the universe through a comprehensive household survey schedule. Further, detailed information in respect of six villages, i.e., two villages from each sub-area were collected, using multiple data gathering devices, to make an indepth analysis of the issues concerning people's participation and development of the target group. Purpose based sampling technique was followed in the selection of the villages.

The key informants for the sample study consisted of (a) the members of SHGs, (b) beneficiaries of different poverty alleviation programmes, (c) members of NGOs, (d) field functionaries of the micro project, (e) other government officials involved in the implementation of developmental schemes, (f) heads of the families, (g) opinion leaders at village level, (h) members of women organisations, and (i) above all the villagers.

The household survey schedule enquired about details of every household spread over 39 Didayi villages regarding family occupation, income and expenditure, savings, family size, age and sex-wise literacy and marital status, health and sanitation, movable and immovable property, etc.

An attitude test battery schedule was also served to study the attitude of respondents towards various welfare activities being implemented by the DDA and effectiveness of the project, etc.

Interviews, both individual and groups were conducted with different categories of informants so as to explore facts pertaining to participation of women in economic activities, benefits of ongoing developmental programmes, people's perception of development, etc. A semi-structured interview schedule was also served to explore the facts pertaining to implementation of various development programmes.

The Focus Group Discussion (FGD) provided the base for intimate interaction with the people in order to explore their perception, attitude, aspiration, success and failure in planning for the future.

In addition to all these, secondary sources of data and information were collected from DDA office, Tahsil office, RI office, Forest Department, etc. Research reports, journals, census hand books and still photographs, etc. were also used for preparing the report.

The data were collected through fieldwork by a team consisting of the Principal Investigator, one Co-Investigator, one Research Associate, four Associate Investigators, and as many as twelve Field Investigators. They visited the field, stayed there, established rapport and came in contact with the people for collection of relevant data in the field situation. The duration of field works in the sub-area, e.g., the plains, the hills and the cut-off areas were five days, twenty days and one month respectively.

The data so collected were processed and analysed after putting to qualitative techniques as well as simple quantitative techniques and percentage.

Demography

The population of the Didayi tribe is 5,727 in 2001-02 as per the detailed household survey conducted by COATS, Koraput. The population was only 1,661 as per the 1941 Census, which increased to 1,978 in 1961; 1,971 in 1981 and 4460 in 1991. The decennial growth rate of the Didayi population does not show uniform positive growth trend. Between 1941 to 1961 Census periods, the growth rate maintained an increasing (+) 9.5 per cent and from 1961 to 1971 it was (+) 9.4 per cent. But this growth rate decreased to (—) 8.9 per cent in the decade 1971-81. Again in the next decade, i.e., 1981-91, it has a sharp increase of (+) 126.3 per cent a favourable trend. The field survey conducted by COATS, Koraput could find a total population of the Didayi as 5,727 in 2001-02 and the decennial growth rate being (+) 28.4 per cent.

The age composition of the Didayi shows that 41.02 per cent of them are in the age group of 0-14 years, 56.16 per cent in the age group of 15-59 years and rest 2.82 per cent in the age group of 60 and above. (Survey by COATS, Koraput)

The sex-ratio among the Didayis also showed some peculiarities in various censuses. The female populations outnumbered the male in 1961, whereas they were nearly 5 per cent less than their male counterparts in 1971 Census. The females again out numbered males in 1981. The same trend is found in 2001-02 survey conducted by COATS, Koraput.

Literacy

The literacy rate which was 2.73 per cent in 1961 decreased to 0.79 per cent in 1971 and subsequently increased to 3.19 per cent in 1981. As per the survey 2001-02, there is an increasing trend in literacy (7.89% in general which consists of 3.61% females and 12.56% of males). This shows that the literacy rate among the Didayi is very low as compared to 16.3 per cent in Malkangiri District (1991) and State average of 48.55 per cent (1991).

Distribution of Population

The population of the Didayi region has been distributed under three sub-areas, i.e., (1) Plains sub-area-6 villages, (2) Hills sub-area-18 villages, and (3) Cut-off sub-area -15 villages, a total of 39 villages in all. There are 326 Didayi households in the plains sub-area with a total population of 1,306 in 296 households.

The Didayi Culture

The tribal culture is intimately interrelated with the economic system of the tribals which can be understood in the purview of cultural factors. The implementation of various development schemes in tribal areas without taking into account the cultural background of a particular tribe, have mostly resulted in failure, and hence, frustration. The case of the Didayi tribe is no exception to it. It is, therefore, necessary to understand the socio-economic organisations and cultural background of the Didayi while suggesting/implementing any alternative strategy for their sustainable development. A detailed discussion of the Didayi culture has been made in Chapter 3 of this report and a brief analysis of it has also been given earlier in the present chapter.

To be brief, the Didayi social organisation consists of a number of clans and there is perfect solidarity and co-operation among the clan members. The family is the primary social institution and the unit of production and consumption. It is normally nuclear and monogamous in nature.

There is division of labour between sexes and ages among the Didayi. Certain activities like fetching of firewood and water, keeping houses clean, cooking and collecting certain roots and tubers are entrusted to women. Men plough the field, cut trees, bushes for shifting cultivation, cut bamboos and timber and go for hunting. Children help their parents in agricultural operations and food gathering. Aged women and girls watch the house and take care of babies.

Boys and girls exercise their choice in selecting their mates only with the condition that they must not choose anyone from their own clan. There were various forms of marriage prevalent among them, but out of this the negotiated marriage is prestigious but cost effective because of the payment of bride price observance of rituals and arrangement of feasts. The widow/widower remarriage and junior leviration are permitted.

The Didayi community has accorded its women and elevated position and granted a good deal of freedom. They play very important role in socio-economic life of Didayi community and shoulder a lot of household responsibilities.

Economic Life of the Didayi

The Didayi economy mostly cluster round the hills and forest and its two important founding pillars are cultivation and forest collection. Their cultivation is mostly forest based, in the sense that they practise shifting cultivation in the hills and forests for their living. The Didayi living in the low lying areas and the plains adopt settled cultivation and mostly raise paddy. In the *podu* fields they grow minor millets like *ragi*, *suan*, *jawar*, and *kandul*, etc. They also grow cash crops like niger in the *dongar* lands.

Shifting cultivation is a very labour intensive type of agricultural practice. From the survey it is now evident that the value of yield per acre of shifting land is lower than that of the settled land, i.e., it is Rs. 1291.49 per acre as against Rs. 2279.10 in settled land. Even the low lying *dongar* land and garden land in hill area show better productivity (i.e., Rs. 1622.74 and Rs. 2093.97 respectively per acre) than that of the shifting land. On the other hand, plough cultivation is gaining popularly among the Didayis living in the plains sub-area, although these people have not totally abandoned their *podu* cultivation. Most of them still practise shifting cultivation in the nearby hill slopes along with plough cultivation. But the yield under plough cultivation is generally more than that of shifting and *dongar* cultivation. Those who live in the cut-off area they are found to adopt shifting, *dongar* and settled cultivation simultaneously. Here also the average yield per acre in settled cultivation is more (Rs. 1182.82) than that of Dongar land (Rs. 1165.25) and shifting land (Rs. 1007.48).

Food Gathering

Although agriculture is the main occupation of the Didayi food gathering and collection of minor forest produce (MFP) constitute important and supplementary source of livelihood. They collect edible fruits plants, leaves and roots in various seasons. Palm wine is drawn and used as a favourable drink by the Didayi. They collect tamarind, *kendu* leaves, fuel wood, bamboo, thatching grass, *Siali* leaves, *siali* creeper,etc., from the nearby forests. The field survey in these villages shows that an average of 27.35 per cent of income of the Didayi comes from forest collection and food gathering taken together.

Hunting has now become a pastime for the Didayi due to depletion of forests and also imposition of regulations in recent times. Now only occasionally they go for hunting and they also take part in annual ceremonial huntings.

Those Didayis who are now living in cut-off areas have to some extent adopted fishing as a supplementary source of living. The Didayi Development Agency (DDA) at Kudumulugumma has been encouraging them by supplying boats and nets for the purpose. These people get only about 2 per cent of their total income from fishing.

Animal Husbandry

Didayis are found to keep various animals like pigs, cattle, goats, sheep, etc. Some of them also rear hens, cocks, etc. But majority of them neither milch their cows nor drink milk. The cattle are reared by them for ploughing and to use as meat occasionally. They are also used as a part of bride price during marriage. The nearby green forests and grass land can support the livestock in the areas. The contribution of livestock to the total annual income of the Didayi comes to be 11.83 per cent.

Almost all Didayi households have kept fowl, which is of considerable economic importance to them. They sometimes exchange or sell fowls in the weekly markets. Fowls are also used for sacrificial purposes.

Didayis, mostly the landless ones, engage themselves as both agricultural and non-agricultural labourers for wages. Wage labour has contributed 17.24 per cent of their annual income.

Level of Income

Didayis get the highest proportion of their total annual income (36.87%) from agriculture. Next to it in importance come forest collections including food gathering (27.35%). Hence agriculture and forest activities taken together have contributed as high as 64.22 per cent of the total income of the Didayi. On an average of Rs. 3893.26 per annum per family has come from agriculture followed by forest produce collection of Rs. 2888.20. Next in importance rank wage earning which contributes 17.24 per cent and livestock (11.83%). Other sources of livelihood like fishing, business and services are of minor importance of the Didayi.

The Productive Factors

In economic analysis land, labour, capital and organisation constitute the factors of production. The available land in the Didayi region may be classified under four broad heads, i.e., (a) shifting or *Podu* land, (b) *dongar* (hill slope dry), (c) settled (low lying paddy) land, and (d) Homestead (including garden) land. There are forests on the hills adjacent to the villages which include reserved, protected and unreserved categories. Didayis exploit these resources both for cultivation and forest collection.

The Didayi mostly engage their family labour in productive activities including cultivation and occasionally hired labour. Co-operative and exchange labour are also marked features in their socio-economic life. There is division of labour between sexes in agricultural and forest activities.

In a subsistence type of economy of the Didayi there is little scope of saving out of surplus income and hence capital formation. The capital formation is at the rudimentary stage.

They have their own plough bullocks and some indigenous tools to be used in agriculture. Now the DDA has started to supply agricultural inputs, like plough, spade, crowbar, sickle, and seeds. Again nets and boats are supplied to the Didayi people for fishing who live in cut-off area and on the bank of river and reservoir.

The Didayi economy basically being a self-sufficient one is at the subsistence level. Organisation of economic activities centre round the family, the basic unit of production and consumption. Profit motive in economic enterprises is rarely found among them. The production decision is mainly taken by the family members and the decision of the head of the family is final.

Consumption Expenditure

The average annual expenditure of a Didayi family comes to

Rs.10038.28; its monthly expenditure being Rs. 836.45, as estimated through the COATS survey made during 2001-02. Out of the total expenditure a major share goes to food (54.78%). Next in the importance comes fuel (10%). A little above 6 per cent of their total expenditure is incurred on clothing and almost the same amount is spent on house building and repairing, etc. In the consumption of tobacco (3.72%), and in drinking (2.26%) combinedly they spend about 6 per cent of their total expenditure. About 4.57 per cent of their total expenditure is made on festivals.

An Analysis of Income and Expenditure

From an analysis of income and expenditure of the Didayi it is found that they maintain a subsistence economy, which is self-sufficient in nature. The average annual income and expenditure nicely balance with each other with a marginal surplus of income (Rs. 520.69) over expenditure. Only 18 households (1.37%) have incurred some loans amounting to Rs. 77,775.

On the basis of an average monthly expenditure of Rs. 250 per month per individual (now the yardstick to select BPL households) about 70 per cent of the Didayis are found to remain below the poverty line.

Exchange and Distribution

With limited wants to be fulfilled by a small number of Didayi people and abundance of forests, forest land and natural resources, they could lead a self-sufficient economy, though at the subsistence level. They derived most of their requirements from their surrounding land, hills and forests.

There was the provision of the direct exchange of goods, animals and services among themselves. They were buying tools and implements mainly from the neighbouring weekly markets, the tools, which they could not produce by themselves.

In course of time changes have taken place. The Didayi have left wearing their traditional bark clothes. Now cotton and synthetic clothes have been bartered. Ornaments have been bought in exchange of chillies, grains, pulses, oilseeds, etc. Cash payments to buy dresses, iron implements, pots and cattle are comparatively recent happenings. Gradually money has become the medium of exchange among the Didayi.

In addition, there are extra-economic exchanges in their community by way of gifts and presentations.

The crops produced in the fields and the items collected from forests are mostly meant for self-consumption at the family level and a small portion of it is meant for exchange in the market. Land areas are mostly self-owned. Labour used in agricultural and forest operations are mostly family labour. Only in case of hired labour wages are paid. There is also system of exchange of labour among them, when loans are incurred for purchase of agricultural implements, plough bullocks, etc., and for other purposes, interest is to be paid.

Political Life

An analysis of the political life of the Didayi has already been made in foregoing paragraphs and more elaborately in Introduction and Chapter Third. Out of all the regional political organisations, the traditional Panchayat or the village council is old and very powerful socio-political organisation. Its functions embrace all corporate activities in social, political, economic and religious spheres of the village. The council functions through its office bearers particularly the headman (Naik) and his assistant, the Chalan and Palasi. All adult male heads of the family are its members.

The statutory Panchayats have already gained confidence of the people and the old system and the new system are complementary to each other.

Religious Life

The religious life of the Didayi centres round the worship of Sun God and Mother Earth. Their pantheon includes several gods and goddesses. The deities are propitiated at regular intervals through a series of religious ceremonies throughout the year. On the occasion of these ceremonies sacrifice of animals is common. These ceremonies are celebrated with dancing, singing and drinking continuously for several days.

Socialisation

Socialisation is a process by which an individual acquires values, ethos and skills essential to live in a society meaningfully. A number of social organisations or agencies, e.g., home, school, peer group, cult, temple, shrine, and church, state, print media, radio, T.V., etc., are involved in it.

In the process of socialisation, the family and the immediate social environment and social institutions like youth dormitories, play important roles. Schools system being in a very bad shape in the Didayi area, majority of the boys and girls at school going age are exposed to their families and other social organisations. They acquire basic life skills through informal verbal instructions and observations. Their behavioural patterns and attitudes are to a great extent are guided by youth dormitories, still functioning in the Didayi villages.

Education

The Didayi are educationally very backward. Out of the 39 inhabited Didayi villages surveyed, it was found that 19 of them do not have even a primary school, Moreover, out of the 20 primary schools existing in these areas, eight are single teacher schools and four are without buildings. It was complained by the villagers that the teachers mostly remain absent from school. Hence, it is not surprising to see that the rate of literacy among the Didayi is as low as 7.89 per cent (i.e. 12.56 per cent for males and 3.36 per cent for females). Another most interesting thing to note here is that the dropout among the Didayi children at primary stage is as high as 90.31 per cent (i.e., it is 87.27 per cent for boys and 94.19 per cent for girls).

Health and Sanitation

Although the Didayi men and women are mostly found to be well built with slim body; still most of them suffer from diseases like malaria, hookworms, dysentery, and conjuctivities. They have still faith in supernatural beings for cure of diseases. The surroundings of the house and village are not kept clean. They mainly use water from the stream that flows within the village boundary.

After working of the DDA, multipurpose workers have been imparted with training and are supplied with some medicines to treat the patients. Medical centres being situated at very long distances from the villages, the villagers face a lot of troubles to avail medical treatment from qualified medical staff.

Value Orientations

One can find mutual love and cooperation among the Didayi. They are more receptive and open minded people; so also frank and honest. Their tolerance helps in conflict resolutions in a reasonable way. They have self-confidence and they do not consider themselves inferior to anyone. They give much importance and prominence to their women counterparts. A woman is the virtual centre of power both inside and outside home.

There are many such growth positive traits in the Didayi value orientation, which can be properly utilised while implementing schemes for their development.

Epistemological Issues

Although the Didayis are mostly illiterate, they possess working knowledge about their environment. They have their own indigenous skills, inherited from their forefathers which they timely utilise to sustain their life.

When the children grow up, they acquire knowledge regarding physical cleanliness, food gathering, cultivation and hunting, etc., and also other behavioural patterns through socialisation and verbal instructions. Their oral literature is very rich in folklore, folktale, myths, songs, riddles and proverbs.

Planned Development Intervention

The development efforts made by the Block authorities was negligible till the end of the Fourth Plan period. Only 5 hectares of land in the Kudumulugumma Block was irrigated and only three service cooperative societies were existing in the Block during 1970-71. The communication facilities were also extremely inadequate. As against 7 kms and 4 kms of road length for 100 square miles for the State and the district respectively, it was as low as 0.27 kms in the project area. The facilities for providing health services were extremely poor. The educational opportunities created in the Block were equally poor. The literacy rate of the Didayi declined from 2.72 per cent in 1961 Census to 0.78 per cent in 1971 Census due to non-availability and non-functioning of schools in the Block.

Educational Institution

After the Fifth Plan period the following socio-economic infrastructure have been created in the Didayi Development Project area. One residential Girls' High School at Purunagumma, one UGME school at Nakamamudi, 16 Primary Schools and three more Primary Schools with hostel have been established by the government for the educational development of the project area.

Health Facilities and Veterinary Services

There is only one PHC at Kudumulugumma Block Headquarters and two A.N.M. centres in the project area. The veterinary dispensary at Kudumulugumma and a L.I. centre at Jantry are the only service centres to look after the domesticated animals.

Co-operative Institutions

The LAMPS at Kudumulugumma is the only centre to meet the credit-cum-marketing requirements in the Block. Due to the absence of sub-centres, it is not able to provide any effective role in extending services in the project area.

Indira Awas Yojana (IAY)

Sixty-eight poor households have been provided with housing facilities under IAY by the Block authorities as a measure of poverty alleviation programme.

Self-Help Groups (SHGs)

In order to empower the women by enabling them to generate income, thirty-three Self Help Groups have been formed in 21 Didayi villages during the period from June 2000 to September 2000. Only 3 out of the 33 SHGs have received incentive grant of Rs. 10,000 recently.

Communication

Only five villages in the project are namely Oringi, Muduliguda, Purunagumma, Chelipadar and Nilapari are approachable by Jeep.

The fifteen villages situated in the cut-off area located across river Machkund are negotiable by boat/launch. The Hills sub-area villages and the villages on the cut-off sub-area are approached by foot only.

Didayi Development Agency Efforts

The Didayi Development Agency was established in August 1986. Initially it was decided by the Project Governing Body to cover up only seven villages. In 1989-90, ten more Didayi villages were included and it is understood that during 1993-94 all Didayi villages were covered up under the development programme.

Important Programmes Implemented

Supply of agricultural implements, like spade, pick-axe, crowbar and M.B. plough; introduction and popularisation of improved and high yielding varieties of crops, introduction of cash crops in the back-yard of their houses and gradual introduction and supply of chemical fertilisers and pesticides are the important programmes implemented by DDA for the development of agriculture sector among the Didayi.

Grafted mango, pineapple, banana suckers, lemon, papaya, coconut and pomegranate were planted in the backyard of the households as well as in the suitable sites to provide a continuous source of income and thereby sustainable development to the beneficiaries.

Check dams, diversion weirs and water harvesting structures have been constructed to provide irrigation facilities and to check soil erosion in limited number of villages. The hilly terrains and the large number of streams in each village provide enough opportunities for construction of water harvesting structures, check dams and diversion weirs.

A number of Didayis living close to both the banks of reservoir are expert in fishing. The D.D.A. has provided boats and nets to around 100 beneficiaries.

More than 100 beneficiaries have been provided with a pair of bullocks at the rate of one bullock per beneficiary in most of the cases. However, they need more of bullock to meet with their necessity. Goat-rearing units, poultry units and sheep units have also been supplied to them.

Thirty-two tube wells have been provided in the project area to meet with the requirement of drinking water. Village paths and link roads have been constructed in few Didayi villages.

Health checks-up programmes have been organised by D.D.A. in the Didayi villages with the cooperation of local medical officers. Medicines have been supplied. However, the absence of sub-centres of P.H.C. in the cut-off and hills sub-areas is creating health problems today also.

Adult education centres, and T.L.C. programmes have been organised. But education programmes in the project area have not come up to expectation mainly due to teacher absenteeism in the schools run by education and H & T.W. Department.

Ongoing Development Process

The D.D.A. is providing input assistance of different kinds of cereals, pulses and oil seeds. Efforts have also been made for promotion of ginger and groundnut cultivation.

Twenty more beneficiaries falling below poverty line have been provided with nets and boats during the last year. During the last year Didayis from different areas have been selected as Health workers and have been imparted with training. These workers have been provided with medicines to meet exigencies in their area.

As goat-rearing scheme has become successful in the project area more funds have been allotted for the purpose during the current year.

Tiles to roof the houses have been provided to the needy Didayis. During the current year 15 beneficiaries selected in the Palli Sabha will be provided by 12 G.C.I. sheet each.

A case study of 51 households on poverty alleviation programme revealed that—

(a) Out of the sample of 51 beneficiary households 41 were assisted through Block and the rest 10 through D.D.A.

(b) Majority of beneficiaries (62.75%) has been assisted in the form of cash. The amount of assistance vary between Rs. 5,000 and Rs. 22,000.

(c) Maximum number of the beneficiaries were selected through the Palli Sabha.

(d) Most of the beneficiaries have reported that they had undertaken the schemes out of their own interest.

(e) As high as 84.35 per cent of the beneficiaries reported that they did never spend any money to get the scheme sanctioned in their favour.

Perceptions of Development

The Didayi are very simple, mild, docile, law abiding, sincere and receptive people. It is because of their cultural apparatus that they eke out their livelihood in spite of ecological, geographical and other odds.

Agriculture is their primary source of livelihood. Scarcity of plain lands and valley lands and absence of other economically viable alternative sources of livelihood force them to take up shifting cultivation practices.

Next to agriculture, which provides them 36.6 per cent of their total income, 27.70 per cent of their income is derived from collection and sale of minor forest produce. Most of the households work as a daily wage earners at least for 30 to 40 days in a year. Survey of COATS in 2001-02 reveals that 86.67 per cent of the households depend on wage earning.

The Didayis on both sides of the reservoir banks with the help of boats and nets. The basket making skill of Didayi is also encouraging.

Most of them are illiterates and due to lack of outside exposure, their awareness is very much limited.

The intervention of Didayi Development Agency has brought considerable change in their perception of development. They have now started feeling the need of agricultural implements, seeds, fertilisers and pesticides. The animal husbandry support provided by D.D.A. has also helped to some extent for improvement in their standard of living.

The Didayi perception of development is now quite favourable for the D.D.A. authorities to inject further development inputs. They now further need better housing facilities, a little education for their children, essential medical services facilities in their own area.

The formation of 33 Self Help Groups in 21 villages with 494 ladies have laid the foundation for the empowerment of women.

Inventory of Resources

The Didayi Development Project area is endowed with abundant natural resources, like land, water and forest. However, the extent of low land available for cultivation is very much limtied. The study conducted by COATS reveals that there are 832.80 acres of low land, and 1362.40 acres of households are forced to follow the pernicious practice of shifting cultivation.

The existence of a number of hills at a higher altitude offer enough scope for extensive plantation of fruit bearing trees and tree having economic value. After the rainy season, the banks of the reservoir offer very good scope for cultivation of tabacco and other cash crops.

There are a large number of natural springs with perennial flow in the project area.

There is approximately 5,000 hectares of reserved land known as Kondakamberu reserved land in the cut-off area, around 2,000 hectares of protected reserve forest known as Balimela P.R.F. in the hill area and approximately 1000 hectares of unreserved land in the plain area villages.

In addition to large number of perennial streams in the hilly and mountainous region, the Balimela reservoir covers deep waterbody of 1,000 sq. kms, providing ample opportunities of pisciculture.

They have learnt from their experience to exploit natural resources to maintain their livelihood. However, without formal education, they lack the knowledge and the skill of scientific use of land, forest and water resources. Health facilities and educational opportunities provided in the area are not adequate. Due to large scale illiteracy in the project area the general level of awareness is very low as a result of which they are exploited by middlemen/businessmen in the weekly markets while exchanging or selling their produce.

Mobilisation of Resources

Natural resources including material resources and human resources need to be properly mobilised for the socio-economic development of the Didayi. Since the inception of the micro project, the government has concentrated on an integrated approach. Mainly having two broad components. The first component is family oriented programme for economic development and the second one is infrastructure development and social services. Agricultural implements, seeds, fertilisers and pesticides were supplied for the development of agriculture. Fruit trees were supplied for the development of horticulture. Bullocks, goat-rearing units, poultry units, etc., were made for the development of animal husbandry section and in the cut off area boats and nets were supplied for fishery development.

An examination of the distribution of these benefits among the beneficiaries reveals that they were not fairly distributed in all villages. Similar is the case with infrastructure development and social service support. This has created a sense of discontentment among the inhabitants of the hill area and cut-off area villages.

Before implementation of any programme in future, resources may be mobilised in a more systematic and equitable manner rather than an on *ad hoc* basis while planning for resource mobilization. Emphasis may be paid on few programmes on extensive basis to a larger number of villages. Similarly, while providing infrastructure development, there is need to be a more or less equal distribution of benefits to all the three sub-areas.

The Challenge and the Response

The micro projects are expected to continue for a definite period of time till the socio-economic and skill development of the people is enhanced to such an extent that they will no more need any external agency to work for them. The project officials may agree to bear this in mind and implement the programmes accordingly ensuring people's participation at each step.

People's Sustainable Development

Didayis were identified as a particularly vulnerable tribal group having small population representing a simple society with rich cultural heritage. Over a period of six decades (1941-2001-02) their average decennial population growth is estimated at +6.81 per cent which is far below the standard decennial growth rate. Among them the most active age-group (15-59 years) is 56.16 per cent of the total population. Their literacy rate is 7.89 per cent for the total population, 12.56 per cent for males and 3.36 per cent for females. The per household and per capita monthly income are estimated at Rs. 884.86 and Rs. 202.95 respectively. The corresponding expenditure comes to Rs. 836.95 and Rs. 191.87 respectively. Thus, the corresponding savings are estimated at Rs. 48.32 and 11.08 respectively. The per household and per capita income are the highest from forest collection, followed by the income derived from shifting cultivation. Out of the total expenditure more than a half, i.e., 54.78 per cent goes towards food only, 1.06 per cent for medicine and less than 1 per cent for education. Around 70 per cent Didayi households are below poverty line, applying the noms of per capita monthly expenditure of Rs. 250.

Sustainable development is possible by prudent combination of natural resources including material resources derived therefrom and human resources. As external development inputs is at least for a temporary period the people have to stand on their own. The socio-structural and techno economic changes around their micro-world will require upgradation of skills and abilities to foster coping mechanisms for future living for themselves and their descendants.

Attitude towards Development

A study of responses of beneficiaries and different programmes undertaken by the DDA in different villages reveal that maximum number of respondents supported the implementation of supply of house building materials, agricultural implements, plough and bullocks and supply of seeds. As regards the assistance received from D.D.A. the responses of beneficiaries revealed that more than 74 per cent of them have received agricultural implements and seeds, majority of them expressed that the officials from DDA paid regular visits to their village.

A study of the attitude towards value orientation among the beneficiaries revealed that majority of the respondents has shown a balanced attitude towards their tradition (90.80%) and change (90.80%). As regards the question whether hard labour or blessing of God is the key to success. Positive response is visible relating to adherence to their core culture, i.e., religious beliefs (71.26%) and 65.52 per cent responded for hard labour is the only key to success as large as 86.21 per cent of the respondents supported for acceptance of new ideas.

Development Inputs Needed

Keeping in view the above considerations and people's prioritisation in selecting development inputs which will facilitate their particitipation, an empirical model has been designed which of course may need suitable modification in the field. Development inputs have been recommended for three sub-areas, which will ensure sustainable development.

PLAINS SUB-AREA

1. Education

Since the literacy and educational status is very low among the Didayi in this area, people have laid emphasis on priority basis for the promotion of literacy and education through provision of necessary infrastructural and personnel components. As in the past lack of school buildings and teacher absenteeism stood on the way of educational development, they have come forward to participate in the construction of school buildings in their locality and provide necessary support for teacher's accommodation in their villages.

2. Health, Nutrition and Sanitation

In addition to the existing ethnomedicinal practices among them they need the help of modern medicines for the prevention and cure of various diseases. They need at least an additional Primary Health Centre at Oringi, the nodal village of this Sub-area. In the context of medical pluralism, there is need for the promotion of tribal medicine, by way of extending support for the growth of herbaria of tribal medicinal plants and herbs. The aged, expectant mothers in their prenatal and post-natal stages and children require nutritional diets. They require good houses to live safe and sanitary toilets to prevent some infectious diseases.

3. Safe Drinking Water

They need safe drinking water supply as water collected from hill streams is not free from contaminations. The tube wells, often defunct, do not provide potable water as it contains some harmful minerals.

4. Communication and Electrification

They have clearly realised that the inadequacy of roads stands on the way of their socio-economic development. They need roads for transportation of men and materials to weekly market places and nearby urban centres. They require street lighting at the initial stage with supply of electricity in their villages.

5. Cultural Centre

In each village they need a cultural centre in the shape of a community hall to provide facilities for the promotion of their histrionic talents through dance, song, performing art, etc., such a community hall will also provide space for community meetings, accommodation of guests, storing of musical instruments, etc.

6. Forests

They need afforestation through social-forestry programme with joint forest management for its optimum utilisation coupled with its conservation for future generation. They realise the ill-effects of *podu* ravaged hill slopes and agree to go for terracing in order to prevent soil erosion by adopting suitable measures.

7. Horticulture

In the context of horticulture, they have already experienced with growing of fruits, vegetables and cash crops and they need massive plantation in *podu* ravaged areas so that their foodstock is supplemented with additional income generation opportunities. They agree to take care of such plantations, which are not only beneficial for the present generation, but also for the generations to come. They also agree to participate actively in raising plants and vegetable seedlings if a nursery is set up in their area. They need to promote the backyard cultivation, as it is felt lucrative economic pursuit for them.

8. Agriculture and Soil Conservation

They need the upgradation of their land resource which includes low land, upland and shifting cultivation or swidden land, by the provision of agricultural implements, plough bullock, improved variety of seeds, fertilizers, pesticides, irrigation facilities and soil conservation measures, etc.

9. Animal Husbandry

They need supply of bullocks, dairy farming, goat-rearing units and poultry units to supplement their income.

10. Co-operation and Marketing

They need establishment of cooperative societies at the village level involving primary producers and it will go a long way in promoting the marketing nexus.

11. Handicrafts and Cottage Industry

They need training for developing various handicrafts and cottage industries, such as bamboo craft, wood craft, mat making, brooms making, food crafts and semi-processing of other consumable goods, provided they are assisted to run such units with funding.

12. Service Sector

In the service sector, they have shown interests in such services as tailoring, cycle repairing, hair cutting, etc.

CUT-OFF SUB-AREA

The Cut-off Sub-area of the Didayi people pose similar felt needs as their counterparts in the plains sub-area in the sectors, such as education, health, nutrition and sanitation, safe drinking water, cultural centre, forest, horticulture and agriculture, soil conservation, cooperative and marketing, handicrafts and cottage industry and service sector. In cases of communication and electrification and fishing and pisciculture, the Didayi people of cut-off sub-area have posed their needs which may be treated as unique and area-specific.

1. Communication and Electrification

They need road from Jantry to Ambilibeda, connected by a bridge and then from Ambilibeda to Oringi by *ghat* road as Oringi village is connected by road with Kudumulugumma, the headquarters of the Block and the D.D.A. as well. Thereafter, electrification of remote villages may be taken up.

2. Fishing and Pisciculture

They need more boats and nets, especially for young and able bodied male youths who intend to earn their livelihood through fishing in the reservoir. They have also shown interests for pisciculture through demonstration and necessary training.

HILLS SUB-AREA

In the hills sub-area, the Didayi have come up with similar felt needs as expressed by their counterparts in the plains sub-area and the unique area-specific need is discussed below:

1. Animal Husbandry

In addition to supply of bullocks, goat-rearing units and poultry units, they need piggery units as they had originally domesticated pigs since the recent past.

RECOMMENDATIONS

1. Education

(i) The Continuing Education Programme of the National Literacy Mission should be implemented intensively in the D.D.A. villages, in order to curb the massive backlog of illiteracy among the Didayi in general and the women of the community in particular.

(ii) There should be mini-Anganwadi centres in each Didayi village, except the nodal villages where Anganwadis are functioning, to strengthen the pre-school education component in order to make the children school ready.

(iii) The D.P.E.P, which has now been sanctioned for the Malkangiri district should take care of the Primary School facilities with all its necessary components to cater to the need of schooling. The chronic teacher absenteeism needs priority attention. This sensitive aspect has to be attended to with all sincerity of efforts so that the teaching-learning situation is invigorated among the Didayis.

(iv) The Educational Guarantee Scheme (EGS) as the latest input should cover all the Didayi villages.

(v) Provision of residential, infrastructural and teacher components, for promoting Upper Primary and Secondary education should be done urgently by pooling the resources of S.T. and S.C. Development Department and School and Mass Education Department.

2. Health, Nutrition and Sanitation

(i) There is need for motivating the tribal medicinemen to continue with their existing ethnomedicinal practices and gradually eschew the magico-religious components. There should be provision for the growth of herbaria for plantation of medicinal plants and herbs, at least one in each nodal village.

(ii) There should be additional primary health centres and mobile health units, keeping in view the geo-physical location of villages.

(iii) There should be provision of supply of nutritional diet to the aged, expectant mothers in their pre- and post-natal stages and children.

(iv) Provision of housing under various schemes should be in accordance with the tribal value orientations with sanitary toilets and good ventilation.

(v) In the Didayi situation, there should be schemes for family welfare rather than family planning for at least a decade. In view of high incidence of the Infant Mortality Rate, the expectant mothers should be given nutritional diet, medicine, medical check-up, etc. The children should also be immunized properly, not simply through pulse polio. Since they constitute a tribal community with very small population, vasectomy/tubectomy should not be insisted upon for at least a decade.

3. Safe Drinking Water

(i) Safe drinking water should be made available through deep tube wells and also pipe water supply taking advantages of gradient particularly in the hilly villages. There is necessity for evolving sustainable designs.

4. Communication and Electrification

(i) Construction of road as per local design and needs may be taken up to minimise the inaccessibility of Didayi villages.

(ii) There should be special efforts for construction of a road with bridge for connecting the cut-off area with the D.D.A. headquarters.

(iii) Provision of electricity in the outreach habitations may be taken up either through RE schemes or alternative energy route.

5. Cultural Centre

The DDA should make provision for a cultural centre in each village.

6. Forests

(i) The Forest Department should take up all measures for the optimum utilisation of forest resources and their conservation for future.

(ii) The Sloping Agricultural Land Technology (SALT) with its three phases, SALT-I, SALT-II and SALT-III should be taken up in the Didayi area as it is eco-friendly and cultural specific ensuring people's participation.

7. Horticulture

The existing horticultural practices should be rejuvenated with necessary inputs as the same is eco-friendly, culture-specific containing the in-built process to ensure participation of the people.

8. Agriculture and Soil Conservation

The Didayi love to promote agriculture as manifested in the low lands, uplands and hill slopes. There should be all-out efforts for the promotion of the primary sector activities with special reference to soil conservation, irrigation, upgradation of skills and material inputs.

9. Animal Husbandry

The existing cattle population is quite good. The bullock for ploughing and the cow for dairy purposes are to be bred and taken care of instead getting any hybrid veriety from outside.

10. Cooperation and Marketing

The Cooperative Department should take steps for the establishment of Cooperative Societies at the village for the promotion of marketing nexus. The Multi-purpose Cooperative Societies will extremely be useful to meet their different needs under one umbrella.

11. Handicrafts and Cottage Industries

The above sector should create avenues for the promotion of various handicrafts and cottage industries, which would help the Didayi in general, and the womenfolk in particular. After the introduction of SHGs, women's propensity to save (both in cash and kind) and desire for taking up handicrafts and cottage industries related activities, such as broom making, semi-processing of tamarind, resin, dry fish, etc., may be started at the initial stage. Other women-related trades would require women's capacity enhancement through demonstration and training. With their existing marketing abilities they will develop gradually their entrepreneurial skill, provided facilities are created.

12. Service Sector

The DDA should create facilities for the promotion of such services as tailoring, cycle repairing, hair cutting, etc. In the beginning, they require at least two sewing machines in each village and these are to be handled by the women folk after receiving training.

13. Fishing and Pisciculture

The existing practice of fishing among the Didayi living by the sides of the Balimela reservoir should be improved by implementing schemes / programmes for pisciculture, by the concerned Department and ogranising cooperatives.

APPENDIX-I

Research Personnel

Overall Supervision:

Shri Pyari Mohan Mohapatra, I.A.S. (Retd.)
Chairman,
Council of Analytical Tribal Studies (COATS)
Koraput (Odisha).
Res: A/111, Saheed Nagar, Bhubaneswar - 751 007,

Principal Investigator:

Professor (Dr.) K.K. Mohanti
Anjaneya, A/152, Saheed Nagar,
Bhubaneswar - 751007 (Odisha).

Co-Investigator:

Dr. P.C. Mohapatro,
Director,
COATS, Koraput - 764 020 (Odisha).

Research Associate:

Professor Dr. V.B. Shastry.
N-1-61A, I.R.C. Village,
P.O. Bhubaneswar (Odisha).

Associate Investigators:

— Dr. Jagabandhu Samal
Reader in Economics, COATS
D.N.K. Road, Koraput - 764 020 (Odisha).

— Dr. Nityananda Pradhan
Senior Lecturer,
P.G. Department of Education,
D.A.V.College, Koraput - 764 021 (Odisha).

— Dr. Kaibalya Behera
Senior Lecturer,
Department of Commerce,
D.A.V. College, Koraput - 764 021 (Odisha0.

— Shri K.C. Meher,
Lecturer,
Department of Economics
D.A.V. College, Koraput - 764 021 (Odisha).

Investigators

1. Shri Gopinath Pradhan, M.A.
2. Shri Ashok Kumar Nanda, M.A.
3. Shri Laxmi Narayan Padhi, B.A., B.L.I.S
4. Shri Kranti Kumar Patnaik, M.A.
5. Shri Rama Krushna Choudhury, B.Com.
6. Shri Mangaraj Mohapatro, B.A.
7. Shri Amulya Sekhar Bagh, B.A.
8. Shri Dipti Ranjan Barik, (A) B.A. (Hons.)
9. Shri Dipti Ranjan Barik, (B) B.A. (Hons.)
10. Shri Kedar Nath Dey, B.A. (Hons.)
11. Shri Bishnu Chetty, M.A.
12. Shri Lambodar Gouda, B.A.

APPENDIX-II

Council of Analytical Tribal Studies (COATS), Koraput

"In Search of a Strategy to build a Field Model to ensure People's Participation for Sustainable Development: Case Study of the Didayi"

(A Particularly VulnerableTribal Group of Malkangiri District of Odisha)

Sponsored by: The Planning Commission, Government of India.

HOUSEHOLD SURVEY

1. Identification:

Name of the Village/Hamlet: G.P.
Block District
Date of Data Collection

2. Household Information

(a) Name of the Head of the family:
(b) Caste/Sub-caste:
(c) Clan:
(d) Religion:
(e) Profession/Trade:
(f) Monthly Earnings:
(g) Monthly Savings:
(h) Mother tongue:

FAMILY PARTICULARS

Sl. No	*Name (in order of age group, eldest to youngest)*	*Age*	*Relationship with head of the household*	*Profession*	*Sex*	*Educational status*	*Marital status*	*Remarks*
1.								
2.								
3.								
4.								
5.								
6.								
7.								
8.								

3. Condition of the House/Sanitation

(a) Number of rooms
(b) Number of rooms having windows
(c) Purpose for which rooms are being used

Room No. 1	*Room No. 2*	*Room No. 3*	*Room No. 4*	*Room No. 5*

(d) Plinth Area of the house in square feet
(e) Is there any provision for drainage of waste water ?
(f) Is there any separate shed for domestic animals ?
(g) Opinion about the cleanliness of the house: (good/manageable/bad)
Please put a (✓) mark in appropriate place

4. Drinking Water Facilities

Source	*Own/Provided by Govt./Neighbours*	*Distance from the house*	*Quality of the water (Satisfactory/ Unsatisfactory)*
Tube well			
Well			
Stream			
River			
Tank			
Any other			

5. Health/Family Welfare regarding

(a) To whom you generally approach for treatment in case of illness ?
(Dissari/Health Worker/Doctor/Any other)

(b) Whom do you approach for treatment of different type of diseases ? Specify.

(c) Has anybody in your family adopted family planning measures ?
(Male/Female/Nobody) put ✓ mark in appropriate place.

(d) Generally from what type of diseases the members of your family suffer ? (Write in order of frequency of attack of the diseases)
(1)
(2)
(3)

6. (a) Information about cultivation (last one year)

Type of land	*Area (approx. in acre)*	*Approximate expenditure in cultivation*	*Name of the crops grown with quantity*	*Value Rs.*	*Net Profit Rs.*
Settled Land					
Dongar (upland)					
Shifting Land					
Garden or Horticultural Land					
Any other					

(b) Type of implements used in the cultivation.

1. 2. 3. 4. 5.

(c) Manure/Fertilisers used in agricultural land:

(Manure/Chemical fertiliser/Both)

7. Collection of Forest Produce and its use (last one year)

Name of the Forest produce collected	*Season*	*Self-use*		*For sale*		*To whom sold*	
		Qty.	value	Qty.	Value	Govt. Organisation	Businessmen/ Traders
Mahua Flower							
Mahua Seed (*Tola*)							
Sal seed							
Tamarind							
Jhuna							
Firewood							
Charcoal							
Wood for agricultural purpose							
Bamboo							
Thatching grass (*piri*)							
Siali Leaves							
Any other							

8. Hunting (last one year)

Name of the animal/bird	*Season*	*Quantity*	*Use*	*Is it related with any festival (if so, name it)*

9. Animal Wealth (present status)

Name of the Domestic animals/ birds	*Quantity*	*Self use*		*For sale*	
		Qty.	*Value*	*Qty.*	*Value*
Bullocks					
Cows					
Buffaloes					
Goats					
Sheep					
Pigs					
Hen					
Ducks					

10. Type of goods collected from domestic animals/birds (milk, curd, Ghee, eggs, etc.). If sold, how much money you have received during the last one year.

11. Poverty Eradication/Economic Benefit Programme

Name of the Beneficiary	*Name of the Scheme*	*Purpose for which received*	*Received in what form*		*Qty./ Value*	*Project cost*		*Present Status*	*Remarks*
			Cash	*Kind*		*Loan*	*Subsidy*		

12. If any family member is engaged in Business/Trade

Name of the family member	*Name of the business*	*Profit during the last one year*	*Present status*	
			Good	*Bad*

13. Movable and Immovable Properties

Type of Asset	*Amount/Qty.*	*How acquired*	*Value in Rs.*
Agricultural Land			
Homestead Land			
Agricultural Implements			
Bullock Cart			
House			
Animal Wealth			
Ornaments			
Utensils			
Furnitures			
Savings			

14. Loans

Source of Loan	*Purpose of Loan*	*Amount of capital borrowed*	*Interest rate*	*Total*	*Amount repaid*
Government Organisation					
Bank					
Cooperative Society					
Money Lender					
Any other					

15. Income from Wage Labour

Type of work	*No. of days worked*				*Total wages*	*Remarks*
	Male	*Female*	*Child Lab.*	*Total*		
(a) Agricultural Labour						
(b) Construction work (Road, Canal, House, etc.)						
(c) Plantation						
(d) Service						
(e) Others						

16. Annual Income

(a) Income from agricultural products	
(b) Income from animal wealth	
(c) Earning from wage labour	
(d) Value of Minor Forest Produce collected	
(e) Hunting/ Fishing	
(f) Service	
(g) Trade/Business	
(h) Loan	
(i) Others	
Total Income	

17. Household Expenditure

Type of expenditure	*Details/ Quantity*	*Amount (Rs.)*
Food		
Dress		
Fire wood/ Fuel		
Kerosene		
Medicine		
Festivals		
Agricultural Implements		
Marriage Expenses		
Birth/death		
House construction/Repair		
Match Box		
Drinking/ Wine		
Other Intoxicants		
Cycle/ Radio/ Watch, etc.		
Others		
Total Expenditure		

APPENDIX-III

Council of Analytical Tribal Studies (COATS), Koraput

"In Search of a Strategy to build a Field Model to ensure People's Participation for Sustainable Development: Case Study of the Didayi"

(A Particularly VulnerableTribal Group of Malkangiri District of Odisha)

Sponsored by: The Planning Commission, Government of India

Views of people about development schemes (Evaluation of the Project(s) now working)

Identification

1. Name of the informant
2. Age
3. Sex
4. Name of the village/ Hamlet
5. Block: Kudumulugumma
6. District: Malkangiri

A. General Information

1. Do you know that an organisation/establishment is working only for the benefit of the Didayi Tribe? Yes/ No
2. If yes, where is that Organisation situated ?
3. From which year the organisation is working ?

4. What type of developmental activities that have been undertaken by the organisation in your village ?
   (a)
   (b)
   (c)
   (d)
5. What types of benefits have been received by your family from the organisation, i.e., D.D.A.?
   (a)
   (b)
   (c)
   (d)
6. Have you received the benefits without any payment or have you paid any amount for that ?
7. Has any officer of that organisation visited your village ? Yes/No
8. If yes, what does he do after coming to your village ?
9. Do the officer(s) discuss about your problems in a meeting of the villagers ? Yes/No
10. If yes, then what are the subject matters of discussion ?
11. Have you been benefited by various activities undertaken by the organisation?
    (a) Yes
    (b) To some extent
    (c) Sufficiently
    (d) Never
12. What more activities, according to you, that should be undertaken by the organisation for your benefit ?
    (a)
    (b)
    (c)
    (d)
13. Besides the Didayi Development Agency, what are the other organisations by whom you have been benefited?
    (a)
    (b)
    (c)
    (d)

14. If yes, what type of benefits you have received ?

Name of the Agency/ Organisation	*Name of the benefits received*	*Amount of the help Cash/Kind*	*Amount of loan*	*Subsidy*	*Present status of the scheme*

B. Specific Information (General)

Please indicate the nature of development works that have been undertaken by various plans/schemes of the Government in your village.

Various Types of Development		*Opinion*	
(i) Children's Education	Yes	No	Not definite
(ii) Medical facilities	Yes	No	Not definite
(iii) Road and communication	Yes	No	Not definite
(iv) Electricity	Yes	No	Not definite
(v) Drinking water	Yes	No	Not definite
(vi) Anganwadi	Yes	No	Not definite
(vii) Marketing	Yes	No	Not definite
(viii) Savings of suplus income (Postal/ Bank etc.)	Yes	No	Not definite
(ix) Facilities of availing loans	Yes	No	Not definite
(x) Vehicles/Transportation	Yes	No	Not definite
(xi) Irrigation	Yes	No	Not definite
(xii) Soil Conservation	Yes	No	Not definite
(xiii) Any other	Yes	No	Not definite

C. Specific Information (Individual)

Please indicate the type of benefits that you (or your family have received from the Government other than the DDA and whether you have been really benefited or not?

Name of the scheme	*Opinion*		
(a)	Yes	No	Not definite
(b)	Yes	No	Not definite
(c)	Yes	No	Not definite
(d)	Yes	No	Not definite

D. Value Based Information

Types of value based information	*Opinion*		
1. Do you think that your children should be educated about the traditions and customs, and way of life, etc., which have been prevailing since long.	Yes	No	Not definite
2. Children should be educated about modern ideas and new ways of life.	Yes	No	Not definite
3. Hard work is the only key of success	Yes	No	Not definite
4. Success lies only on the blessings of the God or Almighty	Yes	No	Not definite
5. Our old/ traditional way of life was good, so let us stick to it	Yes	No	Not definite
6. We cannot live better if we do not accept new innovative ideas	Yes	No	Not definite

APPENDIX-IV

Council of Analytical Tribal Studies (COATS), Koraput

"In Search of a Strategy to build a Field Model to ensure People's Participation for Sustainable Development: Case Study of the Didayi"

(A Particularly VulnerableTribal Group of Malkangiri District of Odisha)

Sponsored by: The Planning Commission, Government of India

Village Survey Schedule

Identification

1. Name of the informant:
2. Age: 3. Sex:
4. Name of the village/ Hamlet: 5. Block: Kudumulugumma
6. District: Malkangiri

SECTION A

1. Geographical location and natural surroundings of the village (River, Stream, Cultivable Land, Mountain, Other village, etc.)

Direction	What are the things existing	Distance from the village
East	(a) (b)	
West	(a) (b)	
North	(a) (b)	
South	(a) (b)	

2. Various Institutions functioning in the village (Put ✓ mark in the appropriate place)
   (a) Schools (Primary /M.E./ High School)
   (b) Club House
   (c) Anganbadi Centre
   (d) Literacy Centre
   (e) Male/Female Dormitory
   (f) Health Centre (ANM Centre/P.H.C.)
   (g) Cooperative Store/Fair Price Shop
   (h) Temple/Church/Masjid
   (i) Panchayat Office
   (j) Village drama/Dance party
   (k) Others (Specify)
3. Other facilities available in the village
   (a) No. of tube wells
   (b) No. of Wells
   (c) Electricity connection
   (d) Village Road connecting to the Main Road (Tar Road, Kuchha Road; Walking Path)
   (e) Common Drainage System
4. Where from water for daily use is brought by majority of villagers — Well/Tube-Well/ River/Stream/ Pond
5. Where does majority of the cattle population take their bath — Well/Tube-Well/ River/Stream/Pond
6. Your opinion on the village sanitation — Good/Manageable/ Bad
7. Distance of P.H.C. from the village
8. In case of minor ailments whose services are required/sought for by the majority for the villagers — Village Dissari/ ANM/ health worker/ Govt. Hospital, Any other institution.

SECTION B

1. What are the different types of cultivation followed in the village — Shifting/Settled/Both
2. Main crops produced in the village
   Write the names of any four major crops in order of priority (Quantity produced)
   (1)
   (2)
   (3)
   (4)
3. Name the three main forest produce available in the village
   (1)
   (2)
   (3)
   (4)
   (5)
4. Main domestic animals reared in the village
   (Name three animals in order of their number)
   (1)
   (2)
   (3)
   (4)
5. Important Poverty Eradication Programme implemented/ being implemented in the village.
   (Write the names of two/three programmes on the basis of the number of beneficiaries benefited)
   (1)
   (2)
   (3)
6. Name 3/4 main occupations in which majority of villagers are engaged.
   (*Example*: Cultivation, Animal Husbandry, Collection of Forest Produce, Fishing Business, etc.)
   (1)
   (2)
   (3)

7. Name 3/4 main habits of the village people
   (*Example*: Drinking, Smoking, Dancing, etc.)
   (1)
   (2)
   (3)
8. Name of the Professional Voluntary Agency working in the village.
9. How the quarrel, litigation, misunderstanding, etc., in the village are generally settled ?
10. Where does the Gram Sabha (Village meeting) take place ? How many times the village meeting is conducted in a Year _______ in a month _____
11. Main festivals observed in the village
    1. Name of the Festivals
    2. When and how these are observed

Full name of the Investigator

Signature with Date

APPENDIX-V

Case Study of Developmental/Poverty Alleviation Programme

1. Name of the Scheme:
2. Name of the Beneficiary:
3. Main Occupation:
4. Subsidiary Occupation:
5. Age: Sex:
6. Marital Status:
7. No. of Children:
8. Educational Qualification:
9. Name of the family members assisting in the activity:
10. Nature of Assistance:
11. Date and Amount of receipt of assistance:
    Date Amount/Kind
12. Source of Assistance:
13. Date of undertaking the activity:
14. Present Status (Extent of success/failure):
15. Reasons of success/failure:
16. Basis of your selection as a beneficiary:
17. Whether you were interested to undertake the scheme ?
18. If yes, state the reasons:
19. If no, what made you to accept the scheme:
20. Total amount of money/kind received:
    (a) Loan Component
    (b) Subsidy component
21. Have you spend some money to obtain this scheme ?

APPENDIX-VI

Proceedings of the Focus Group Discussion — 1

The main objective of the present study is to design a suitable strategy of development of 'Didayi' tribe situated in three different sub-areas with different geo-physical and ecological conditions. Therefore, the problem of research is designed to explore and establish empirical models to ensure active participation of the people (including women) in their own development where optimum use of locally available resources, human as well as natural, shall be made. In order to make this model operational, adequate care has to be taken to ensure cultural as well as geographical sustainability in eco-friendly situation and fit into the locally available resources.

In view of the above objective focus group discussions (FGDs), were conducted in study villages.

Village	: Dhakadpadar
Date	: 25.11.2001
Time	: 4 P.M.
Participants	: 26 Adult males, 6 Ladies and 15 Children.
Moderator	: Dr P.C. Mohapatro
Rapporteur	: Dr. N.N. Pradhan
Facilitator	: Sri K.C. Meher

Issues Discussed

- Income and Savings.
- Enrolment and dropout at Primary stage.
- Common Diseases and their methods of prevention.

- Family Planning.
- Protection of Natural Environment, including Soil, Forest and Wild Animals.
- Forest Produce and their economy.
- Women's Participation.
- Plantation of Economic species.
- Benefits of Poverty Alleviation Programme.
- Occupation and Occupational Hazards.
- Economic needs and Demands.
- Other related matters and additional information.

Common Views/Issues

1. There is interest in saving in terms of cash as well as kind to meet the future contingencies.
2. Quality of Primary Education is poor. The teacher appointed rarely comes to school. Teacher absenteeism has almost made the school non-functional.
3. Majorities have faith in the allopathic medicine supplied by the government through a Health Worker. However, they still have confidence on the *disari* (the indigenous medicineman). Scabies, Malaria Fever, Diarrhoea, Stomach troubles are the common ailments.
4. Villagers are aware of the Family Planning measures. However, only nine males in the village adopted it. The male vasectomy is preferred instead of female tubectomy.
5. Watershed project/water harvesting structure like one at Jantry would help development of agriculture of the inhabitants. There is demand for training on terracing and terrace cultivation.
6. The villagers are aware of the evil effects of shifting cultivation, but practise them due to scarcity of cultivable low lands for settled cultivation. During the discussion the villagers took interest to follow scientific methods of shifting cultivation so as to reduce soil erosion in the sloppy lands. They opined that provisions of alternative employment opportunities may refrain them from such practice.
7. The minor forest produce like fuel wood, wood for making plough share and house construction, different types of edible

roots, leaves and fruits, honey, etc., are mostly used for their own consumption and are rarely sold in the market.

8. There is a great demand for supply of diesel motor pumps for lift irrigation.
9. Women play equally important role in doing economic activities. This is in addition to their regular household chores including cooking, fetching water for drinking and caring babies. The women are found to occupy an important status in the family discussion making process.
10. A great interest has been shown by the inhabitants for plantation of economic species like Mango, Cashew, *Kusum*, Guava, Lichi, Coconut, Lemon, Pomogranate, Tamarind, etc. Hence, the Didayi Development Authority has to make adequate provision for these plantations.
11. During the iast ten years only four persons have received housing facilities under Indira Awas Yojana. Only three have received boat and net. Four persons have received tile for roofing their houses, four persons have received each a pair of bullocks and ten families have received seeds for cultivation.
12. Every household possesses kitchen garden with mostly hybrid varieties of papaya and banana plants supplied by the Didayi Development Agency (DDA).
13. Cash crop cultivation which includes ginger, chilly, potato, tobacco are well accepted whereas the proposals for leaf-plate making, rearing of buffaloes, installation of *Gobar* Gas plant are resented.
14. As the school is not properly functioning a pre-school centre may be established with the provision of mid-day meal. A local educated boy may be entrusted to impart education at the pre-school stage. The Anganwadi worker may be entrusted with the responsibility of supplying mid-day meal to pupils.
15. Two SHG groups have been promoted in the village consisting of 12 to 14 tribal women. These SHG groups have not received any funds so far from the Block authorities.
16. Boat and net are to be provided to the needy people for improving their economic conditions through fishing.
17. The villagers took interest in the provision of subsidiary/ alternative employment opportunities, which can be

sustained. One villager came forward with the proposal of supplying sewing machine to one or two persons in each village in the cut-off area.

18. Most of the villagers look clean, cheerful and healthy.
19. Milking cows are not preferred.
20. The government officers have shown little interest for their development. The Sarpanch has collected RoR of land from Khillo and Khilla of the village with a promise to provide bullock back last two years. But they have neither received back the RoR, nor the bullocks so far. Similarly, D. Khillo, A. Khillo and K. Muduli were selected to receive housing facility under Indira Awas Yojana. But they have been asked to get cement and G. C.I. Sheets from the Block office at their own cost.
21. The proposal for dairy farming, goat-rearing and poultry farming are well accepted by the people.

APPENDIX-VII

Proceedings of the Focus Group Discussion — 2

Village	: Orapadar
Date	: 24.11.2001
Time	: 6.30 P.M
Participants	: 35 Adult males, 10 Females and 10 primary school children
Moderator	: Dr P.C. Mohapatro
Rapporteur	: Dr. N.N. Pradhan
Facilitator	: Sri K.C. Meher

Issues Discussed

- Income and Savings
- Enrolment and dropout at Primary stage
- Common Diseases and their methods of prevention
- Family Planning
- Protection of Natural Environment including Soil, Forest and Wild Animals.
- Forest Produce and their economy.
- Women's Participation
- Plantation of Economic species
- Benefits of Poverty Alleviation Programme
- Occupation and Occupational Hazards.
- Economic Needs and Demands
- Other related matters and additional information.

Common Views/Issues

1. There is interest in savings in terms of cash as well as kind to meet the future exigencies.
2. They show interest in education of their wards. Teacher absenteeism, however, results in low attendance of children in Primary Schools. Only 13-14 children out of approximately 60-70 children in the age group of enrolled 6-11 years attend Primary Schools.
3. Quality of Primary Education is poor. Children promoted to Class-III, count numbers up to 20, put their signatures with much difficulty. The children who are interested to study beyond Class - III are sent to the residential schools.
4. Many people have learnt to put their signatures through adult literacy programme. These people, however, are not able to read or write simple Odia.
5. Majorities have faith in medicine supplied by Government through mobile unit. They too respected *disari* (the village medicineman). Scabies and Malaria fevers are the common diseases.
6. Awareness of modern family planning measures is as low as 9-10 households. Males have adopted vasectomy which is preferred than tubectomy for females.
7. The average family size is four (i.e., two numbers of children per couple) which is not encouraging.
8. The villagers look clean, cheerful and healthy. Many participants are found to joke or laugh with open mind during the discussion.
9. They are aware of the negative impact of shifting cultivation, but practise them out of necessity. Alternative provisions, therefore, may refrain them from such practice.
10. The non-timber forest produce, such as leaf, fuel, bamboo, etc., are used for household purposes. In other words these are not collected to sale in the market to earn money.
11. Watershed Project, like the one at 'Jantari', would help in agricultural development of the inhabitants. There is demand for training on terracing and terrace cultivation.
12. Women take equal part in economic activities with their male counterparts. This is in addition to their regular household

chores including cooking and caring of babies. Therefore, the women occupy a prestigious position in the family.

13. The proposals for economic activities, like duckling, ginger cultivation, potato cultivation, fishery, cow rearing are well accepted, whereas the proposals for leaf plate making, rearing of buffaloes and installation of Gobar Gas Plant are resented.
14. The welfare measures being implemented by the Government of Andhra Pradesh in nearby villages are better as compared to those followed in Odisha State in their village.
15. Interested in listening to and accepting suggestions pertaining to agricultural activities. Majority of the villagers have planted varieties of fruit-bearing trees including mango, coconut, etc., supplied by the Didayi Development Agency.
16. Every household possesses kitchen garden with mostly hybrid varieties of papaya and banana plants supplied by the Didayi Development Agency (DDA).
17. Evinced resentment in milking Cows.
18. Government officers are partial in implementing development schemes in the village. The nearby villages have been benefited more as compared to theirs.
19. The assistance of Government in terms of bullock would enhance the economic status of the people most. Many families hire bullocks, mostly from their neighbouring Bondos at Rs. 300 to Rs. 400 per bullock per year and it is not cost effective.
20. Government Officers have little interest in supplying bullocks to them. Four persons, namely Sadar Muduli, Gopa Muduli, Pandu Muduli, and Lacha Bisoyi had applied for bullock loan by submitting their record of right about five years back. But they have neither been provided with bullocks nor returned back their record of rights so far. The solar light systems and two out of three tube wells in the village are defective since long. The concerned officials do not bother about this.
21. There is high demand for supply of motor pumps for lift irrigation.
22. Majority of the villagers have enjoyed the benefits of different poverty alleviation programmes being implemented through Block and DDA. Some households have enjoyed even more than one or two benefits.
23. The boys marry between 16 and 20 years of age and girls between 13 and 17 years.

APPENDIX-VIII

Proceedings of the Focus Group Discussion — 3

Village	: Dabuguda
Date	: 26.11.2001
Time	: 4 P.M.
Participants	: 22 Adult Males, 8 Adult Females
Moderator	: Dr P.C. Mohapatro
Rapporteur	: Dr. N.N. Pradhan
Facilitator	: Sri K.C. Meher

Issues Discussed

- Income and Saving
- Enrolment and dropout at Primary stage
- Common Diseases and their methods of prevention
- Family Planning
- Protection of National Environment, including Soil, Forest and Wild Animals.
- Forest Produce and their economy.
- Women's Participation
- Plantation of Economic Species
- Benefits of Poverty Alleviation Programme
- Occupation and Occupational Hazards.
- Economic Needs and Demands
- Other related matters and additional informations.

Common Views/Issues

1. There is interest in saving both in terms of kind as well as cash to meet with the future needs/contingencies.
2. The educational opportunity provided is not adequate. There is a primary school building. But the teacher posted has not come to the school for the last two months. Teachers' absenteeism at present is the main factor of loss of interest on the part of children to attend schools regularly.
3. Majority have faith in the allopathic medicines supplied by the Government through a health worker for common ailments. However, they still go to the *disari* (their traditional for medicineman) for medical aid. They visit Hospital or Primary Health Centre only when the *disari* fails to cure them. Scabies, diarrhoea, malaria, fever, and stomach troubles are the common diseases in their locality.
4. All of them came with the view that a P.H.C. should come up through the Government efforts either at Jantry or Totaguda to serve the villages and habitats in the cut-off area.
5. Villagers are aware of the Family Planning method. But they wait for a male child to be born. Male vasectomy is preferred and only six males have undergone vasectomy operation.
6. The villagers are aware of the evil effects of shifting cultivation, but they practise it due to scarcity of lands and due to non-availability of alternative employment opportunities. During the course of discussion when they were explained about the indigenous practices followed in parts of NEFA and Nagaland (i.e., placing of the cut-off tree trunks across the slope to reduce soil erosion and to form a rudimentary terrace). They accepted our suggestions very much. They requested for a demonstration of the process in one or two villages, so that they can follow the practice in future in a better way.
7. Non-timber forest produce, like fuelwood, wood for making plough share and constructing/repairing house, a variety of edible roots, leaves and fruits are exclusively used for their own consumption and are rarely sold in the market.
8. Women play a very important role in performing outdoor economic activities. This is in addition to their regular household chores including cooking, fetching water from

the tube well and caring babies. The women are found to occupy an important status in the family also in the decision making process.

9. After the establishment of DDA, almost all the cultivators have received agricultural implements, Paddy, Ragi, Maize, and Suan seeds, vegetable seeds, oil seeds, coconut sapling and cashew saplings have been provided to few households. Some of them have received housing facilities under the Indira Awas Yojana, boat and net, a pair of bullocks and tiles to roof their houses.
10. An intensive programme of agricultural development is the need of the hour. The DDA authorities should provide a pair of bullocks to each cultivator who do not have it, and provide cereal, pulses, oil and vegetable seeds in such quantities as each cultivator needs for taking up cultivation.
11. Watershed projects, water harvesting structures, diversion weirs would facilitate development of agriculture of the inhabitants. There is also a great demand for training on terracing and terraced cultivation in the hill slopes. They also agree to provide community labour for the preparation of terraced plots.
12. Boat and net need to be provided to the deserving persons from amongst the villagers to improve their economic standard through fishing. They are also eager to go for pisciculture, provided infrastructure facilities are created and training is made available for the Didayi youths.
13. A keen interest has been shown by the villagers for plantation of economic species, like Mango, Cashew, Tamarind, Lichi, Lemon, Coconut, Guava, Pomegranate, etc. The success of lemon plantation done by DDA in certain villages of the cut-off area and hilly area has provided impetus for plantation.
14. Every household possesses kitchen garden with hybrid varieties of papaya and banana plants supplied by the Didayi Development Agency.
15. The proposals for cow and goat-rearing and poultry farming are well accepted by the people.
16. Cash crop cultivation, like ginger, chilly, potato, tobacco, papaya, banana and vegetable cultivation are well accepted wherseas the proposals for leaf plate making, rearing of buffaloes, installation of Gobar Gas Plant are not accepted.

However, once such a plant is introduced through governmental efforts and the benefit of the plant will be experienced by the villagers, it will create interest in them, so that they will come up in future without external aid.

17. Almost all the villagers' evinced resentment in milking cows. The villagers apprehended milking of cows would affect the health of the calves. However, when explained about the use of milk for the healthy growth of their own children, a few of them accepted the proposal.
18. Most of the villagers look clean cheerful and healthy. Villagers were found to take hot water bath in the evening everyday after the days work.
19. Villagers in the cut-off area are in large demand for water pumps for lift irrigation. In the absence of electric power they are prepared to use the diesel sets for watering their fields. This will facilitate them to go for a second crop during the winter.

APPENDIX-IX

Proceedings of the Focus Group Discussion — 4

Village	: Jantari
Date	: 20.11.2001
Time	: 7.00 P.M
Participants	: 40 Adult males
Moderator	: Dr. N. Pradhan
Rapporteur	: Sri. K.C. Meher
Facilitator	: Dr. P.C. Mohapatro

Issues Discussed

- Income and savings pattern.
- Enrolment and dropout at Primary stage.
- Common diseases and their methods of prevention.
- Family Planning.
- Protection of Natural Environment, including Soil, Forest and Wild Animals.
- Forest Produce and their economic in implications.
- Women's Participation.
- Plantation of Economic species.
- Benefits of Poverty Alleviation Programmes.
- Occupation and Occupational Hazards.
- Economic Needs and Demands.
- Other related matters and additional information.

Common Views/Issues

1. People are interested in saving both in terms of cash and kind for the unseen future. But lack of surplus of foods and lack of other alternative sources of income bring them to the old subsistence level living or living from hand to mouth. On the other hand investment of inputs on agriculture is much more than their output. Most of the people are hiring bullock from the Bonda neighbour at high cost. Traditional types of cultivation also give them low level of output. Stored seeds of last year, which are affected by fungi and give them low level of production. In addition, their traditional habit of consumption of country liquor and smoking renders them spend thrift.
2. People in general are interested in education. Parents wholeheartedly participated in this issue. They expressed that the "teacher absenteeism" is the main cause of low attendance in school. Simultaneously they require a girls school with hostel facility (*kanyashram*) in the region.
3. For all kinds of common diseases, they need the help of *disari* or village medicineman, who gives some medicinal plants, roots, etc., for treatment and in exchange of that he collect cash and kinds (cloth, paddy, suan, etc.) People have also developed faith in the government supplied medicines. They are using Government medicines supplied through mobile health workers for malaria, stomach pain, headache, knee pain, etc., which are the common diseases. The villagers requested for the establishment of a Primary Health Centre with a permanent doctor either at Jantari or at Totaguda.
4. The average family size of the people is comparatively larger. Most of the people have four/five children, which is a issue against the health and economic development. Early marriage is common practice of these people. Generally the boys marry at the age between 15 to 20 years and girls between 13 to 18 years. Preference of large family size is one of the reasons because of the high Infant Morality Rate (IMR). The people are aware of the family planning programme and some women have adopted tubectomy not only from the Odisha Government but also from the Andhra Government as the incentive provided by the A.P. Government is higher than that in the Odisha Government.

5. All festivals are related to their social life and their relation with forest eco-system. Both males and females participate in different festivals. They perform different festivals, i.e., before they start cultivation perform *puja* on land, before using new fruits they first offer that to their local deities. During *Chaita Parab* they go for hunting and at night perform dance together in the open-air platform.
6. Forest is the source of their livelihood. All their economic and social implications deal with the forest and its produce. Almost throughout the day, they spend in the forest for different purposes, i.e., collecting fire wood, fruits, bamboo, leaves, roots, etc. They use these forest produce for their own purpose and not for commercial purpose. Most of the villagers have a little knowledge or awareness about deforestation and its effects on their children. They are practising shifting cultivation only due to necessity, as they have no other alternative source of income for earning livelihood.
7. Poultry farming, Dairy farming and making of leaf plates are welcome by the villagers, especially women folk. In addition to their domestic chores of cooking and caring of babies, they participate in all other activities, i.e., cultivation, collecting fruits, fire wood, bamboo, etc., with their male counterparts. Women occupy a dignified position in the society, which is also reflected at the time of marriage. Bridegroom pays bride-price in terms of cash or kind to the parents of bride to marry her.
8. About the development programmes/schemes, the government officers have little interest for the development of tribal people. They are not informing them about the different programmes of the government in general and family benefit programmes in particular. The Didayi Development Agency (DDA) and Block have intervened some of the villages and supplied fruits bearing trees in kitchen garden, i.e., hybrid papaya, and banana plants. In spite of prime demand for bullock or bullocks loan they have not been provided by the government till now. As a result they are hiring bullocks from the Bondo neighbours by paying Rs. 300 to Rs. 400 per annum and some additional charges, and it is very expensive.

9. Most of the villagers are active in the cultivation and they are seeking suggestions and accepting different views for the development of their agriculture. They are more enthusiastic in the plantation of fruit bearing trees, i.e., mango, coconut and cashew, etc. Some of the plants are also supplied by the Didayi Development Agency (DDA). They face irrigation problems and require government help to supply pump sets for this purpose, so that areas adjacent to reservoir can be cultivated. There is also demand for training facilities on the modern methods of better cultivation.
10. Economic needs/demands of these people are very limited. They live simple life, and their first priority goes to food, shelter and clothing. But we have marked some changes in the younger generation, they have developed attraction for the modern clothes and modern style of living, i.e., purchasing of radio or tape recorder, watch, etc. They are not only ready to accept this new type of cloth or instrument but also more widely accept the new occupation, i.e., fishing, cultivation of modern fruits and vegetables which have much demand in the markets.
11. Drinking water facility is almost nil in these villages. Government has supplied 2 tube wells in this village but they are out of order since last 3 to 4 months and even the water of these tube wells are not potable. So they purely depend on hill stream water for all purposes, i.e., drinking, bathing, animal bathing, etc., and it is available roughly half a kilometre away from their village.
12. Problems of transportation and communication are the key issues of these people. There are only two motor launchers supplied by the Odisha Government for the people of the whole region and these launchers are frequently getting out of order. There is absence of adequate communication facility to have contact with District Headquarters, except by tracking mountainous range, which is very difficult and dangerous also.

APPENDIX-X

Proceedings of the Focus Group Discussion — 5

Village	: Badankhiguda
Date	: 20.01.2002
Time	: 6.30 P.M.
Participants	: 27 Male Adults, 9 Children (7 Women listening to the discussion from a short distance)
Moderator	: Sri K.C. Meher
Rapporteur	: Dr. K.K. Behera

Issues Discussed

- Income and Savings.
- Enrolment and dropout at Primary stage.
- Common Diseases and their methods of prevention and cure
- Family Planning.
- Protection of Natural Environment, including Soil, Forest and Wild Animals.
- Forest Produce and their economy.
- Women's Participation.
- Plantation of economic species.
- Benefits of Poverty Alleviation Programmes.
- Occupation and Occupational Hazards.
- Economic Needs and Demands.
- Other related matters and additional information.

Common Views/Issues

1. Source of income is only from sale of agricultural or minor forest produce. The income is so less that it fails to meet their basic needs. Temporary surplus income, if any, is hoard up in the house only. Institutional saving practice is nil.
2. Primary occupation of all the villages is agriculture. The related hazards consists of problems of hill slope farming, wild animals eating away and damaging the standing crops, lack of bullocks and the scarcity of sufficient farming land.
3. Hunting, which was once an important activity, has been sizeably reduced due to lack of game animals on account of large scale deforestation. However, hunting of forest cock is popular among the young people.
4. The economic demand is not much. They just need a pair of bullocks each, seed and agricultural implements. And when they do not have anything to eat, they may be provided with food for work.
5. Development through poverty alleviation programme is not noticeable. The assistance available from the Didayi Development Agency (DDA) was very limited. They have not heard of IRDP, ERRP, PMRY, etc. However, some people admitted that they had worked in Food for Work Programme once in the recent past.
6. Demand for old age pension has increased. Nobody in the village was getting such assistance.
7. Minimum infrastructural support they need is tube well and a road connecting the plains area. The existing tube well is insufficient to meet the requirement of the entire village.
8. They are not very conscious about their environment and its protection. Felling of trees are rampant and widespread for "Podu Cultivation". Rapid soil erosion is common.
9. Forest produce includes roots, stem, leaves and fruits of a number of plants, most of which enter into their daily dietary menu. Surplus items, if any, are taken to weekly market for sale.
10. Participant's major grievance was on schooling of their children. The village "Gyan Mandir" runs with a teacher who does not come to the school. The children have interest to learn. There was a feeling that with a regular teacher their children will be able to read and write.

11. Two children of their village are reading in Mudulipada School.
12. The adults are not able to read or write.
13. Malaria and cold related fever, joint pains are common in the area. People have strong belief in *disari*, the village medicineman. He is always contacted first for treatment of any disease. In case of failure, medical help is sought for.
14. A family on an average has four children. Thereafter, they adopt their traditional measure for birth control. Use of the root of a plant (given by the *disari*) was shown as a measure of family planning. Only two men admitted to have undergone family planning operation.
15. Drinking of liquor is too much. This has disturbed their economic base.
16. In course of discussion they told that no top level official, either from Block or DDA had visited their village.
17. In spite of all the hardships in the village they do not want to go beyond their ancestral home to any other place even if they are provided with better houses, farm lands and other income generation opportunities.
18. They have fair idea about the market price of their useable products.
19. Women are considered as better partners. They do maximum labour for their household management. On financial and other matters, their opinions are honoured in the decision making process.
20. Pre-marital physical relationship among young boys and girls may be tolerated, but not the post marital adultery.
21. Hills area Didayis have rare matrimonial relationship with the plains area Didayi who are under-estimated by the plains area Didayis in terms of socio-economic status.

APPENDIX-XI

Proceedings of the Focus Group Discussion — 6

Village	: Oringi
Date	: 25.12.2001
Time	: 4.30 P.M.
Participants	: 50 persons (males and females) including members of two women SHGs.
Moderator	: Prof. K.K. Mohanty
Rapporteur	: Dr. N.N. Pradhan.

Issues Discussed

- Income and Saving.
- Enrolment and dropout at Primary stage.
- Common Diseases and their methods of prevention.
- Family Planning.
- Protection of National Environment, including Soil, Forest and Wild Animals.
- Forest Produce and their economy.
- Women's Participation.
- Plantation of Economic species.
- Benefits of Poverty Alleviation Programme.
- Occupation and Occupational Hazards.
- Economic Needs and Demands.
- Other related matters and additional information.

Common Views/Issues

1. People have concern for future and, therefore, go for savings in terms of cash in the bank at Kudumulugumma.
2. Children are not attending schools regularly because of teacher absenteeism. Teachers coming from far off places do not stay in the village. People are committed to send their children if the teachers stay in the village and become regular in running the school.
3. The common diseases among the villagers are scabies, malaria and cold fever. The nearest medical facility is available at Kudumulugumma, i.e., three kms away from the village.
4. There is no practice of shifting cultivation. There is of course little scope for it. People are aware of the environmental implications of shifting cultivation being practised in the hilly area.
5. The village is surrounded by trees, like mango, tamarind, kendu, *sal*, *bija* etc. Fruit bearing trees like coconut, guava, mango, jackfruit, banana, papaya, tamarind, etc., are found in large numbers within the village. There is greenery in and around the village.
6. People collect minor forest produces, like *pitkanda*, *cherkanda*, *badapitkanda*, etc.
7. Three women S.H.Gs formed by the D.D.A. and OSCARD are there in the village since 1997. These S.H.G.s are almost defunct by now. The members are not paying their monthly contributions regularly, but the amount collected so far is lying in the bank account.
8. Women are co-workers of their male counterparts in the agricultural field. The women, however, are shy as compared to men before the outsiders.
9. Majority of the households have received financial assistance from D.D.A. as well as Block for land development and purchase of bullocks, seeds, plough, etc.
10. Didayi Development Agency (D.D.A.) at Kudumuluguma supplies hybrid variety of seeds, like groundnuts, paddy, blackgram, greengram at subsidised price. The same agency, however, does not provide fertilizers. There is demand for fertilizers.

11. People have never tried cultivation of turmeric, ginger and cashew. They, however, are interested to try them on experimental basis consequent upon the success of groundnut cultivation since last three years. They need demonstration by the experts in the line.
12. Irrigation is the major deterrent on the way of agricultural development. However, there is scope for water harvesting structure and weir dam as well as M.I.P. at Tentulimunda and Ambabeda.
13. There are three M.I.P.s out of which one is defunct. People raise cash crops, like groundnuts, tomato, brinjal, onion, etc. in addition to paddy. There is, however, no scope for double crop because of water scarcity.
14. The villagers observe festivals like Pandu Sankranti, Nandi Parab, Chait Parab, Osa Parab (Nuakhia), etc. Besides, they worship Nisani Hundi (village deity) every month by offering eggs and cow milk. The Bhirubhairo installed near the village is a very famous deity of the area and a big festival is arranged once a year. Bhirubhairo to which people from far-off places attend and sacrifice goats, cocks, coconut, etc., to propitiate her for blessings.

APPENDIX-XII

Proceedings of the Focus Group Discussion — 7

Village : Bayapada
Date : 14.12.2002
Time : 6.30 P.M.
Participants : 12 adult males and 5 children
Moderator : Dr. P.C. Mohapatro.
Rapporteur : Dr. N.N. Pradhan
Facilitator : Dr. J. Samal

Issues Discussed

- Income and Savings.
- Enrolment and dropout at Primary stage.
- Common Diseases and their methods of prevention.
- Family Planning.
- Protection of National Environment, including Soil, Forest and Wild Animals.
- Forest Produce and their economy.
- Women's Participation.
- Plantation of Economic species.
- Benefits of Poverty Alleviation Programme.
- Occupation and Occupational Hazards.
- Economic Needs and Demands.
- Other related matters and additional informations.

Common Views/Issues

1. A number of households are living hand to mouth. But every household takes interest in saving in terms of cash as well as kind to meet the future contingencies.
2. Teacher absenteeism is the root cause of failure of the primary education system. The teacher appointed stays at Kudumulugumma and rarely comes to the school.
3. The Anganwadi workers do not attend the centre regularly. Sometimes uncooked food materials are distributed among the children for a week. Thus, the pre-school centre is almost defunct in the village.
4. Villagers are aware of the family planning measures. However, everyone of the household wait for a male child to be born. The male vasectomy instead of female tubectomy is preferred in the village.
5. They have two checks dams in their village for irrigation and soil conservation purposes. They need diversion weirs and mini watershed projects to expand irrigation facilities in the village.
6. The villagers are very much conscious about the pernicious practice of shifting cultivation. But they cannot abondon the practice due to their necessities of producing food articles. The Naik opined that provision of suitable employment opportunities may wean them away from this practice.
7. The minor forest produce like fuel wood, wood for construction of houses and making ploughs, different types of edible roots, leaves and fruits, etc., are mostly used for their own consumption and are seldom sold in the market.
8. Cash crop cultivation, which includes ginger, chilly, tobacco are well accepted in the village.
9. Each and every household possesses kitchen garden mostly with hybrid varieties of papaya, banana, chilly, jack fruits, etc., supplied by the Didayi Development Authorities.
10. The inhabitants have shown interest in the plantation of economic species, like mango, cashew, kusum, guava, lichi, coconut, lemon, pomegranate, tamarind, etc. They are not satisfied with the number of plants supplied by the D.D.A.
11. The villagers have received tiles for roofing their houses, argicultural implements, seeds and bullocks from the D.D.A.

12. Many of them have received the benefits of different poverty alleviation programmes implemented through the D.D.A. and the Block.
13. They still have confidence on the *disari* (the indigenous medicineman) though they have started using allopathic medicine supplied by the government through a Multipurpose Health Worker.
14. Women play a very important role in doing economic activities. This is in addition to their regular household chores including cooking, fetching water for drinking, caring of the babies and looking after the domestic animals.

APPENDIX-XIII

Proceedings of the Focus Group Discussion — 8

Village	: Karkaguda
Date	: 21.01.2002
Time	: 6.00 P.M.
Participants	: 15 males and 5 females
Moderator	: Dr. Jagabandhu Samal
Rapporteur	: Dr. N.N. Pradhan.
Facilitator	: Dr. P.C. Mohapatro.

Issues Discussed

- Income and Savings.
- State of Education.
- Enrolment and dropout at Primary stage.
- Common Diseases and their treatment.
- Family Planning
- Protection of Natural environment, including Soil, Forest and Wild Animals.
- Forest Produce and their economic implications.
- Women's Participation.
- Benefits of Poverty Alleviation Programme.
- Economic Needs and Demands.
- Plantation of Economic Species.
- Occupation and Occupational Hazards.
- Other related matters and additional informations.

Common Views/Issues

1. Participants in discussion expressed that they had interest to save in terms of kind and cash to meet their future requirements/categories, but many of them have no real capacity to do so due to their very subsistence level of living.
2. There is no school in the village, even though it is a village consisting of 41 hosueholds. The nearest Primary School is at about a distance of 8 to 10 kms away. Nobody in the village is literate. However, some 5/6 could write their names, which they had learnt by their own efforts while going outside the village. They want that a primary school should be established in their village.
3. There is a Multi Purpose Health Worker in village. He has been provided with tablets like Chloroquine, Lariago, and some other tablets for use in diarrhoea, common cold and fever, etc. However, they still depend upon village *disari* (their traditional medicineman) for treatment. They generally suffer from diarrhoea, malaria, fever, stomach troubles, etc.
4. Most of them are aware of family planning methods. Only about 10 male persons have undergone the operation of vasectomy. They generally wait for a male child to be born. They do not consider that more children are burden to them.
5. Villagers expressed the view that lack of communication facility is the most important problem. The nearest *hat* (weekly market) Jabaghat is about 15 kms. from the village and the Panchayat Headquarters at Nakamarnudi is still far away. It took a whole day to go to Panchayat Headquarters to receive rations on BPL cards and kerosene, etc. Hence, most of them do not avail such facilities, though 32 households have been provided with BPL cards. They preferred to get rice, kerosene, etc., from Somanathpur Gram Panchayat which is about 10 kms away, but they do not get facilities there, as their village comes under another Gram Panchayat. To reach any of these places one has to cross very difficult hill paths on foot only.
6. Almost all the households in the village practise shifting cultivation on the nearby hills. When they were told about the evil effects of shifting cultivation like depletion of forest, soil erosion, etc., they admitted it, and told that they have no

other alternatives to stop it. Hence, it is inferred that until suitable alternative sources of living is available, it is impossible for them to do away with shifting cultivation. One thing they admitted that the proceeds from the shifting cultivation was just sufficient to maintain themselves for a year if weather conditions remained normal and no other natural calamities occur and crops are free from the damages by wild animals and birds.

7. Majority of them knows that Didayi Development Agency is functioning at Kudumulugumma. They have admitted that the Agency is helping them in providing agriculture implements, seeds, etc., some helps they have so far, received personally after going to Kudumulugumma. They confessed that no officer so far personally visited their village.
8. The Non-Timber forest produce and items of food collection from hills and forests are mostly meant for self-consumption; and rarely these are sold in the market. But they have ample confidence in nature, i.e., Forest on which they fall back upon almost everyday for their very survival. One lady participant of the Group told, "we know "Dongar Dian and Karadikhia" which means, "We move on the hills and in the forests and eat the roots and fruits, etc., form it that is our lifestyle".
9. Women in the Didayi society has an important place, both in economic and social fields. They participate in households management, transactions, treatment of guests, etc. In addition to it cooking, cleaning, caring of children and old persons are also their responsibilities. They extend helping hands to their male counterparts in outdoor economic pursuits in the fields and forests.
10. There is a well with tube well fittings in the village, which is not functioning properly. With much of pumping whatever water comes out, it is found to be unfit for drinking purpose. as a odour of iron content is there and water is not clean at all. So the villagers, as usual, are solely depending upon the water of the flowing hill stream found inside the village.
11. They demand (a) good road, (b) a tank, (c) a school with building and (d) an Anganwadi Centre, immediately.
12. Villages showed keen interest for planting of fruit bearing trees like mango, jackfruit, papaya, guava, lemon and also

tobacco. They admitted that the DDA is showing interest for horticultural development in their area, but it has not been quite successful till today. If proper guidance is given they are ready to go for cash crops like ginger, chilly, potato, tobacco, banana, etc.

13. It is against the Didayi culture to milch the cows. Like many other tribal groups, they think that the milk of the cow is solely meant for the calf. It seems with spread of education and extension activities, they will accept the idea of commercial use of milk and also consumption by them for better health of their children and of themselves.
14. They admitted that the food and fodder available in the forest were sufficient to rear animals like cattle, goat, sheep, etc. They are rearing pigs since time immemorial. Similarly, every household has reared poultry, which helps them for exchange of goods in weekly markets, in ceremonial offering and in festivals and feasts.
15. Last, but not the least, the Didayi people of this village are found to be friendly, co-operative and hospitable in nature.

APPENDIX-XIV

Council of Analytical Tribal Studies (COATS), Koraput

"In Search of a Strategy to build a Field Model to ensure People's Participation for Sustainable Development: Case Study of the Didayi"

(A Particularly VulnerableTribal Group of Malkangiri District of Odisha)

Sponsored by: The Planning Commission, Government of India.

A comparative study between the Traditional Panchayat and Modern Panchayat Systems)

Identification

1. Name of the informer:
   Age: Sex:
   Name of the village/hamlet: Block: Kudumulugumma
   District: Malkangiri
2. Name of the person reporting
   Age: Sex: Status:
3. Is the Traditional Panchayat System (Which was functioning before in your village functioning nowadays ?
   If yes, what are the offices/posts existing ?
   (viz., Nayak, Pujari, Jani, Barik, etc.)
   A. B. C. D.
4. (a) How many times do the traditional panchayat meetings at the village level sit in a year ?

(b) What are the matters/problems discussed in these meetings ?

A.

B.

C.

D.

5. Please give an account of the matters/problems discussed in the Traditional Panchayat meetings in your village during the last one year (viz., Land Problems/marriage related/ Litigation and quarrels/observance of festivals/village development works/any other)

Name of the Problem	No. of times	Result
(a)		
(b)		
(c)		
(d)		

6. Please indicate the posts for which elections were conducted to the Panchayat (modern) in your village/area during the last Panchayat election.

Post	Number of posts	No. of contestants
Sarpanch		
Ward Members		
Samiti Member		
Any other		

7. How many voters of your village did cast their votes in the last Panchayat (modern) election ?

Total Number of voters	Number of voters did Cast their votes	Percentage

8. Please give an account of the matters/problems that have been brought before the Panchayat (modern) meetings for consideration in your village.

Type of problem	Total Number	Result
(a)		
(b)		
(c)		
(d)		
(e)		

9. Do the views/opinions of the functionaries of the Traditional Panchayats (*viz.* village Naik, disari, pujari, Barik and other

important persons) are taken into account in the modern village Panchayat meetings? if yes, then on which subjects?

(a) Identification of poor beneficiaries Yes/ No
(b) Forest protection/conservation Yes/ No
(c) Management and functioning of school Yes/ No
(d) Health services Yes/ No
(e) Anganwadi Yes/ No
(f) Drinking water Yes/ No
(g) Road and Communication Yes/ No

10. To which organisation do large number of people prefer to go for justice if any quarrels/misunderstanding or litigation arise among the households/people in the village. ?
(a) Modern Panchayat ( )
(b) Traditional (old) Panchayat ( )
(c) Police/courts etc. ( )

11. The decision of which organisation is generally given more weightage or respect in case of quarrels among families, marriage and related problems, litigations, etc. ?
(a) Traditional (old) Panchayat at village level ( )
(b) Modern Panchayat ( )
(c) Police/Courts, etc. ( )
(d) Any other, if so, please specify

12. Do you feel (or face) any difficulty or problem in the functioning of the modern Panchayat ? Please give specific views
(a)
(b)
(c)
(d)

13. Do you think that the value or importance of the traditional Panchayat is being undermined or degraded after functioning of the modern Panchayats ? Yes/ No
If yes, in which respect ?
(a)
(b)
(c)

14. Do you feel that the level of indiscipline has gone up (on account of party politics) in your village with the holding of elections to the modern Panchayats? Yes/No

If yes, on what accounts ?
(a)
(b)

15. Has "Palli Sabha" meetings are being held in your village? Yes/No
16. If yes, what type of problems are being discussed in these meetings?
(a)
(b)
(c)
17. Have you heard about the conduct of "Gram Sabha" meetings in your Panchayat ? Yes/No

Signature of the Investigator

APPENDIX XV

Interventions of Activities/Schemes for Socio-Economic Development of the Didayi People based on People's Felt Needs as Recommended by COATS

As the Didayi, a numerically small particularly vulnerable tribal group living in a small and contiguous area, represent a cohesive social group. They prefer to have community organisation such as a grain-*gola* to meet the exigencies of food scarcity in each village and a community centre to have meetings, recreational activities for boosting their histrionic talents, games and sports activities, education/literacy endeavours, community based religious festivities, storage of common assets of the village, etc. The management of such common institutions shall rest with the people themselves. It is noticed during the study that in spite of their craze for individual property rights, they have realised that the benefits which, would accrue out of such common endeavour would have sustainability and provide them enormous scope for standing on their own, even if, in course of time, pumping of money through development efforts is stopped. This is certainly a growth-positive cultural trait found among the Didayi. Further, a revolving fund for each village created out of contribution of at least 10 per cent of benefits received by them under different schemes/ programmes would render help to the needy households while facing difficulties. This would reduce dependence on the moneylenders and exploitation thereof. Thus, each village would march towards self-sufficiency and the Didayi people as a whole would become self-reliant. Such common endeavours, some of which have not been tried earlier require immediate attention. Further, in the context of human resource development, capacity building activities have been neglected so far. The training component for upgradation of skills is essential in such fields as agriculture, horticulture, soil conservation animal husbandry, forestry, poultry, semi-processing of minor forest produce, pisciculture, food processing, etc. The same is in case of decision-making, management of community-based organisations/ institution and the like. There shall be follow up action to invigorate the existing SHGs in order to boost the confidence of women folk and to encourage establishment of required additional number of SHGs in each village by creating awareness through Government/ N.G.O. efforts.

DEVELOPMENT OF AGRICULTURE

Agriculture is the mainstay of the Didayi economy. As per the survey conducted by the Council of Analytical Tribal Studies (COATS), Koraput during 2001-2002, 96.85 per cent of Didayi households (1273 out of 1313 households) depend either on settled cultivation or on shifting cultivation or on both. They were using old and outdated agricultural implements, traditional varieties of seeds and following primitive methods of cultivation before the establishment of D.D.A. in 1986. It was rightly decided by DDA to give topmost priority for improvement and development of agricultural practices though the achievements are limited. The important programmes/schemes which may be implemented for development of this primary sector in the project area are as follows:

I. Supply of Bullocks

The DDA authorities have provided a pair of bullocks to needy Didayi households at one bullock per household. In other words, a pair of bullocks have been supplied to two Didayi households. This practice has created two main problems. After the death of one of the bullocks of any one beneficiary, both the households face the problem of cultivation of their land. This practice has also created discontentment among the other cultivators who have not been provided with bullocks by the DDA.

The available records from DDA reveals that bullocks have been supplied only to 90 beneficiaries during the period from 1992-93 to 1995-96. The survey conducted by COATS revealed that out of 985 cultivating households of settled land, only 601 households own 1256 bullocks and ten households own 24 buffaloes, 374 cultivating households do not have any cattle population and many of them are hiring a pair of bullocks from their neighbours at a cost of Rs. 700 to Rs. 800 per annum.

All these 374 households who do not own any cattle population need to be provided with a pair of bullocks. Among these households having bullocks, around 100 households need a pair of bullocks to replace their old ones which are not fit to be used for cultivation, as they have not yet become economically strong enough to purchase the same. In addition, out of 533 landless households 20 per cent, i.e., 106 households need to be supplied with a pair of bullocks and a cart to enable them to use them on hire basis on other's farms or transportation purposes where communication facilities are available. Thus, there is the need for supply of total number of 580 pairs of bullocks in the Didayi villages.

It may be relevant to point out that according to clause (b-2) of Section 2, of Odisha Government Land Settlement Act of 1962, a landless person means any person, the total extent of whose lands exçluding homestead together with lands held by all the members of the family who are living with him in common hearth is less than one standard acre and whose total annual income, together with all members of the family who are living with him in common hearth does not exceed rupees three thousand and six hundred. The application of this clause in the study area will increase the landless households from 533 to 1253.

All the assets including livestock population provided to Didayi households need to be properly covered by insurance with a one time premium at the time of supply so as to cover the risk of losses on account of pre-mature death or theft of assets including animals. Unless the assets created or acquired are maintained properly, sustainability in the development efforts and results would be a myth than reality.

II. Supply of Agricultural implements

Agricultural implements, like spade, pick-axe, crowbar and M.B. Plough (an improved type of hand driven plough) have been provided by the DDA to the Didayi households to acquaint them with these tools and to raise their productive efficiency. Between the period

1987-88 and 1995-96 agricultural implements have been provided on three instalments. The survey made by COATS revealed that only 792 households have been covered under the programme in a piecemeal manner. None of the beneficiaries have been provided with a full set of agricultural implements. Adequate provisions have to be made for supply of these implements to all the needy Didayi households. At least 521 sets of agricultural implements need to be supplied to the households who have never received them.

In order to initiate comparatively new and improved production technology, provision may be made for supply of hand operated power tillers in all the three pockets of the area. Young cultivators need to be provided with proper training facilities to handle and take care of these hand operated power tillers. Past experiences has shown that this has succeeded in the Kutia Kandha Development Agency, Belghar, Phulbani district in the State and hence can be initiated in the Didayi area.

III. Introduction of High-yielding Varieties of Seeds and Cash Crops

It has been found that introduction and popularization of high-yielding varieties of seeds and cash crops have yielded better return per unit area and per unit labour in place of low-yielding traditional crops in Didayi area. The popularisation of high-yielding varieties of seeds, i.e., cereals, like paddy, maize and ragi, pulses like *arhar*, green gram (*mung*) and blackgram (*biri*), oil seeds like mustard, niger and groundnut and other vegetables like chilly, soyabean, lady's finger, pumpkin, watermelon, cucumber and bittergourd in the area have proved successful. Efforts need to be made to use newer varieties of high yielding seeds which are better suited to the agro-climate conditions of the area for higher return per unit area and labour through intensive demonstration. Steps may be taken to motivate the tribal farmers of the area for accepting new methods.

IV. Backyard Kitchen Garden

Most of the Didayi households are in the habit of maintaining a kitchen garden at the backyard of their houses. They usually grow tobacco, mustard, some roots and tuber crops. The DDA has taken advantage of this practice and have introduced cultivation of chilly, ginger, turmeric and vegetables like brinjal, lady's finger, potato, tomato, onion etc. It has been found during the survey that chilly, ginger, and vegetable production both in the backyard and in the nearby lands around the villages have been successful. The per acre average yield of backyard kitchen garden is found to be the highest in the Didayi area (i.e., Rs. 2027 as against Rs. 1873 in case of settled cultivation)

Supply of improved variety of seeds and saplings suited to the agro-climatic conditions have to be ensured to intensify this programme in all the Didayi households.

V. Chemical Fertilisers and Pesticides

Gradual and systematic introduction and supply of chemical fertilizers and pesticides have been made by DDA to ensure more and assured return in cultivation. Simultaneously, the farmers have been encouraged by DDA to continue compost manuring in a more scientific way. However, the efforts made by the DDA was found to be very much limited in these directions. During the year 1991-92, 114 qtls. of Syamala, 40 qtls. of DAP and 165 qtls. of urea were distributed to 357, 185 and 335 beneficiaries respectively. During the year 1992-93 and 1993-94 pesticides like Demicran, Endotaf, Bavisthin and Dethen-45 were distributed to farmers in limited quantities.

Provisions have to be made for expansion of these programmes to more and more households. Compost manuring in a scientific way has also to be expanded to all the villages by providing them encouragement by way of subsidy for digging pits.

VI. Horticulture

Development of horticulture in the backyard kitchen garden of the households, in suitable high lands and *podu*-ravaged areas, besides reducing the evil effects of soil erosion can provide a continuous source of income and sustainable development of the beneficiaries. The efforts made by the DDA in case of backyard plantation has led to positive results in case of banana, lemon and papaya plantations. The success story is very much limited in the Hills sub-area and cut-off sub-area villages. Cashew plantation, which is a profitable type of cultivation, is still to pick up in the area. Grafted mango, coconut, guava, lemon, *salap*, jack fruit and tamarind plantation need to be properly encouraged both in the backyard and other suitable lands in the area. Mango and coconut plantations have been made in few villages in the area. The guava, lemon and the coconut plantations taken up in plains sub-area by few households have started yielding fruits and now the demand for these seedlings have increased.

There are 1814.50 acres of shifting land and 1362.40 acres of *dongar* land in the project area, which are put under cultivation during the year 2001-2002. If we include the shifting land, which were not cultivated and were put to rest in the *podu* - cycle/ fallow period, the total land under shifting cultivation will be around 5,000 acres. Out of 1362.40 acres of *dongar* land around 500 acres are sloppy land with small stones all over the field. Plantation of fruit bearing trees can be taken up on the lands between 10 degrees to 30 degrees slope and beyond 30 degrees slope some fast growing species, like Acasia, *Chakunda*, etc., can be planted in *podu* ravaged lands which can maintain the ecology of the area.

VII. Checking the Evil Effects of Shifting Cultivation

The villagers are aware of the evil effects of shifting cultivation, but they practise it due to scarcity of plain lands and absence of alternative means of livelihood. In order to check the evil effects of shifting cultivation primarily washing away of topsoil through soil erosion, stone terracing methods may be encouraged by engaging the beneficiaries under the "food for work" programme. Simultaneously, plantation of economic species other than fruit bearing trees may be taken up on the land beyond 30 degrees slope and fruit-bearing trees may be planted on the land below 30 degrees slope. This is another version of the Sloping Agricultural Land Technology (SALT, Phase I, II and III) or agro-forestry method which will be suitable for the project area. Cultivation of cereals and pulses can be undertaken till the fruit bearing trees bear fruits and the shade of the plants will not hamper the crops to grow. After this period, the cultivators can get a greater amount of income from the sale and use of fruits. This can gradually wean the Didayis away from the shifting cultivation practices without affecting their livelihood. The land below 30 degrees slope can be recorded in the name of the beneficiaries as has been done in case of Kashipur area of Rayagada district in Odisha. This will provide further incentive to the cultivators to give up shifting cultivation.

VIII. Land Reclamation

The *dongar* lands (high lands) of the Hills sub-area and cut-off sub-area are sloppy with 20 degrees to 40 degrees slope. More than 50 per cent of land in the Hills sub-area and 25 per cent of the land in cut-of sub-area are sloppy. In addition, the *dongar* lands of Hills sub-area are covered with small stones all over the land. These lands need to be properly reclaimed and developed. There are around 1000 acres of land, which need to be reclaimed.

IX. Irrigation Facilities and Soil Conservation Measures

As the lands in the project area are very much undulating and a number of hill streams are there in almost all the villages, mini-watershed can be initiated in each of the sub-areas in suitable places, for assured irrigation facilities and prevention of soil erosion. The check dams, water harvesting structures and diversion weirs provided in few villages have become old and need renovation at least ten mini-watershed projects can be constructed in the area with the provision of irrigation channels to assure irrigation facilities.

An earth dam between the two hillocks, i.e., between Gojia *dongar* and Jiramali (about 500 metres length) can be constructed at Muduliguda to reserve the water coming from the hill streams during the rainy season. This minor irrigation project, besides helping to control soil erosion and flood can help to irrigate the lands of three villages, i.e., Muduliguda, Oringi and Purunagumma.

A guard wall of about half a kilometre need also to be constructed to protect Oringi village from flood water. The water from the hill streams and the rain water coming from the mountains creates a threat to the villages, and the standing crops are destroyed. The construction of a guard wall will help to protect the village, the cultivable lands and will act like a water harvesting structure.

X. Provision of Diesel Pump with Accessories

The lands of the villages situated on the banks of Balimela reservoirs can be irrigated with the help of diesel pumps till electrification facilities are provided in the area. A diesel pump of 5 h.p. to 10 h.p. depending upon the size of households in the villages can be provided to enable the cultivators to irrigate their lands by lifting water from the reservoir. The people are willing to bear the running cost of these diesel pumps. During the focus group discussions conducted in Orapadar, Totaguda, Jantry, Dhakad Padar in cut-off sub-area villages the villagers showed a lot of interest for supply of diesel pumps to irrigate their lands.

XI. Fishing

The vast stretch of water surface on Balimela reservoir offers plenty of scope for fishing through boats and nets. A number of Didayi villagers living close to both sides of the banks of reservoir have become expert in fishing. During the period from 1993-94 to 1995-96, only 30 units of Boats and nets were provided to 60 beneficiaries of cut off area. Few villagers on the hills-sub-area close to the reservoir are interested to avail the benefit of fishing. There is the need for providing at least 100 sets of nets and boats to 200 beneficiaries at one unit per two households, as has been the practice with the DDA.

XII. Drinking Water Facilities

Thirty two tube wells have been provided in the Didayi inhabited villages in the DDA area to cater to the need of drinking water, i.e., seven tube wells in the plains sub-area villages, eleven in the hills sub-area villages, and fourteen tube wells in the cut-off sub-area villages. The number of tube wells provided is not adequate to meet with their requirement. Calculated at of one tube well for 20 households there is the need for providing 40 additional tube wells in the DDA area. In addition, 10 out of 32 tube wells are not functioning properly as there is no provision for maintenance of tube wells. A mechanic needs to be appointed at least for a period of three years in the DDA area for timely maintenance of these tube wells. In the mean time the educated Didayi youths may be trained for maintenance of these tube wells in order to take care of the tube wells after a period of three years.

Further, where favourable gradient is naturally available, sump for storage, preservation/purification of water can be made and water can be supplied to villages with pipeline and taps. They have already succeeded in 3 villages, such as Jantry, Disariguda and Dabuguda in the Cut-off area. Such facilities may be extended to Damodarbeda in the Hill sub-area Orapadar and Taberu in the Cut-off sub-area and Oringi, Chilipadar and Tikarapara (A) in plains sub-area villages.

XIII. Communication Facilities

Absence of communication facilities in the Cut-off sub-area and Hills sub-area is one of the biggest problems the Didayi's face. Only once or twice in a week they attend the nearby weekly markets to dispose of their surplus produce and purchase their necessities. In order to overcome this problem a jeepable tar-felting road from Oringi village in the plains sub-area to Bayapada, i.e, the central village in the Hills sub-area will provide a vital link road. The minimum requirement of roads, bridges, culverts and causeways has been listed out at Appendix XV (1) and XV (2) to ensure the link among other villages. A link between the cut-off sub-area with Hills sub-area villages can be ensured through construction of a bridge on the reservoir to connect Jantry village in the Cut-off sub-area with Amblibeda village on the hills.

XIV. Cooperation and Marketing

LAMPS at Kudumulugumma Block Headquarters is the only cooperative institution established to meet with the credit-cum-marketing requirements of the Didayi project area. Due to the absence of Sub-centres in the inaccessible pockets, it is not able to play an effective role in providing these services in the project area. Hence, it is necessary to establish two sub-centres, i.e., one on the Hills sub-area and another in the Cut-off sub-area to enable the LAMPS at Kudumulugumma to play an effective role.

XV. Indira Awas Yojana (I.A.Y.)

Only sixty-eight poor Didayi households have been provided with housing facilities under Indira Awas Yojana by the Block authorities as a measure of poverty alleviation programme. However, it has been calculated on the basis of the Survey by COATS, 2001-02 that 70 per cent of the households are living below the poverty line. Hence, at least 460 (i.e. 50%) of the households out of 919 households living below the poverty line who have no suitable dwellings may be provided with dwelling houses under the IAY programme within a period of five years.

XVI. Self Help Groups (SHGs)

As a measure to empower the women by enabling them to generate income, thirty-three SHGs have been formed in 21 Didayi villages within a record time, i.e., between June 2000 to September 2000. The members in these SHGs vary from 11 to 20 and there are 494 women members. An interview with some of the these members revealed that they have planned to start business in the collection of tamarind, brooms, supply of kerosene oil and other necessities to make the SHGs viable. However, only three out of 33 SHGs have received incentive grant of Rs. 10,000 each. At least 60 SHGs can be formed in the 39 Didayi villages to empower the women through effective participation in income generating activities.

XVII. Health Services

In the absence of Medical services in the Didayi area they continue to depend upon the traditional medicinemen. Due to the lack of additional P.H.C. in the Cut-off and Hills sub-areas the inhabitants of these areas are facing a lot of health problems. In order to provide them health services in the vicinity of their villages at least four additional PHCs, four ANM centres and a Mobile Health Service facility need to be provided in the area. In the cut-off sub-area a motor launch has to be provided with all emergency treatment facilities with medical personnel made available there.

The existing Health workers in all the three sub-areas require further training for capacity enhancement to cater to the needs of the ailing villagers. The medicines for common ailments, such as fever (including malaria), diarrhoea, headache, cold and cough, etc., are supplied at present, through the health workers. But they need more medicines for treatment of gastrointestinal disorders, skin diseases etc. Hence, provisions have to be made for supply of these medicines to meet with the needs of the area.

XVIII. Electrification

There is no provision of electricity in the Cut-off sub-area and Hills sub-area. Electricity line has been taken up to Oringi village in the plains sub-area. This line can be extended up to Bayapada village in the Hills sub-area which is only 4 kms away from Oringi village.

Once the Bayapada village will be connected with electricity line, the villages located in both the sides of Bayapada can be provided with electric lines. Bayapada village on the Hills sub-area is at a distance of 15 kms from Amblibeda which is on the side of Balimela reservior in the Hills sub-area. The electric line can be taken to Jantry village in the Cut-off area from Amblibeda. Provision of electricity has to be taken up on priority basis to provide lift irrigation facilities to the villages situated on both the sides of the reservoir at the minimum cost.

XIX. Handicrafts and Cottage Industries

Promotion of handicrafts and cottage industries in the Didayi area can open viable employment opportunities to both the men and women folk. Bamboo craft, woodcraft, rope making, broom-making, semi-processing of tamarind, resin, dry fish, etc., may be started at the initial stage. After the introduction of SHGs, women's propensity to save has increased and many of the office bearers like Presidents and Secretaries of SHGs have started taking keen interest to develop their talents in different trade activities. If women's capacity building can be enhanced through demonstration and training at this stage, the SHGs can become viable trading units as well as centres of cottage and handicrafts industries.

Eleven households in the cut-off sub-area and 13 households in the plains sub-area are presently engaged in bamboo craft. They are making mats, baskets, fish catching devices, winnowing baskets and storage baskets out of bamboo available in their area and sell them in the weekly market. These households earn an income of Rs. 8000 Rs. 12000 per capita per annum from this bamboo craft trade which is only a subsidiary income source. This area can be properly developed through training for capacity building.

XX. Animal Husbandry

As the Didayi like other neighbouring tribes generally do not milk their cows, the supply of dairy unit may not help them at present for their economic development. This may be tried at a later stage with proper education and motivation. Smaller animals like goat, sheep, pig and birds like fowl, will besides providing portion for their food will meet their requirement of festivals and their daily necessities which they can purchase by sale of these animals and birds in the markets.

It has been found in the field that goat-rearing units supplied by the DDA has proved to be successful. At present 669 households possess 1,577 goats and bucks.

Out of the 533 landless households only 50 households have been provided with two goats each and a buck for their households. Hence, 483 households need to be provided with goat-rearing units consisting of 5 goats and a buck. The local variety of goats which can easily be maintained by them need to be supplied. The hybrid bucks available in the neighbouring Andhra Pradesh can be supplied to improve the quality of goats. The Didayi area is rich in forest and grazing fields which are suitable for rearing of smaller animal units. Pigs are the domestic animals only in limited villages of hills Sub-area. Piggery units may be supplied only in those villages where the people are experienced in the rearing of pigs.

Poultry units are common in the Didayi villages. 886 households possess 2,650 hen and cock. The DDA has provided improved variety of cock in every village. Poultry units have not been provided as yet. Poultry units consisting of 10 hens and a cock can be supplied to 300 landless and marginal farmers which will go a long way to improve their standard of living.

XXI. Establishment of Revolving Fund

A Revolving Fund can be created in every village to come to the aid of households at the time of their need. This fund can be created through the contributions made by the villagers. Initially any villager who receives some benefit as a beneficiary under any programme/ scheme from the DDA/Block authorities/NGOs would contribute ten per cent of the value of the benefit received towards the Revolving Fund. The percentage of contributioin can be progressively raised from 10 per cent to 50 per cent gradually as and when the paying capacity of the beneficiary increases. In the Didayi area as all the households of village are beneficiaries under one scheme or the other, all the heads of the households will become members of such Revolving Fund.

In the DDA area this proposition can be easily implemented as the DDA authorities are collecting 10 per cent of the value of the benefit given to the beneficiary in terms of cash. This system has been introduced after taking a decision in the governing body meeting of DDA in 1977 to distribute the limited resources available with DDA to the beneficiaries who actually need them. In other words, each beneficiary will receive the benefits as much as he really needs only if he has to pay a part of the price of the benefit. This system can be replaced with the creation of a Revolving Fund.

As in the case of SHGs the DDA/ DRDA can provide an incentive grant of Rs. 10,000 after the creation of a Revolving Fund. The fund can be deposited in a bank in the name of Revolving Fund of a particular village. The traditional Naik/headman of a village and the elected Ward member of the Panchayat or a selected educated youth in the village meeting, in the absence of a Ward member in a village can be the President and Secretary of the fund respectively who will jointly operate the account of the fund.

The establishment of such a fund can come to the help of any villager at his difficult times in the shape of a loan at a lower rate of interest. Grant of a loan to a villager can be decided by the villagers themselves in a village meeting taking into account the need of a borrower. An educated villager may be asked to maintain the account on payment of a monthly honorarium to be met out of the interest money.

The establishment of such a fund and entrusting the day-to-day management of the fund to the villagers themselves will be of utmost importance to the villagers from the point of view of sustainable development. This will help the villagers to be free from the exploitations from various quarters.

XXII. Grain Banks

Tribals usually borrow in terms of cash and kind at the time of their needs from the moneylenders. Village *mahajans* and businessmen exploit them in a number of ways. To save the tribals from the clutches of the moneylenders and traders, the establishment of grain banks will play an important role.

A grain bank can be established in every village in the Didayi Development Project area. All the heads of the Didayi households in a village can become members of the grain bank by contributing a share either in the form of grain or cash. The DDA will take up the responsibility of construction of the building to house the grain bank and will provide an incentive grant of Rs. 20,000 after the grain bank is established in a village through collection of contribution from each household.

Any member can take a loan in the form of grain to meet with his consumption needs or seed purpose to meet with his cultivation needs at the rate of 25 per cent interest to be returned after harvesting of crops in case of a cultivator or within a period of six months in case of a landless labourer.

The traditional Nayak and the elected Ward member or elected villager in the absence of a elected Ward member in a village can become President and Secretary of the grain bank respectively. Another three members can be elected from the village in a village meeting to form an executive committee to perform the management functions of a grain bank.

In Odisha State such a scheme known as graingola was introduced in the year 1951-52. But the system did not work and died a natural death due to lack of participation of the people in the management of graingola. However, grain banks established by the agragamee, a leading NGO working in the Kashipur area of Rayagada district has proved to be successful.

The establishment of grain banks in every village, where people's participation can be ensured in their management will act as another stepping stone for sustainable development.

XXIII. Village Community Centre Complex

Every village needs a community centre complex to meet with varieties of needs of the community. The villagers need such a complex to house community organisations such as Grain Bank, education and literacy centre place for performance of community-based religious festivities, storage of common assets of the village, meeting place, recreational activities and the like. Instead of constructing separate buildings for each of these community organisation, efforts can be made to provide a community centre complex to accommodate all such community organisations including a primary school, Anganwadi centre and ANM centre, etc. In the community centre complex, there should be a provision for separate room to house a girls' dormitory. The boys can accommodate themselves in the room meant for their recreational activities.

Each community centre complex should be provided with a radio set-cum-tape recorder, one *durry*, one steel almirah, one steel table wth five plastic chairs, reference books for primary passed out students, photograph of some national leaders, kerosene lantern and one covered bucket and few glass tumblers. The provision of all these will attract the villagers to spend their evening in the community centre and expose them to various informations of the world.

The management of such common institutions shall rest with the people themselves. The benefits which would accrue out of such common endeavours would have sustainability and would provide the villagers enormous scope for standing on their own.

Education

1. Family plays a vital role in the process of socialisation during childhood. A Didayi child at his school going age, assists his parents in their occupation as well as in harvesting, caring for younger siblings and other household chores.
2. The process of socialisation, during adolescence and youth is regulated by youth dormitory (*Dhangda/Dhangdi Basa*). It is not only a sleeping room for the youths, but also provides facilities for acquiring life skills through training, recreation, learning and the living together boosts mutual help, cooperation; and exchange of skills, knowledge and ideas.
3. The rate of drop-out among the Didayi children in the elementary schooling stage is too high (90.31%). It is 87.27 per cent in case of boys and 94.19 per cent in case of girls.
4. Majority of the Didayi children do not have access to primary education. Out of 39 Didayi inhabited villages of Malkangiri district 21 villages do not have Primary Schools within the habitation nor within a distance of one kilometre (see Table 3.8). The distance of the nearest schools in such villages vary between 2 to 12 kms.
5. As many as 7 out of 18 primary schools of the Didayi inhabited village, are single teacher schools.
6. Four out of 18 Primary Schools of the Didayi inhabited villages do not have school buildings. Further, 2 out of 15 primary schools building of the area need minor or major repair.
7. The percentage of literacy among the Didayi is as low as 7.89 per cent. It is 12.5 per cent among the males and 3.36 per cent among the females. As many as 14 out of 39 Didayi inhabited villages are found to be zero literacy villages.

Implications for Sustainable Development

For their sustainable development, education, which is the key input has to be given top-priroity attention:

(i) Provision of community centres, in every village, will fulfil the requirement of youth dormitories.
(ii) School timing and vacation may be made liberal in view of local rituals and festivals.
(iii) In order to make the school environment congenial and bridge the gap between home environment and school environment, the school building should be attractive, with spacious campus, which can accommodate playground, orchard, and a backyard.
(iv) Establishment of new primary schools, alternative schooling centres and *sevashrams* are necessary.
(v) Appointment of additional teachers in single-teacher schools may be taken up.
(vi) Repair of school buildings—minor or major—is a dire need.
(vii) Establishment of literacy centres/*chetana kendras* for illiterate adults is also necessary.

Suggested Inputs

1. The proposed community centres in the villages with more than 100 population are mentioned below.

Hills sub-area	*Plains sub-area*	*Cut-off sub-area*
Bayapada	Tikarapada(A)	Dabuguda
Bedankhiguda	Muduliguda(A)	
Tikarapada(B)	Chelipadar	
Niringjhola		
Khajuriguda		
Karkaguda		
Damodarabeda		

Further community centres in the following uniethnic Didayi villages with population below 100 may also be constructed so as to serve multiple purposes, e.g., adult literacy Centre, alternative schooling centre, place of recreation, meetings etc.

Hills sub-area	*Plains sub-area*	*Cut-off sub-area*
Suripoda	Chelipadar	Totaguda
Bataguda		Maribeda
Anguriguda		Disariguda
Muduliguda(B)		Arlingipada
Burulibandh		Nadimanjori
Bamaring		Kantamanjari
		Sanyasiguda

2. The Primary School buildings of the following villages need immediate repair and maintenance:

Minor repair	Major repair
Purunagumma	Damodarabeda

3. Additional teacher (one to each school) may be provided to the following single teacher primary schools:

Bayapada	Dabuguda
Bedankiguda	Jantry
Damodarbeda	Sanyasiguda

4. New primary school may be opened in the following three Villages:
   Ghisingbeda (Hills sub-area)
   Dhakapadar (Cut-off sub-area)
   Tikarpada(A) (Plains sub-area)
5. Residential facilities may be provided at Jantry (cut-off area) to cater to the need of the following nearby schoolless villages:

Maribeda	Kantamanjari
Disariguda	Arlingpada
Nadimanjari	Ramaguda
Bhojaguda	

6. Residential facilities may be provided at Bayapada primary school to cater to the need of the following nearby schoolless villages in the Hills sub-area:

Bataguda	Anguruguda
Suripada	Muduliguda(B)

7. Residential facilities may be provided at Nilapari Primary School to cater to the need of the following nearby schoolless habitation:
   Bamaring
   Burulubandh
8. All the 39 villages may be covered under Adult Literacy Programme during Continuing Education (C.E.) phase through mopping up operation in view of low rate of literacy in 25 villages and zero literacy in as many as 14 villages.
9. In order to prevent teacher absenteeism moderate residential quarters may be provided in the school campus for teachers.
10. As it is an inaccessible area (facilities of communication, health facility, higher education, absence of electricity etc.) a teacher may be assured that he would be posted to a place of his choice if he continuously work there for a period of six years.
11. Selected Sub-Inspector of schools be posted in the area for better supervision.
12. As per the National Education Policy 1986 (as amended in 1992) local persons with lower educational qualification may be recruited for primary schools. These teachers will be given in-service training from time to time so that their deficiency due to lower qualifications could be done away with. While recruiting dedication and commitment of persons to serve the people for promotion of their education shall be the primary objective.

In course of fieldwork among the Didayi for the present study it was also revealed that there are as many as 50 persons (both males and females) specially in the plains and cut-off sub-areas for the above purpose. But in the hill sub-area in the absence of such educated persons, candidates from the plains and cut-off sub-areas who are willing for the work may be appointed for the purpose.

The above mentioned arrangement will eradicate teacher absenteeism in the Didayi area.

APPENDIX-XV-(I)

Infrastructural Facilities to be created—Construction of Roads

Sl. No.	*Name of the Road*	*Length in kms*
1	Jantry to Kantamanjari *via* Maribeda and Nadimanjari villages	10
2	Ghisingbeda to Amblibeda village	4
3	Khajuriguda to Tikarpada(B)	3
4	Khajuriguda to Naringjhola	3
5	Bayapada to Oringi village (mountainous track)	4
6	Somnathpur to Karkaguda	7
7	Tikarpada(B) to Amblibeda	3
8	Chelipadar to Tikarpada(A)	4
9	Domodarbeda to Karkaguda *via* Burlubandha and Bamaring	15

Source: Survey by COATS, 2001-2002

APPENDIX-XV-(2)

Infrastructural facilities to be created—Bridges, Culverts and Causeways

Sl. No	*Name of the Road*	*Type of infrastructure*	*Nos.*
1	Jantry to Kantamanjari	Bridge	1
		Culverts	2
		Causeways	1
2	Bayapada to Damodarbeda	Submersible bridge	1
		Culverts	4
3	Khajuriguda to Tikarpada (B)	Causeways	1
4	Tikarpada (A) to Chelipadar	Causeways	2
5	Ghisingbeda to Amblibeda	Submersible bridge	2
6	Sanyasiguda to Totaguda	Submersible Bridge	2
7	Jantry to Amblibeda	Bridge	1
8	Damodarbeda to Karkaguda *via* Bamaring and Burlubandh	Causeways	6

Source: Survey by COATS, 2001-2002.

APPENDEX-XV-(3)

Infrastructural Facilities to be provided

M.I.P, Guard-Wall and Diesel Pumps

Sl. No.	*Name of the project*	*Description of the work*
1	Muduliguda M.I.P. Earth Dam	An earth dam of 10 feet breadth and 15 feet height between two mountains, i.e., Gojiadonger & Jiramali
2	Oringi Guard wall to protect Oringi village	A guardwall of about half a kilometer
3	Renovation of a old pond at Oringi village	—
4	Diesel pump at Jantry, Orapadar, Totaguda and Dabuguda	10 H.P. each with accessories and a shed for keeping motor.

Note : Survey by COATS, 2001-2002.

Bibliography

Arya, Swarn Lata and J.S. Samra (1994). "Determinants of People's Participation in Watershed Development and Management—An Exploratory Case Study in Shiwalik Foothill Villages in Haryana", *Journal of Rural Development*, Vol. 13(3) pp. 411-422, NIRD, Hyderabad,

Atal, Yogesh (2000). "Sustainable Development of Human Settlements: A Social Science Perspective", in *Prashasnika* – A Journal of Administrative Processes of the HCM Rajasthan State Institute of Public Administration, Jaipur, Vol. XXVII, No. 1, Jan-June, 2000, pp. 13-23.

Baker, Therese L. (1988). *Doing Social Research*, McGraw Hill Book Company, New York.

Barth, Fredrik (1969). *Ethnic Groups and Boundaries*, George Allen & Unwin, London.

Behura, N.K. and K.K. Mohanti (1998). Vulnerable Ethno-cultural Groups (VEGs) *Adivasi*, Vol. XXXVIII, No. 1 & 2, The Journal of the S.C. and S.T. Research and Training Institute, Odisha, Bhubaneswar.

—— "Culture and Development: The Tribal Scenario" (unpublished)

Best, J.W. and J.V. Kahn (1995). *Research in Education*, 7th Edn., Prentice Hall of India Pvt. Ltd., New Delhi.

Bose, N.K. (1972). *Anthropology and Some Indian Problems*, Institute of Social Research and Applied Anthropology, Calcutta.

Cernea, Michael M. (ed.) (1985). *Putting People First*, Oxford University Press.

Chein, P. (1988). "*An Introduction to Sampling in S.B. Merriam* (ed.), 1988.

Chowdhury, B. (1990) "Didayi" in Tribes of Odisha, Tribal and Harijan Research-cum-Training Institute, Odisha, Bhubaneswar, pp. 98-102.

Coser, Lewis A. (1977). *Masters of Sociological Thought: Ideas in Historical and Social Context*, Second Edition, Harcourt Brace Jovanovich, Inc. New York.

Das, J.K. (1972). "Didayi" in the report on Scheduled Tribes of Odisha, Book One, *Census of India*, 1961 Volume - XII - Odisha - Part - V-B, Odisha Government Press, Cuttack, pp. 44-49.

Denzin, N.K. (1988). "The *Research Act: A Theroretical Introduction to Sociological Methods*", Chicago: Aldine, p. 308 in S.B. Merriam (ed.), Case Study Research in Education — A Qualitative Approach, Jossey - Bass, Inc. New York.

Devi, Laxmi *et al* (eds.) (1996). *Encyclopaedia of Economic Planning and Development*, Vol. 2 & Vol. 4, Anmol Publications Pvt. Ltd., New Delhi (Institute for Sustainable Development, Lucknow).

Furer-Haimendorf, C. Von (1982). *Tribes of India — The Struggle for Survival*, Oxford University Press, Delhi.

Gengaje, Rajan K. and E. Desingu Setty (1992). "A Model for Developing Agro-Enterprises among Farm Women in Asia", in *Journal of Rural Development*, Vol. 11(5), pp. 545-571, NIRD, Hyderabad.

Ghosh, R.N., R. Gabbay and K.C. Roy (eds.) (1999). *Sustaining Development—Human Resources, Gender and Environment*, Atlantic Publishers and Distributors, New Delhi.

Goetz, J.P. and M.D. Le Compte (1988). "*Ethnography and Qualitative Design in Educational Research*", Orland Flair Academic Press (1984) in S.B. Merriam (ed.), 1988.

Gopalan, Sarala "Monitoring and Evaluation of Training Programmes for Women Functionaries in Rural Development", in *Journal of Rural Development*, Vol. 11(5) pp. 573-599, NIRD, Hyderabad.

Government of Odisha (1958). Review of Plan for Community Projects and National Extension Service, Draft Second Five Year Plan of Odisha, 1956-57 to 1960-61: p. 79.

Government of Odisha (1999). Didayi Development Agency, Kudumulugumma, Information Sheet (unpublished).

Government of Odisha (1966). *Tribal and Rural Welfare Manual*, Vol. II, Tribal and Rural Welfare Department, pp. 97-103.

Government of Odisha (1974). *A Handy Reference Book*, Tribal and Rural Welfare Department, pp. 17-18.

Government of Odisha (2000). *Integrated Tribal Development Agency*, Malkangiri, S.C. & S.T. Development Department (Memiographed).

Government of Odisha (2002). Regional Workshop on Fiscal Governance Reforms and Poverty Reduction Strategy, NISWASS-CEDEL Press, Bhubaneswar-13.

G.R. Varma (2002). *The Odisha Government Land Settlement Manual*, The Law House, Cuttack and The Law House, Bhubaneswar.

Guha, Uma *et al.* (1970). *The Didayi — A Forgotten Tribe of Odisha* (Anthropological Survey of India), The Manager of Publications, Government of India publication Branch, Civil Lines, Delhi.

Gupta, N.L. and R.K. Gurjar (eds.) (1993). *Sustainable Development*, Vol. I. Rawat Publications, Jaipur.

—— (1993). *Sustainable Development*, Vol. II. Rawat Publications, Jaipur.

Harijan and Tribal Welfare Department, Government of Odisha (1990). *Tribes of Odisha,* Tribal and Harijan Research-cum-Training Institute, Odisha, Bhubaneswar.

Holsti, O.R. (1988). "*Content Analysis for the Social Sciences and Humanities,* Reading Mass, Addition - Wesley (1981) in S.B. Merriam (ed), 1988.

Hui, Jianguo and Patricia E. Mclean Meyinsse (1994). "Food Shortage Models in a Developing Economy: China's Experience" in *Journal of Rural Development*, Vol. 13(1), pp. 1-8, NIRD, Hyderabad.

Iqbal Narain (1989). *Development, Politics and Social Theory*, Sterling Publishers Pvt. Ltd., New Delhi.

Mahapatra, L.K. (1986-87). "Evolving a plan for Social Inputs in Rural, Tribal Blocks with People's Participation", *Manav,* Vol. II, No. 1, Anthropological Society of Odisha.

Mann, R.S. (1987). *Social Change and Social Research—An Indian Perspective*, Concept Publishing Company, New Delhi.

Meier, Gerald M. and Robert E. Baldwin (1961). *Economic Development—Theory, History, Policy,* Asia Publishing House, Bombay.

Merriam, S.B. (1988). *Case Study Research in Education—A Qualitative Approach*, Jossey—Bass, Inc. New York.

Mishra, B. and P.C. Mohapatro (1980). *Evaluation Report of Malkangiri*, I.T.D.A., Koraput District, Odisha, Utkal University, Bhabaneswar.

Mohanty, S.C. (1981-82). "Didayi, A Picturesque Tribe of Odisha", in *Adivasi*, Vol. XXI, Nos. 1-4, pp 1-10, THRTI, Odisha.

——(1992). "Didayi and Their Development", in *Adibasi*, Vol. XXXII, No. 2, pp. 10-18, THRTI, Odisha.

Mohapatra, P.K. (1963-64). "Didayi" in *Adibasi*, Vol.V No. III (Special Issue), pp. 127-130, THRTI, Odisha.

——(1963-64). "The Didayi—A Hill Tribe of Odisha", in *Adibasi,* Vol. No. 2, pp. 63-66, THRTI, Odisha.

Mohapatra, P.M. and P.C. Mohapatro (1997). *Forest Management in Tribal Areas: Forest Policy and Peoples Participation*, Concept Publishing Company, New Delhi.

Morris, Freilich (ed.) (1970). *Marginal Natives—Anthropologists at Work*, Harper & Row Publishers, New York.

Mukherji, S. (1985). *Modern Economic Development—An Elementary Text*, Wiley Eastern Limited, New Delhi.

Nayak, P.K. and Anil Mahajan (eds.) (1991). *Human Encounter with Drought*, Reliance Publishing House, New Delhi.

Pelto, Pertti J. (1970). *Anthropological Research—The Structure of Inquiry*, Harper & Row Publishers, New York.

Rayappa, P. Hanumantha (1993). Issues in Tribal Development—A Study of Selected Tribes in Dakhina Kannada District of Karnataka in *Journal of Rural Development*, pp. 123-144, Vol. 12(2), NIRD, Hyderabad.

S.C. & S.T. Research and Training Institute, Government of Odisha (1997). "Tribal Medicine and Medicinemen: An Exploratry. Study of Didayi of

Odisha", *Adibasi*, Vol. XXXVII, No. 2, Dec. 1997, pp. 72-101, S.C. & S.T. R & T.I., Bhubaneswar.

——(1996). *Development Hand Book for the Bondo of Bondo Development Agency Area*, Mudulipara, Malakangiri District.

——(1996). *Development Hand Book for the Kutia Kandha of K.K.D.A. Belgarh*, Phulabani District.

Sen, Amartya (1999) "Hunger in the Modern World in *Yojana*, Vol. 43, No. 1, January, 1999, New Delhi.

Sharma, B.D. (1978). *Tribal Development—The Concept and The Frame*, Prachi Prakashan, New Delhi.

Sharma, H.S. and S. Chattopadhyay (eds.) (1998). *Sustainable Development—Issues and Case Studies*, Concept Publishing Company, New Delhi.

Shrivastava, M.M.P. (1994). "Sustainable Development with Special Reference to Environment and Agriculture" in Journal of *Rural Development*, Vol. 13(1), pp. 47-55, NIRD, Hyderabad.

Sinha, B.N. (1999). *Geography of Odisha*, (1971), National Book Trust, India, Third Edition (revised).

Vidyarthi & B.K. Rai (1985). *The Tribal Culture of India*, (1976), Concept Publishing Company, New Delhi.

Vidyarthi, L.P. (ed) (1968). *Applied Anthropology in India (Principles, Problems and Case Studies)*, Kitab Mahal, Allahabad.

Wilkinson, T.S. and P.L. Bhandarkar (1992). *Methodology and Techniques of Social Research*, 9th Edn. Himalaya Publishing House, New Delhi.

Yojana (1999). "Amartya—The Pride of India" and Sen's Key Contribution to Welfare Economics" in *Yojana*, Vol. 43, No. 1, January, 1999, Ministry of Information and Broadcasting, New Delhi, pp. 5-7.

Yugandhar, B.N. (1991). *Methodology and Database for Decentralised Planning*, Lal Bahadur Shastri National Academy of Administration, Mussoorie, Heritage Publishers, New Delhi.

Index

Adult education centres, 86, 144
Adult literacy programmes, 179, 223
Afforestation, 106, 150
Agricultural development, 179, 183, 194
Agriculture and Soil Conservation, 106, 150, 154
Agro-forestry methods, 211
Alternative schooling centres, 221–222
Amblibeda village, 214
Amended Panchayat Act, 67
Anganbadi Centre, 86, 170, 200, 219
Animal husbandry sector, 96
Animal husbandry, 55, 107–108, 136, 150, 152, 154, 171, 216
Anthropological Survey of India, 48
Anthropology, action, 14–15
Attitude test battery, 26, 100, 132
Auguste Comte's formulation, 4
Austro-Asiatic tribes, 23

Balimela Dam Project, 54
Balimela Hydro-Electricity Project, 24, 127
Balimela reservoir, 19, 23, 80, 84, 92, 95–96, 146, 155, 212–213
Bamboo, 44, 54, 58, 86, 90, 95, 134, 136, 179, 187, 216
Bamboo craft, 107, 151, 216
Bari land, 52
Baskets, 63, 86, 90, 145, 216
Bayapada village, 215–216
Behavioural patterns, 77, 140–141
Biotechnology, 11
Block Development, 78, 110
Bondo Development Agency, 30
Bondo hills, 23
BPL, 61–62, 68
Bri land, 50–51
Bride price, 44, 136
    payment of, 44, 55
Brundtland Commission, 12
Buffaloes, rearing of, 92, 176, 180, 183

Capital formation, 19, 58, 129, 137
Capitalism, 2, 4
Capitalist system, 2
Caring of babies, 180, 187
Cash crops, 83, 95, 106, 135, 143, 146, 150, 194, 201, 209
Cash payments, 49, 63–64, 138
Cashew, 59, 83, 92, 176, 183, 188, 194, 196, 210
Census of India Reports, 31
Ceremonies sacrifice of animals, 70, 139
COATS Survey, 36, 59, 62, 90–91, 138, 145
Coconut, 59, 83–84, 92, 143, 176, 180, 183, 188, 193–194, 196, 210

Coffee, 61
Common Drainage System, 170
Communication facilities, 24, 79, 85, 93, 141, 199, 208, 214
Community centres, 206, 219–221
Community development approach, 8
Community Development Blocks, 78
Community organisations, 206, 219
Compost manuring, 83, 210
Conditioning elements, 14
Conflict resolutions, 16, 76, 141
Constitutional Amendment Act, 66
Continuing Education, 152, 223
Co-operative Institutions, 81, 142
Co-operative labour, 58
Co-operative society, 79, 107
Cooperative store/Fair price shop, 170
Corporate activities, 65, 139
Cottage industries, 107, 151, 155, 216
Council of Analytical Tribal Studies (COATS), 30–32, 34, 36, 38–39, 56, 82, 133, 145, 165, 169, 202, 207
Country liquor, 53, 186
Credit-cum-marketing requirements, 81, 142, 214
Crop rotation, 76
Cultivable land, 18, 43, 49, 212
Cultivation
- of cereals, 211
- extension of, 94–95
- method of, 52, 92

Cultural centres, 106–107, 149, 151, 154
Cut-off and Hills sub-areas, 214–215
Cut-off area, 12–13, 17–19, 23–24, 59, 62, 94–95, 97, 127, 133, 135
Cut-off sub-area villages, 85–86, 91, 213

Dairy project, 129
Darwin's theory, 4
Deforestation, 18, 92, 187
Development
- of agriculture sector, 82, 96, 143
- all-round, 8
- educational, 105, 142, 149
- fishery, 96, 146
- horticultural, 201
- inputs, 13, 91, 105, 110, 145, 148
- intellectual, 4
- mental, 4
- national, 7
- perception of, 10, 27, 90, 132, 145
- personal, 100
- planned, 125
- schemes, 16, 128, 165
- speedier, 9
- technological, 12
- tribal, 6, 8–10, 126
- wasteland, 19

Developmental programmes, 27, 100, 132
Developmental schemes, 132
Diarrhoea, 75, 87, 175, 182, 199, 215
Didayi
- cut-off area, 13, 127
- devotees, 20
- economy, 49, 58–59, 82, 129, 135, 137, 207
- families, 43, 49, 59, 63, 71, 137
- farmers, 58–59
- food gathering, 135
- hills area, 191
- making skill of, 90, 145
- opinion milk, 19
- plain, 13
- poor, 13, 127
- separated, 36
- tribe, 30, 42, 133–134, 174

Didayi Development Agency (DDA), 75, 81, 84, 87, 110, 127, 136, 143, 148, 176, 180, 183, 207, 210, 218
Didayi Development Project, 90
Disasters, 21
Diseases, common, 26–27, 174, 179, 182, 186, 193

Dissimilar methods, 25
Dongar land, 51, 211
Dormitory, 26, 72, 219
Drainage, 75, 159
Drought Prone Areas Programme (DPAP), 8
Dual organisation, 43

Economic activities centre, 59, 137
Economic analysis land, 137
Economic benefit schemes, 64
Economic determinism, 2
Economic development, 1–3, 5, 96, 146, 186, 216
Economic factors, 5
Economic groups, 48
Economic organisations, 42, 110
Economic pursuits, 18, 43, 56–57, 99, 106, 129, 150, 200
Economic resources, 65
Economy, pre-agricultural level of, 13, 127
Education
  basic, 4
  formal, 71, 96, 146
  higher, 223
  informal, 39
  middle school, 39
Educational attainment, 11
Educational Guarantee Scheme (EGS), 152
Educational profiles, 72
Electric power, 184
Electrification, 80, 105, 107, 149, 151, 153, 215
Elementary schooling stages, 220
Elwin Committee, 78
Emotions, 46
Entrepreneurial activities, 48
Environment, quality of, 9, 100, 126
Ethno-cultural groups, 13, 98, 109
Ethnographic case study, 22, 131
Expectant mothers, 105, 149, 153
Experimental method, 15
Extra-economic exchange, 48, 63, 139

Family benefit programmes, 187
Family income pool, 48
Family labour, 64, 137, 139
Family planning measures, awareness of, 179
Family planning operation, 191
Family planning programmes, 186
Farm land, 191
Felling of trees, 190
Fertile land, 48
Fertilisers, 96, 106, 145–146
Fertility, 50
Field survey, 31, 133, 136
Firewood, fetching of, 43, 134
Fisheries department, 84
Fishing, 13, 18–19, 48, 54–55, 59, 84, 90, 108, 129, 137, 151, 155, 213
Five Year Plans, 78
Floods, 212
Focus Group Discussion (FGDs), 21, 27, 91, 112, 132, 174, 178, 181, 185, 189, 192, 195, 198
Food crafts, 107, 151
Food for Work Programme, 190, 211
Food gathering, 13, 18, 47–48, 53–54, 57–58, 61–62, 77, 127, 129, 134–136, 141
Food scarcity, 206
Forest
  activities, 57, 136–137
  authorities, 63
  clear, 62
  collection, 49, 53–54, 58, 99, 135–137, 147
  contractors, 49
  deity, 20, 130
  depletion of, 18, 21, 54, 129, 136, 199
  eco-system, 187
  non-timber, 19, 47, 179, 182, 200
  operations, 64, 139
  villages, 50

Fox Indian model, modified, 16
Fox Indian Reservation, 14
Fuel wood, 59, 136, 175, 196

Gangapada village, 41
Garden land, 135
Gastrointestinal disorders, 215
General Theory of Employment, 2
Goat-rearing schemes, 87, 91, 144
Goat-rearing units, 85, 87, 91, 96, 107–108, 143, 146, 150, 152, 217
Gobar Gas Plant, installation of, 180, 183
Governmental efforts, 17, 184
Grain banks, 218–219
Gram Panchayat, 66–67, 199
Gram Sabha, 66–68, 172
Gram Sasan, 66–67
Grass land, 56, 129, 136
  availability of, 56
Grinding of pulses, 46
Guava, 59, 92, 176, 183, 193, 196, 200, 210–211

Handicrafts and Cottage Industries, 107, 151, 155, 216
Harmony, 12, 110
Harrod-Domar model of growth, 3
Harvesting, 23, 47, 51, 58, 71–72, 219–220
Health centres, 26, 68, 170
Health workers, 27, 87, 144, 175, 182, 215
Herbaria, growth of, 153
Hereditary, 20, 65, 129
Hill areas, 17–18, 43, 51, 58, 63, 94–95, 97, 129, 135, 146–147
Hill tops, 92
Hired labours, 64, 137
Horticulture, context of, 106, 150
Household management, 16, 44, 191
Household survey schedule, 26, 132–133
Human Development Index, 3
Human resources development, 16
Human-centred development, 5
Hunting, 13, 18, 44, 48, 54–55, 58, 62, 70, 77, 127, 129, 134, 136, 190

Ideological subsystem, 14
Immunisation programmes, 48
Imperialism, 2
Indigenous skills, 19, 77, 110, 129, 141
Indira Awas Yojana (IAY), 81, 142, 176–177, 183, 214
Industries, handicrafts, 216
Inequalities, 3
Infant Morality Rate (IMR), 186
Institutional framework, 5
Institutional saving practice, 190
Institutional transformation, 5
Institutions
  cooperative, 214
  cultural, 7
  primary social, 43, 134
  social, 71, 140
  traditional socio-political, 69
Integrated socio-economic development, 8
Integrated Tribal Development Agencies (ITDA), 8
Intensive programmes, 183
Irrigation, 10, 26, 76, 154, 194, 196
Isolationism, 7

Jantry village, 84, 216
Junior leviration, 44, 135

Kerosene, 199
Keynesianism, 3
Kitchen garden, 18, 49, 58, 83, 129, 176, 180, 183, 187, 196, 209
  backyard, 83, 209–210
Kutia Kandha Development Agency, 209

Land reclamation, 48, 212
Land revenue, 64

Landless families, 56
Landless labourers, 49, 91, 219
Law of Parsimony, 15
Lendi Pande, festival, 70
Lift irrigation, 176, 180, 184
Lineage groups, 43
Literacy and Educational Status, 38
Literacy Centre, 170
Livelihood
  primary source of, 88, 145
  source of, 55, 57, 137
  supplementary source of, 53–54, 136
  viable alternative sources of, 88, 145
Livestock, 26, 55–56, 136–137
  rearing, 56–57
  contribution of, 55
Local markets, 19, 129

Maize, 59, 83, 183, 209
Malaria, 75, 87, 140, 182, 186, 191, 193, 199
Manures, 50
Marginal Farmers and Agricultural Labourers Development Agencies, 8
Marx's theory, 2
Marxian analysis of economic development, 2
Max Weber's theory, 4
Medical centres, 75, 80, 85, 140
Medical pluralism, 105, 149
  context of, 105, 149
Medical treatment, 140
Medicinemen, 18, 128
Micro project, 9, 25, 98, 132, 146–147
Mid-day meal, 176
Milching cows, 55
Mini-Anganwadi centres, 152
Mini-watershed project, 212
Minor forest produce (MFP), 67, 90, 95, 135, 145, 175, 190, 193, 196, 207
Minor irrigation project, 68, 212
Minor millets, 50, 135
Modified Area Development Approach (MADA), 8
Moneylenders, 206, 218
Mother Earth, 69–70, 139
Multiethnic villages, 49, 109
Multi-purpose Cooperative Societies, 154
Multipurpose Health Workers (MPHW), 87, 197
Multipurpose Workers (MPWs), 18, 75, 128, 140
Mustard, 59, 83, 209
Mutual distrust, 110

National Education Policy, 223
National Literacy Mission, 152
Nehru, Jawaharlal, 7
Neighbouring tribes, 216
New leaders, emergence of, 20, 129
New Panchayat system, 69
Non-agricultural labourers, 136
Non-economic factors, 42
Non-Governmental Organisation (NGOs), 25, 111, 132
Non-kinship association, 72

Odisha Government Land Settlement Act, 208
Odisha Gram Panchayats Act, 66
Odisha Panchayat Samiti Act, 66
Odisha Zilla Parishad Act, 66
Operational design, 104
Organic evolution, 4
Organisation of economic activities centre, 137
Oringi village, 107, 151, 212, 214–215

Paddy, 44, 46, 49, 52, 59, 83, 86, 135, 137, 183, 186, 193–194, 209
  husking of, 46
Paddy land, 49, 52
Panchayat Samiti, 67, 79

Panchayati Raj Institutions (PRIs), 17, 48, 128
Participant observation, 26
Participatory development, 9–10, 125–126
Patriarchal society, 110
Peer groups, 140
Personal interview, 27, 112
Personality, 76
Plain area villages, 97, 146
Plains land, 49, 52, 95
Planning Commission, 165
Plantation of fruits, 146, 188
Podu cultivation, 90, 135, 190
Podu land, 50–51, 58, 72, 137
Policy enunciation, 8
Political life, 64, 139
Political organizations, 19
Poor beneficiaries, identification of, 204
Potable water, 105, 149
Pots, 63, 138
Poultry farming, 177, 183, 187
Poverty alleviation programmes, 25, 27, 87, 132, 144, 175, 190, 197
Poverty Line, 61
Power tiller, 16
Pre-agricultural modes, 8
Pre-agricultural stages, 13, 127
Pre-school centres, 176, 196
Primary education, 39, 73–74, 175, 179, 220
  quality of, 175, 179
Primary Health Centre, 80, 105, 149, 153, 182, 186
Primitive tribe, 36
Professional Voluntary Agency, 172
Programme formulation, 10, 126
Protestantism Calvinism, 5
Psychosomatic disorder, 20

Rapid soil erosion, 190
Regional groups, 65
Religion, 129
Religious life, 69, 139
Remote villages, 107, 151
  electrification of, 107, 151
Research design, 22, 131
Reserved land, 95, 146
Resources mobilisation, 96, 146
Revolving fund, 217–218
Rich alluvial soil deposits, 95
Rich farmers, 49
Rituals, 44, 48, 65, 70, 135
Rural communities, 78
Rural development, 78

Schumpeter's theory, 2
Second World War, 5
Sectors, non-agricultural, 48
Self-Help Groups (SHGs), 17, 25, 48, 81, 91, 132, 142, 145, 155, 207, 215–216, 218
  participation in, 48
Self-sufficient economy, 60, 62–63, 138
Service centres, 80, 142
Service sector, 107, 151, 155
Settled agriculture, 49, 64, 127
Settled cultivation, 18, 24, 47, 49, 52, 58, 82–83, 129, 135, 175, 207, 210
Sex Group, 32–35
Sex ratio, 34
Shifting cultivation, 13, 18, 23–24, 47, 49–52, 82, 92, 129, 135, 200, 211
  economics of, 51
  evil effects of, 175, 182, 199, 211
Shifting land, 49, 51–52, 106, 135, 211
Skill development, 9, 98, 147
Sloping Agricultural Land Technology, 154, 211
Sloppy land, 175, 211
Small Farmers Development Agencies (SFDA), 8
Smith, Adam, 1–2
Social change, 3, 5–6, 14–15
Social development, 1, 4, 6
Social environment, 71, 140

Social forestry schemes, 19
Social organisations, 12, 20, 42, 130, 134, 140
Social sector, 67
Social-forestry programmes, 106, 150
Socialism, 2
Socialization, 72, 77
  process of, 72
Social-structural subsystem, 14
Society Registration Act, 81
Socio-economic development effort, 8
Socio-economic life, 58, 135, 137
Socio-economic order, 11, 126
Socio-economic organisation, 42
Soil conservation, 26, 106–107, 150–151, 154
  animal husbandry, 207
  measures, 106, 150, 212
  purposes, 196
Soil erosion, 18, 21, 83–84, 95, 143, 150, 175, 182, 199, 211–212
  evil effects of, 92, 210
Soil fertility, 18
Solar light system, 180
South-eastern border, 23
Special campaign, 17
Special Central Assistance (SCA), 8
Special development measures, 6, 125
Spices, 46, 63, 95
Staple food, 61
Statutory Panchayats, 66–69, 139
  functionaries of, 68
Stone terracing methods, 211
Storage facilities, 19
Subsistence economy, 58, 61, 138
Supernatural elements, 76
Surplus income, 58, 137
Survey, 30, 32, 34, 36, 38–39, 56, 60, 62, 67, 82, 99, 133, 135, 207
Sustainable development processes, 11, 126
Synchronic ethnographic case study, 22

Teacher absenteeism, 71, 86, 92, 96, 105, 144, 149, 175, 179, 186, 193, 196, 223
Techno-economic subsystem, 14
Terracing, 106, 150, 175, 179, 183
Territorial organisations, 65
Test battery, 100
Threshing, 47, 51
TLC programme, 86
Traditional Panchayats, 44, 67, 139, 203–204
Transportation, 106, 149, 188
Tribal Development Agencies (TDA), 8
Tribal development Blocks, 8, 78
Tribal Development Co-operative Corporation (TDCC), 79
Tribal development intervention, 125
Tribal Sub-Plan (TSP), 8, 12, 67
Tuber crops, 83, 209
Turmeric, 59, 83, 194, 210

Unreserved land, 95, 146

Value of freedom, 15
Value-orientations, 104
Vasectomy operation, 182, 199
Vegetable
  cultivation, 183
  production, 210
  seasonal, 18, 129
  seedlings, 106, 150
Vegetation, 50
Village
  council, 65, 67–68, 70, 139
  deity, 20, 194
  drama/Dance party, 170
  elders, 70
  forests, 54
  mahajans, 218
  markets, 67
  medicineman, 179, 186, 191
  meetings, 87, 106, 172, 218–219
  messenger, 67

naik, 203
organisations, 64
centres, 141
Vocational skill development, 16

Wage earnings, 56–57, 145
Wage labour, 56, 136, 163
Wage-earner, 47–48
Water harvesting structure, 84, 92, 143, 183, 194, 212
Water resources, 21, 77, 96, 146
Water scarcity, 194
Watershed project, 92, 179, 183, 196
Weeding, 47, 51
Well-being index, 11
Wet land, 47, 49, 71
Widowers, 17, 36, 46
Widows, 36, 46
Women
development, 9
empowerment of, 9, 91, 145
household affairs, 76
organisations, 25, 132
participation of, 27, 132
tribal, 9, 176
World Commission on Environment and Development, 12

Youth dormitories, 48, 72, 140, 220–221

Zero literacy, 220, 223